PLACE

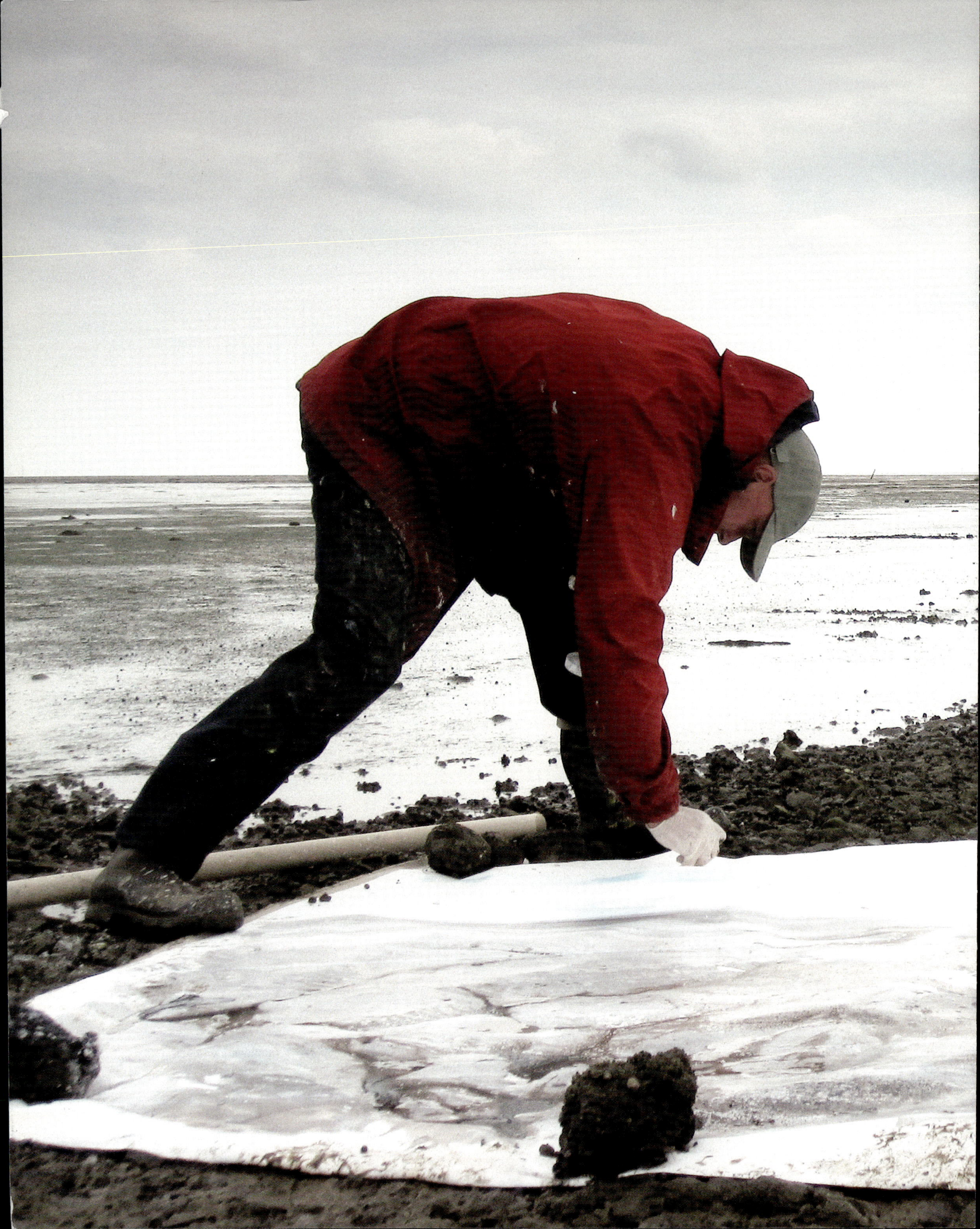

PLACE

KURT JACKSON

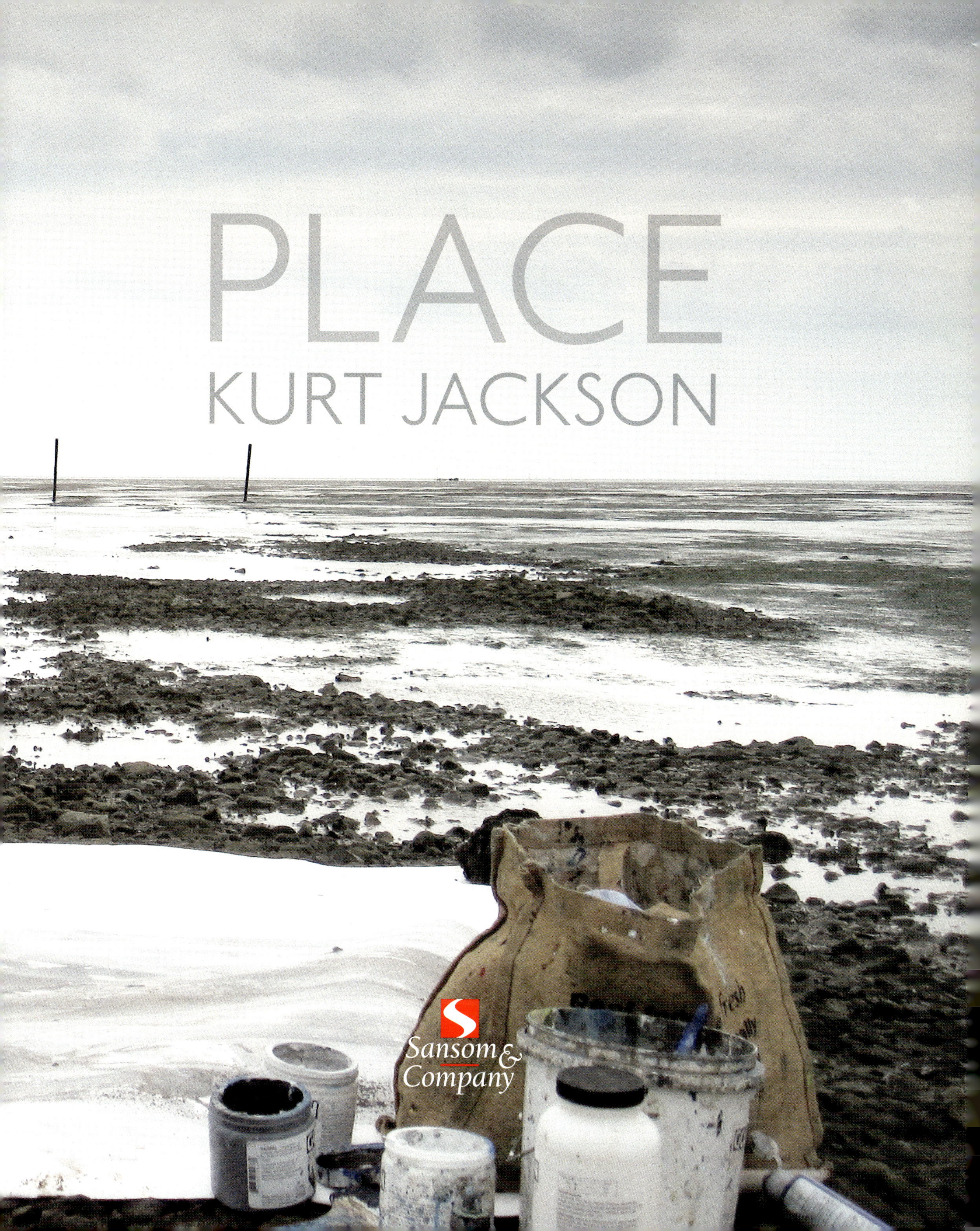

Sansom & Company

First published in 2014 by Sansom & Co.
an imprint of Redcliffe Press Ltd.
81G Pembroke Road, Bristol BS8 3EA
www.sansomandcompany.co.uk • info@sansomandcompany.co.uk

ISBN 978-1-908326-54-6

British Library Cataloguing-in-Publication Data
A catalogue record for this book is available from the British Library

Design and typeset (Johnston) by E&P Design • Printed by Zenith Media
Sansom & Co is commited to be being an environmentally-friendly publisher.
All our books are printed on sustainably sourced paper.

Listen to Tim Hubbard, journalist, reading *Place*
(content subject to change and availability)

Contents

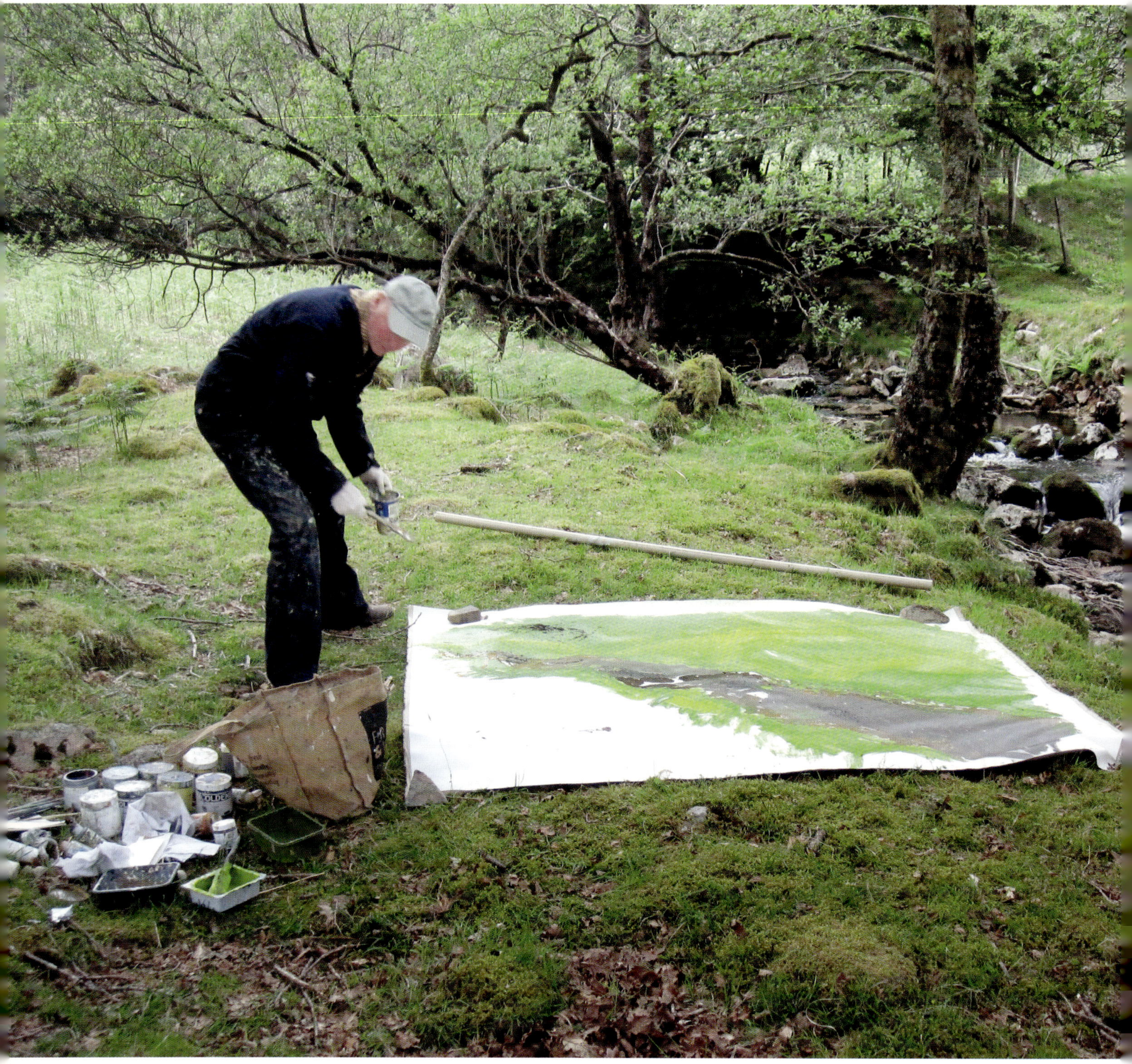

Introduction

Kurt Jackson

Over the last 30 years as my working practice has evolved, I have become more and more conscious that I need a reason for visiting a location for my work to happen there. I have a paranoia that when I attempt to paint, sculpt or respond to a particular part of the world my response may fall into that of simply a tourist, like the brief snapping of an image, producing a fleeting trivial record that has no depth or link to anything other than the desire to visit.

With that self-imposed constraint in my mind, with that prerequisite; my making and creating of the work will then normally take the form of a project, a body of work based upon previous research. I need to be previously informed – the physical experience and immersion comes later, with the elements and the setting feeding my mood and energy and determining the nature of the work.

The location may exist as a memory from other times or be one of a series, a string of locations forming a route, a course or journey across the land. To follow a river, ancient track-way or path through the landscape slowly and repeatedly: over, across and through (and occasionally even under) the countryside using the practice of making (visual imagery) is the ultimate way to discover, understand and ultimately become intimate with a place.

These links, these reasons to work in particular 'places' are therefore not simply topographic i.e. choosing the 'interesting' or 'pleasing' or panoramic view for a starting point, that is the lie of the land, but they can be topophilic resulting from the investment of time through ones life or family rooted into that land with nostalgia, fondness, attachment or connection. There are also those places that are the locations of specific events, times, occasions or fauna and flora; that beckon and attract ones attention, maybe a nature reserve, a colony of rare plants, a historical site, someone else's community.

Everyone has a link to somewhere special. For this project, Place, I turned my normal methods of working upside down and looked for a more unsystematic way in order to relinquish control and to funnel new sources into my working practice; broadening my access into the landscape, opening up new potential avenues and venues for my work. I decided to ask other people for their own choice of a preferred location, with them choosing where to 'send' me to make work at their own personal place within Britain. This site, this locale would then become the focus for my response in situ and then subsequently in the studios back home. The parameters became not my connections to a place but my connections to the people who chose the place.

Once the project was underway it took on its own momentum and it was then that I realised the enormity of the task I had undertaken – the distances involved, the logistics, the accessibility, the geography; an undertaking made the more enjoyable and sometimes bearable by the constant companionship and sharing with Caroline. I feel privileged to have had an insight into the personal lives of the 32 contributors as well as having had the opportunity to explore and connect with this disparate and diverse part of the world we call the British Isles.

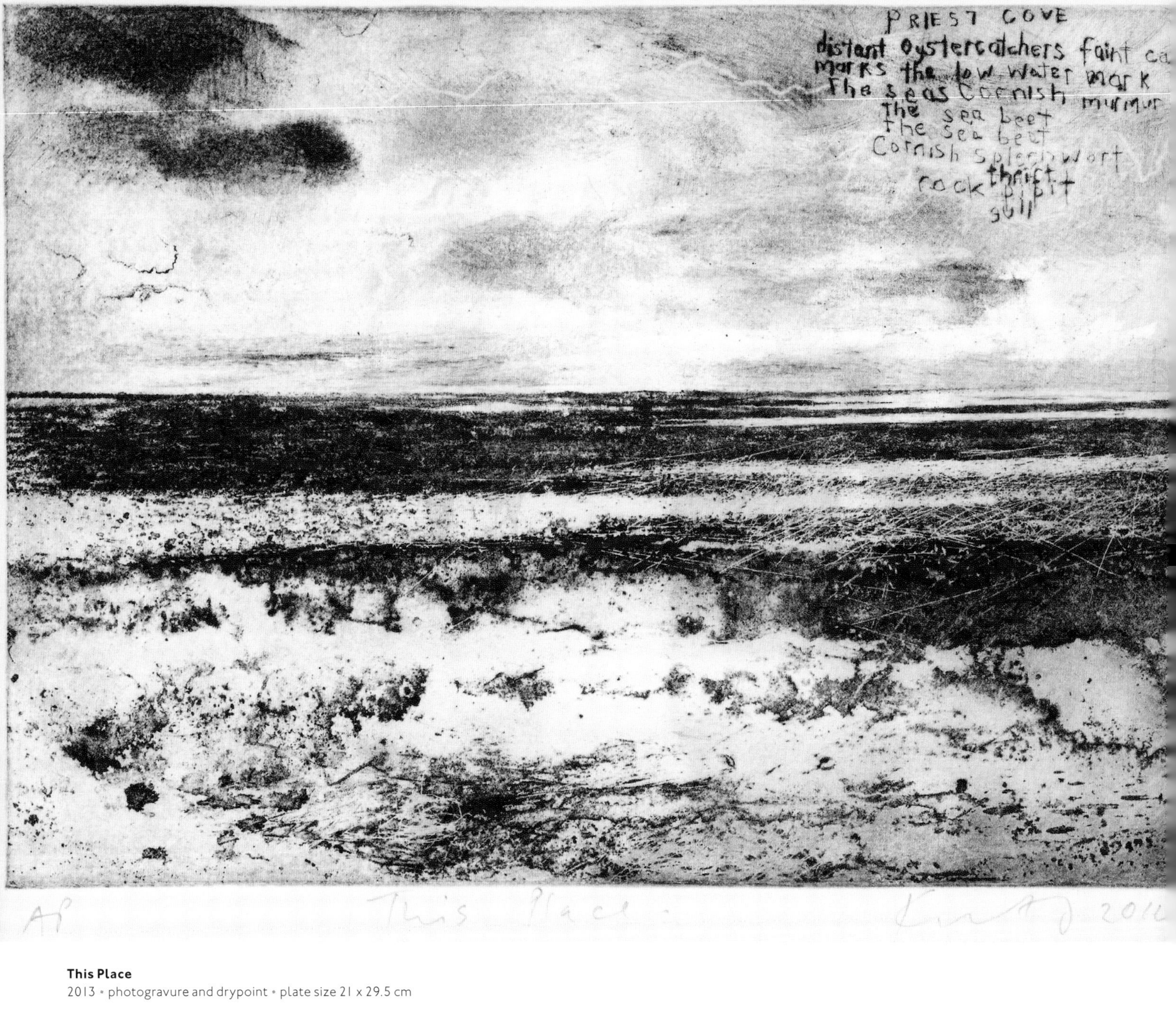

This Place
2013 • photogravure and drypoint • plate size 21 x 29.5 cm

Friends, colleagues and admired writers were all sent the following letter:

St Just-in–Penwith
Cornwall
21st of August 2012

Dear …

I'm writing to ask if you'd be interested in being part of my latest project – for the moment I'm calling it 'Place'. I'm asking thirty or so people to take part – some you'll know, some you won't. I want you to each choose a location somewhere in Britain that has a special meaning to/for you. I need you then to write a page about why that place is important to you, (reasons/feeling/history/description/narrative etc etc whatever angle you want). I will then visit that setting to paint/draw – try and capture it for myself; I'll need any clues – time of year or season or even time of day and how to find it! Ideally these pieces of text will then be put with my images in the form of a publication and an exhibition.

So first of all I need a yes or no that you're up for being involved. Then if you're in, I need the location and details. The text can happen at a later date – I don't need to see it before I paint.

In return I'll make a limited edition etching of 'my place' one each for everyone taking part.

Cheers,
Kurt

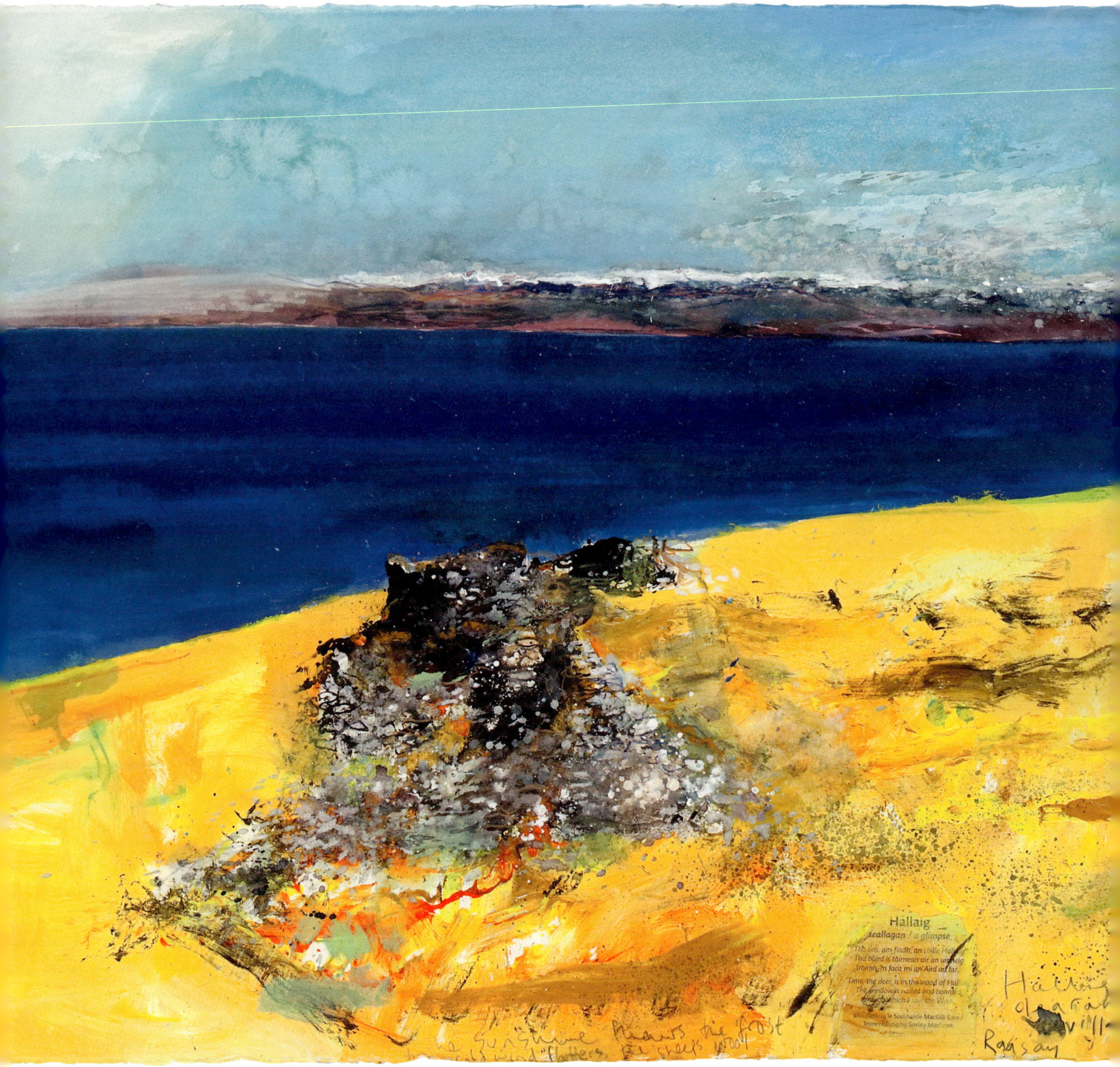
Hallaig
seallagan / a glimpse
Time, the deer, is in the wood of Hallaig
Raasay

PLACE

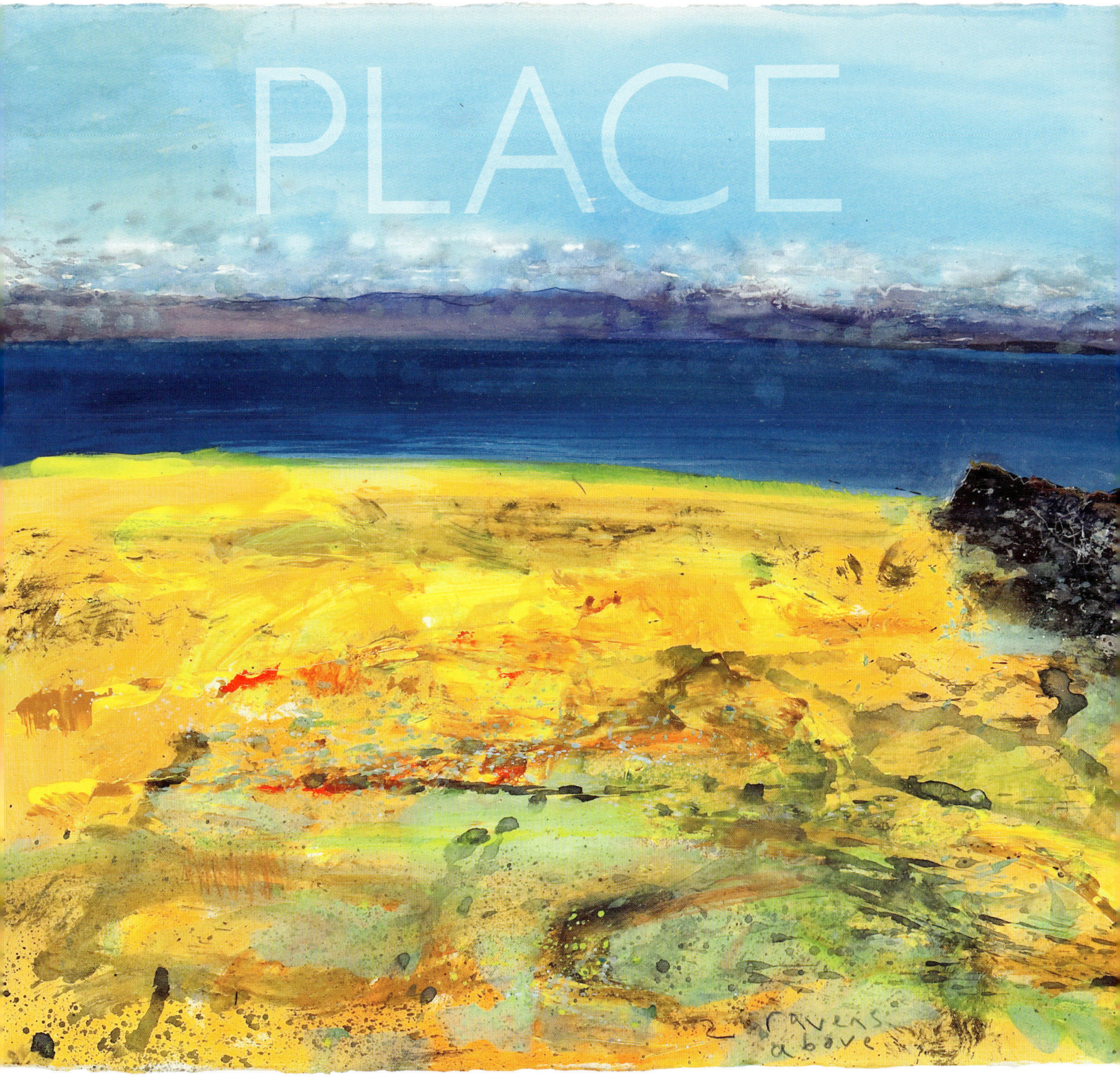

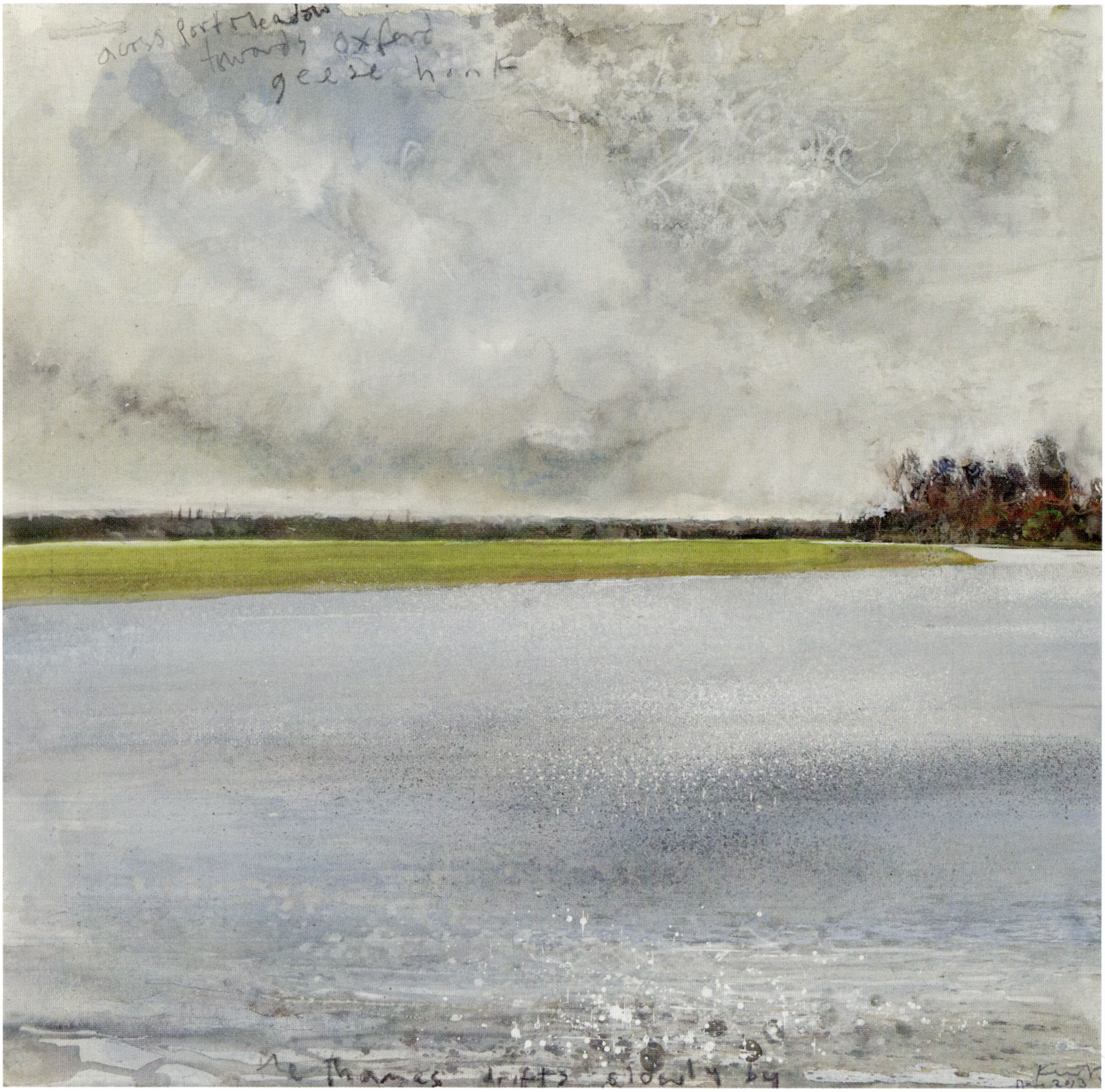

1. **Across Port Meadow towards Oxford. Geese honk. The Thames drifts slowly by**
March 2013 • mixed media on paper • 57 x 60 cm

1. Port Meadow, Oxford

Cathy Anderson

I first discovered Port Meadow entirely by accident. I'd been in Oxford only a few months, knew no one except my boyfriend, who I was about not to marry, and I was lonely and depressed. It was in this state that I wandered up Walton Well Road, through that old scrappy car park and out …

It was late spring, and unusually warm. The first thing that struck me was the skylarks' song, and the fact that I could hear them, not the city behind me, which had faded away the instant I'd walked onto the meadow. Flanked by trees to the right and the Thames to the left, Port Meadow rolled away from me, drawing me in with its beautiful grasses, flowers, insects and bees. In the distance I could even see cows and horses grazing.

At that point I looked behind me to Oxford, entirely confused that this rural idyll was actually in the centre of the city. This confusion entirely bumped me out my self-indulgent depression (and regret) at the state of my non-impending marriage, and the moment firmly established itself as the time Port Meadow saved me from what would have been a disastrous marriage to the airline pilot.

Thankfully life in Oxford moved on to happier times, and I returned probably weekly to the meadow, watching it change across the seasons and enjoying what it generously gave to me …

Summer nightswimming there in the river on the way back from the pub, kissing a friend for the first time in the dark, cool water. Sleeping off the night before on a picnic rug and waking shivering as the evening sun went down behind the trees. Boating through on the river on a day so hot that all the horses seemed to be standing in the water to cool off, and even trying (and failing!) to skate in one of those rare moments it floods and freezes, and the whole of Oxford seems to come out to enjoy it. For all those great times though, I still think spring on the meadow can't be beaten; when I'm sure I can actually see things growing, when the green is that beautiful just-grown green, and the sun seems new and extra bright.

But … Today that wonderful detachment from the city has been ruined by encroaching developments, with the claim that student accommodation is more important than the magic of this place that was here even before Oxford University; common land, for everyone, and a place left wildish in the ordered development of England's south east. That seemingly distant view of Oxford n ow wrecked by flats that say you're in a city, you're in a city … You can't escape.

Port Meadow is a rare, ancient, beautiful, space. It deserves respect for the bronze-aged people buried there, it deserves protection for the nature that flourishes there every spring, and it deserves the space to be common land for common people, like me. Save Port Meadow.

***Cathy Anderson** came originally from Durham, but left at the age of 18 for the bright lights of the south. She has spent most of her working life in the charity sector, working for Oxfam and Greenpeace. Cathy is deeply committed to the difference that charities can make in the world.*

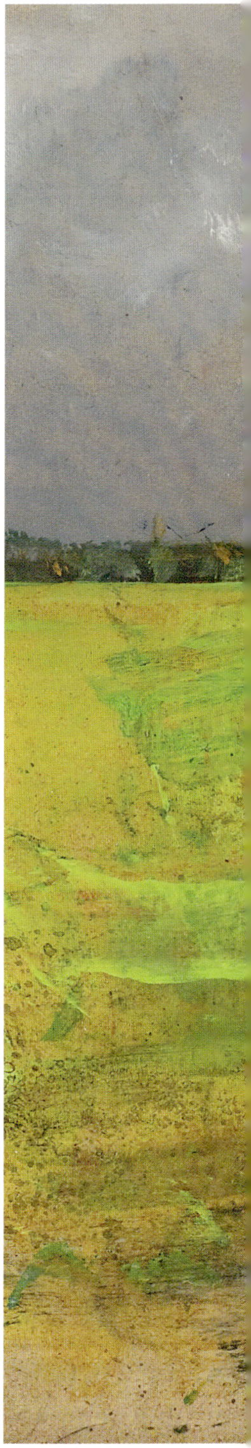

2. **Port Meadow cattle and sunshine and cold winds**
May 2013 • mixed media on wood panel • 19 x 25 cm

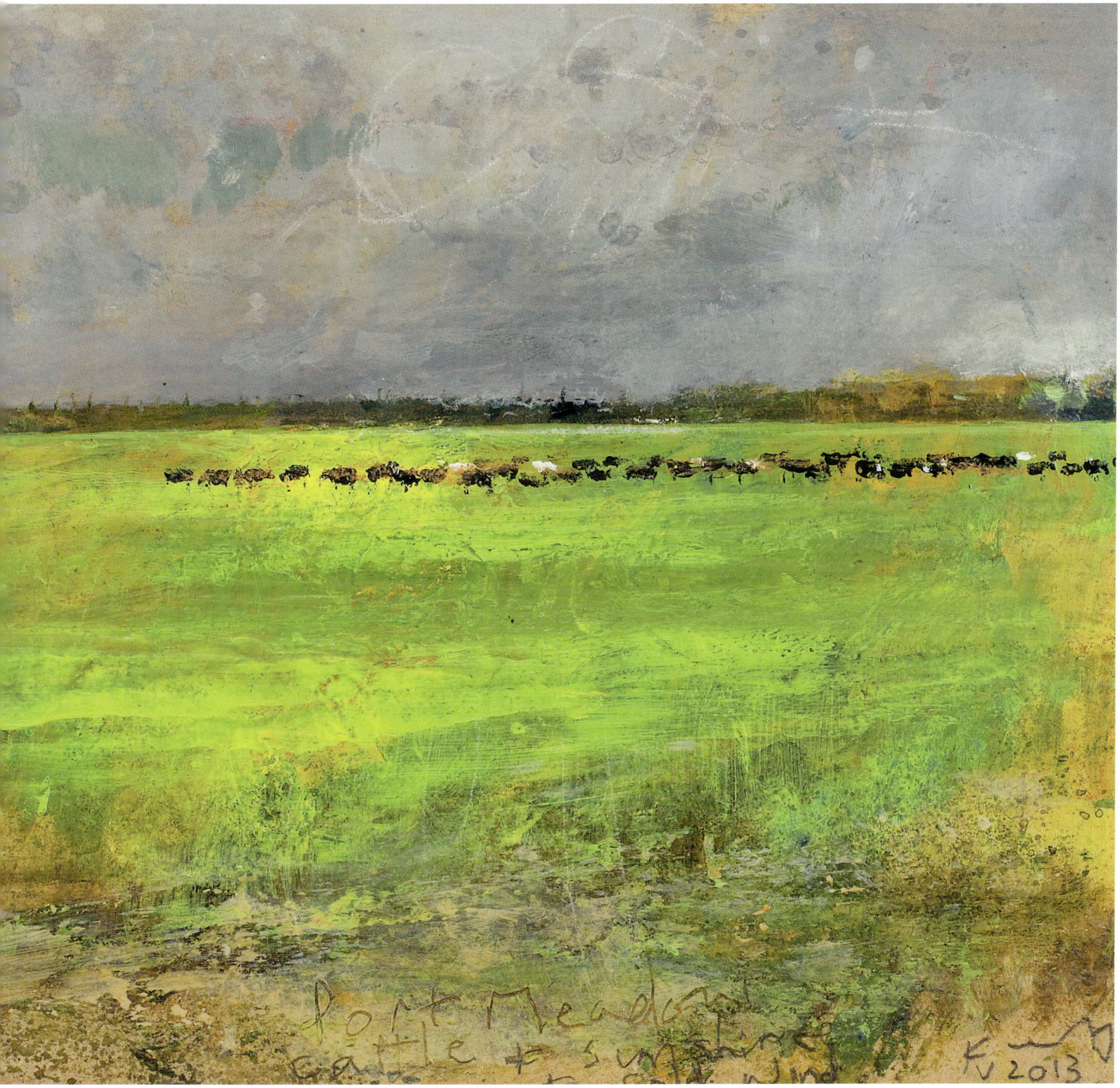
Port Meadow
cattle + sunshine
2013

3. **Black headed gulls scream, swallows skim the grass. Hot sunshine, distant warbler song. Port Meadow**
2013 • mixed media on linen • 138 x 140 cm

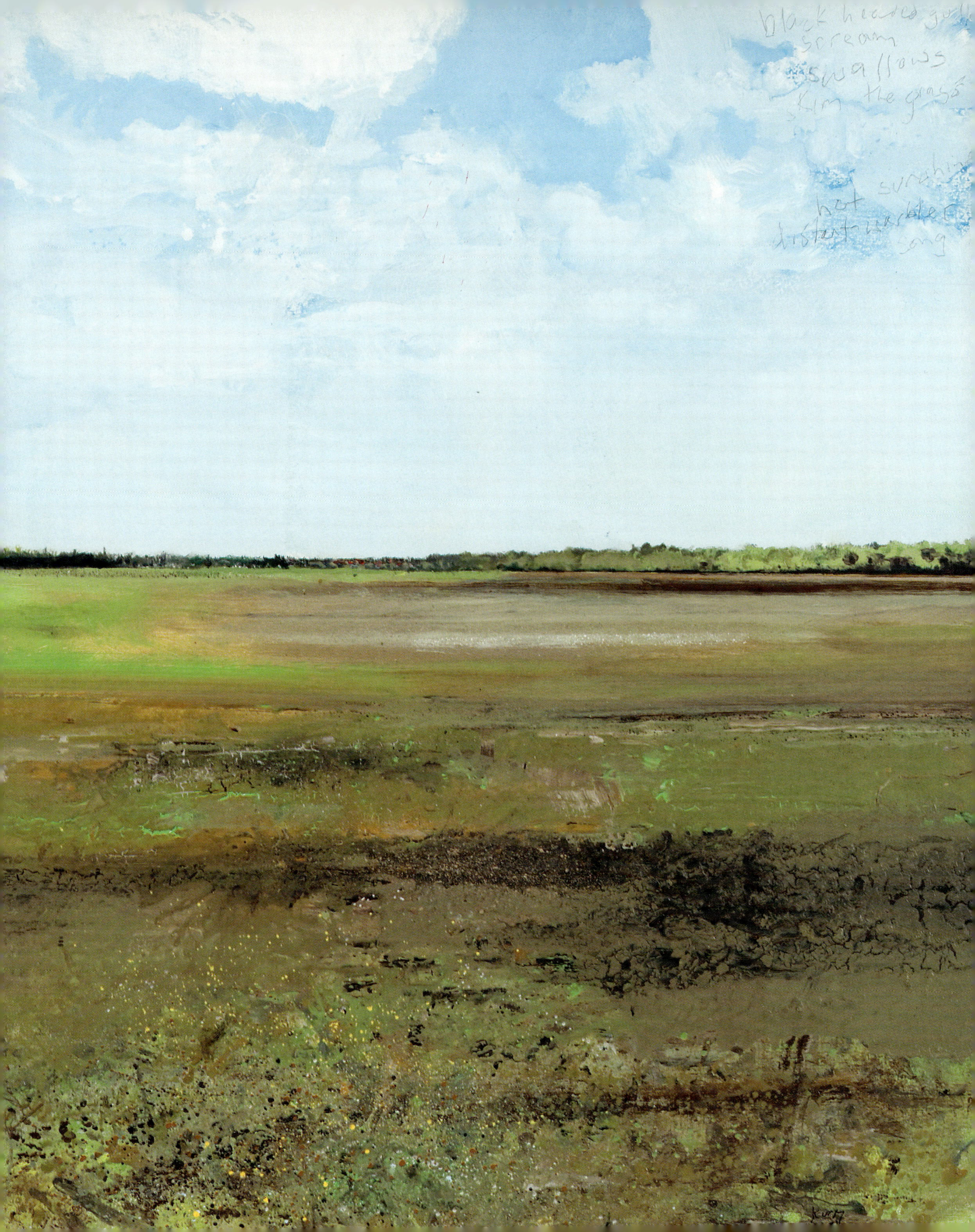
black headed
scream
swallows
kim the grass
hot
song

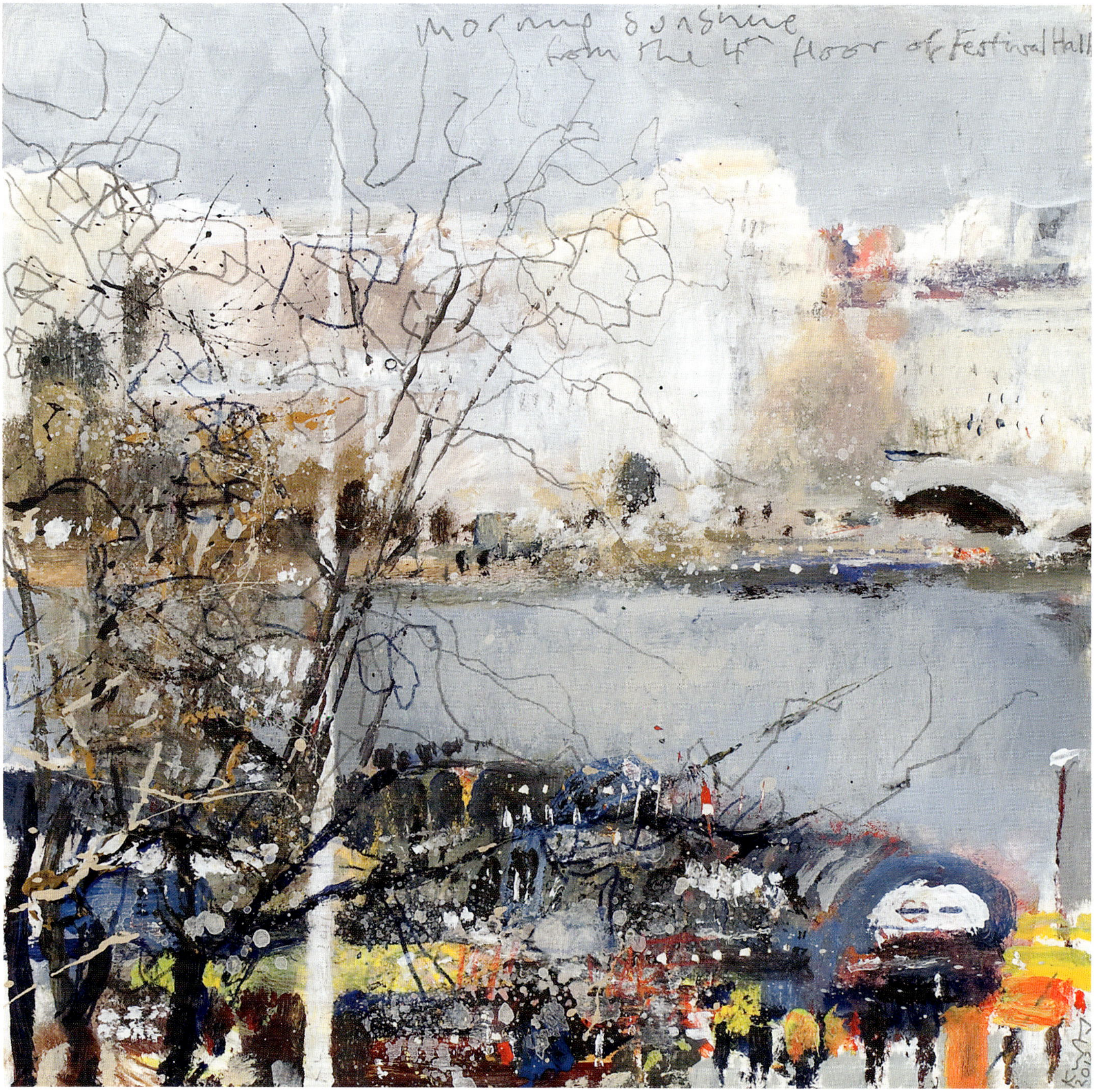

4. **Morning sunshine from the 4th floor of the Royal Festival Hall**
2012 • acrylic on board • 18 x 18.5 cm

2. Royal Festival Hall

Andy Atkins

I often work at the Royal Festival Hall. I emerged from deep concentration one day suddenly aware of a world of sounds around me. At a table nearby, a group of East European construction workers watched a football match on a laptop. Snippets ofsymphony leaked from an orchestra rehearsing in the auditorium behind me. Further round the gallery, an earnest young man was getting a German lesson from a tutor. A mother, in a sari, emerged on the landing between floors to recapture her renegade toddler. That's one thing I love about the Festival Hall: it's a safe and spacious space in the heart of London, open and free to all, wrapped around a world-class centre for music and the spoken word. An average day there reminds you just how culturally diverse London is.

Sometimes I go up to the 6th floor overlooking the Thames. From there I see symbols of so much of my daily world. The river has been dramatically cleaned up in my lifetime, showing that environments can be restored. Commuter waterbuses, river barges, pleasure boats and police launches cruise by, making great use of this natural transport link through the capital. Across the river, just off picture to my left, lies Westminster, Parliament, Millbank studios. I can be there in 20 minutes by foot for a meeting with an MP or a TV interview.

Directly across and inland from Embankment gardens is the West End – celebrated not only for its entertainment but for its tradition of social commentary which goes with theatre. Away to the right is the City, so critical in its influence not just on our economy but on the global environment, through investment in dirty fossil fuels or clean renewable energy.

Yet, if need be, I can also be back at Friends of the Earth's office, near the Oval, in just 15 minutes on my fold-up bicycle. With a backdrop of the living Thames, the West End, blue sky or 'weather' above, I'm stimulated to think, read and write. Usually it's for campaigns to protect the environment for people and nature.

Access to a healthy environment, including safe water and food, clean air, a stable climate, pleasant places to work, play and just be, is critical to human wellbeing. Many are basic human rights which too many people can't enjoy. London could do better on many fronts but it's got some great public spaces. These are so vital for urban populations and the UK is now 80% urban. The Royal Festival Hall is a hugely important public space. Every town should have one – and preferably a river running through it too.

Andy Atkins is executive director of leading environmental charity Friends of the Earth. Andy was previously policy and campaigns director at relief and development agency Tearfund. He was part of the original group of charity campaigners who started the high profile Make Poverty History campaign in 2005.

Andy has been a leading advocate of the need for the development sector to understand the critical importance of environmental issues. Under his leadership Tearfund became the first major UK development NGO to campaign on climate change.

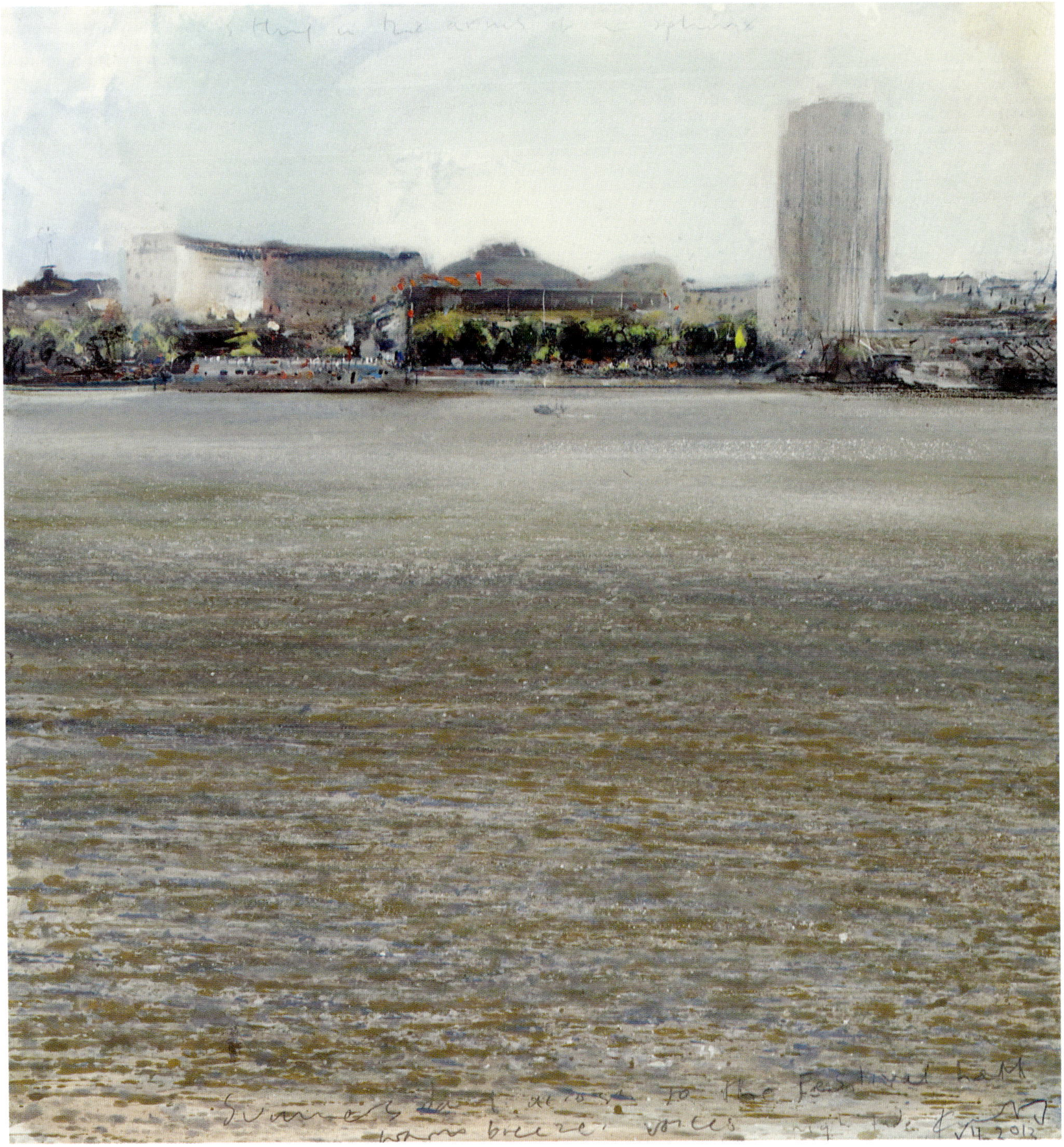

5. **Sitting in the arms of a sphinx. Summers day looking across to The Festival Hall**
July 2013 • mixed media on board • 51 x 49 cm

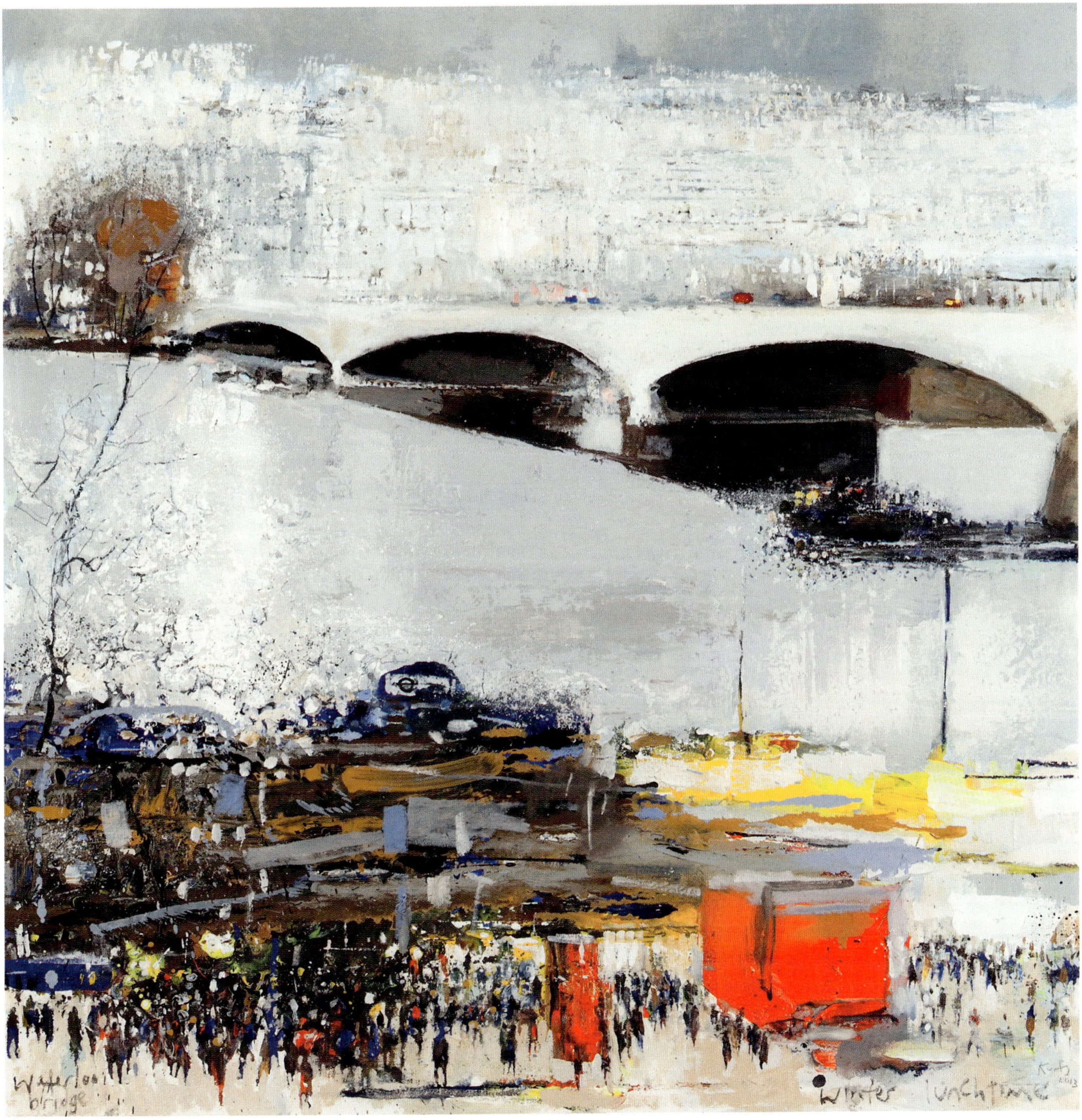

6. **Winter lunchtime, Waterloo Bridge**
2012 • oil on canvas • 81.3 x 81.3 cm

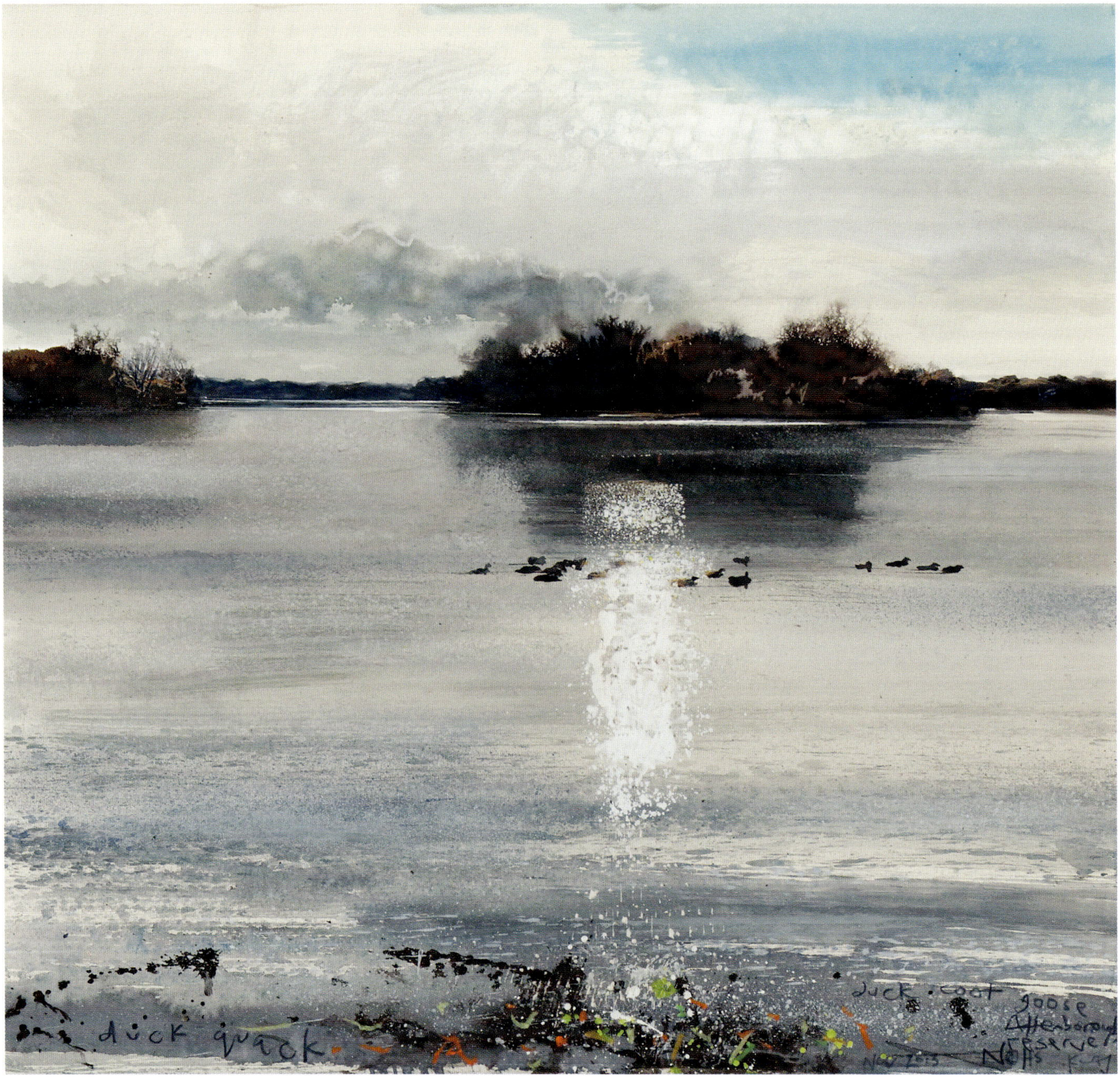

7. **Duck, coot, goose. Attenborough Nature Reserve, Nottinghamshire**
November 2013 • mixed media on paper • 57 x 61 cm

3. Attenborough Nature Reserve

Jeff Barrett

We called it The Gravs and for a few formative years in the 1970s it was my favourite place. I went there to play, cycling the two miles from home in Chilwell, down into Attenborough, across the railway tracks and into a wetland jungle so different to anywhere I'd ever been before that it took many visits to honestly believe I wasn't trespassing.

Originally the Gravs were my short cut to the river. We'd cycle through it to get to the Trent where, if there was a match on, we'd watch 100 or so anglers filling their keep nets with roach and bream. But soon it was all about the Gravs. It became the destination, its wildness capturing my mischievous youthful imagination as a place to explore, my curiosity only heightened by the signs that read DANGER. QUICKSAND. KEEP OUT.

On either side of the throughway there were gravel pits, their banks dotted with dug-in anglers doing their best to hide from life beneath green canvas umbrellas. The pits all had names: Myfords, Plessey, Boots, The Depot. These were names of local factories and workplaces, names I'd heard spoken of by grown-ups, given to the pits whilst their social clubs held the lease.

Fishing was becoming a thing for me. My Dad was an angler and so was my brother, and this was where I decided to learn how to do it for myself. How better to learn that than by moving into the swims of local legends as they packed up their kit and went home for their tea, or in the morning after a night-fishing session, being given leftover bait, maggots tipped from an Efgeeco box belonging to a proper angler.

This all happened a long time ago and I now call my childhood place of refuge by its 'real' name, the Nature Reserve. Attenborough Nature Reserve. No doubt it was called that back then but those vast deep pits, dug from the gravel that went to build the A52, were simply The Gravs. Today there are no anglers. The factories are gone, the social club membership cards lie blank, the lakes are silted up. Now my Mum's name can be added to the list of names that haunt the landscape, another ghost of Beeston's past. That's the main reason I go there now, to say hello and have a quiet moment.

Today it's recognised as a Site of Special Scientific Interest and the birdwatchers have replaced the anglers. It's a shame, because there are still monster fish in there. I'm sure of it.

***Jeff Barrett** was born Chilwell, Nottingham 1962 and has lived in Shepherds Bush since 1985. Married to Wendy, two teenage boys, Sonny & Danny. Always music, always 'Caught by the River'.*

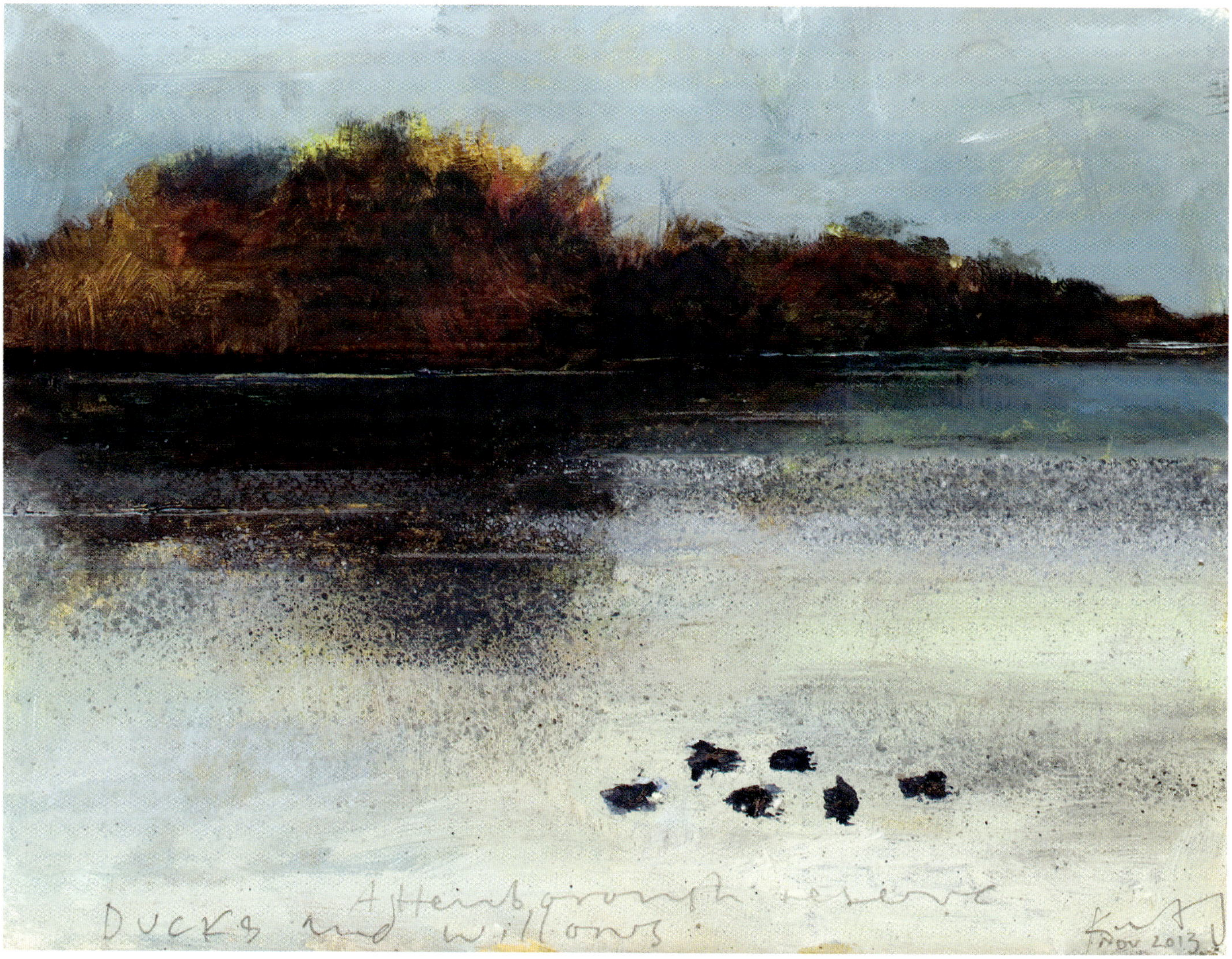

8. **Ducks and willows. Attenborough Nature Reserve**
November 2013 • acrylic on board • 18 x 24 cm

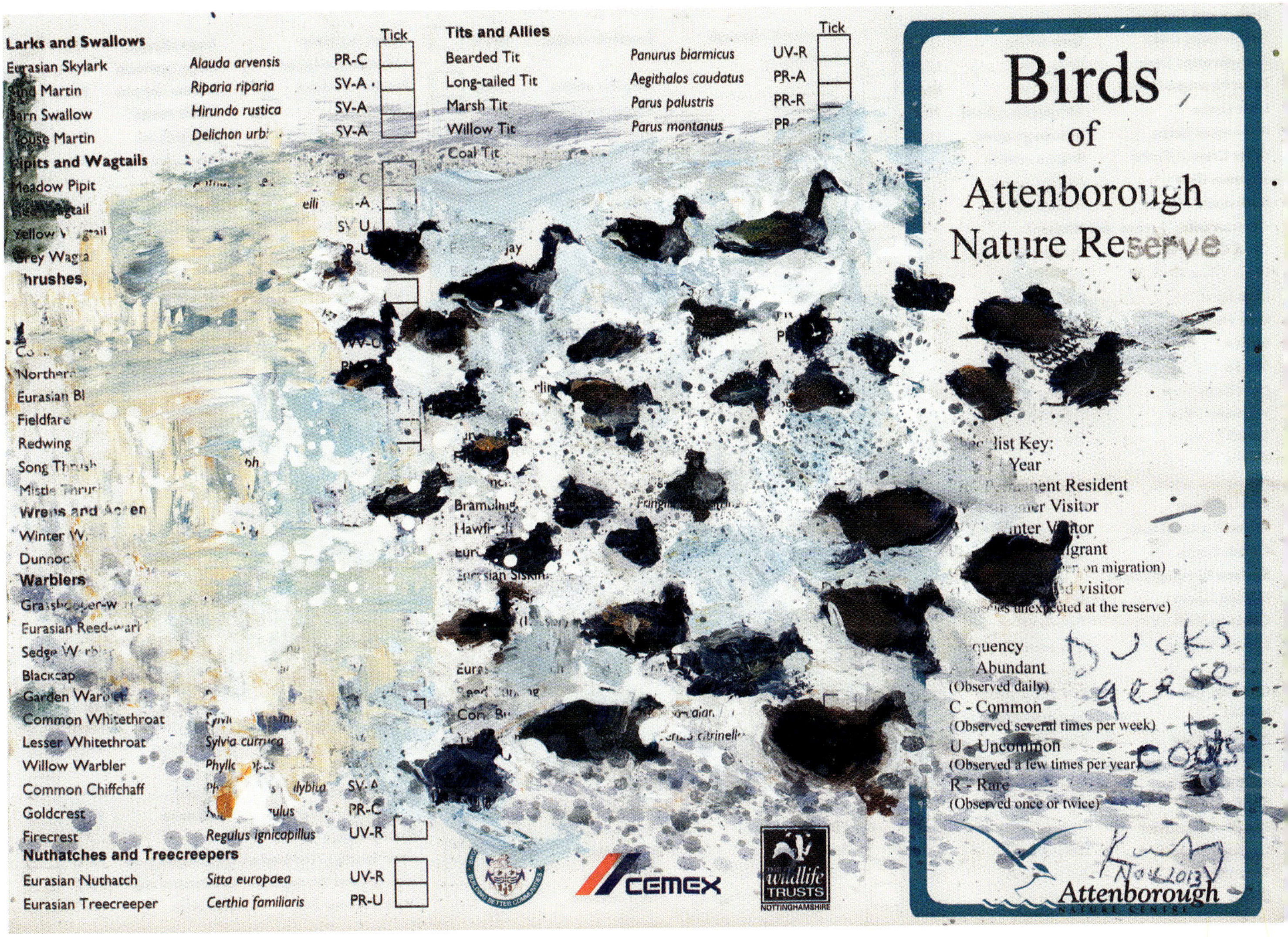

9. **Birds of Attenborough Nature Reserve**
November 2013 • mixed media on paper • 21 x 30 cm

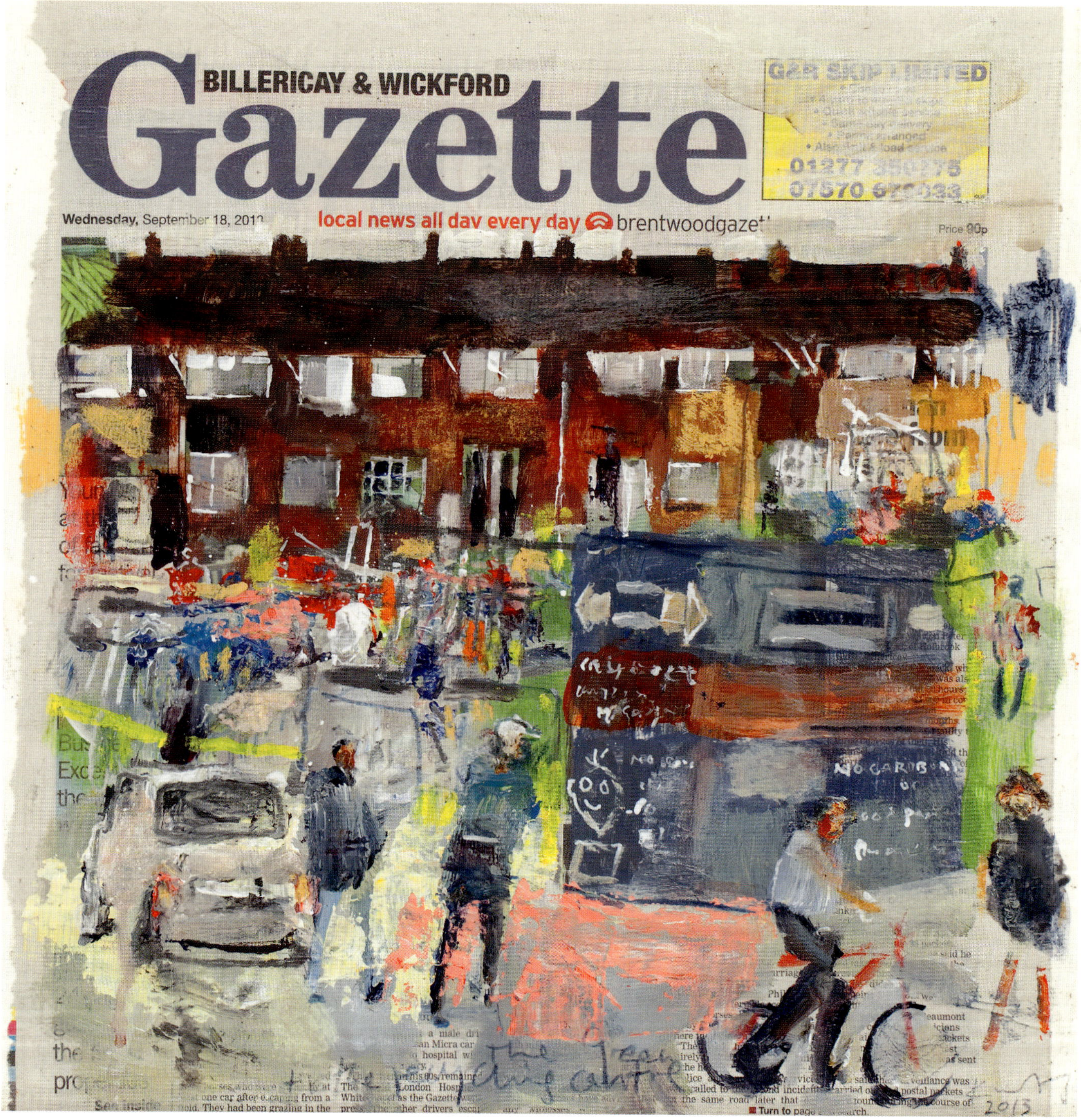

10. **The Green and the Recycling centre**
September 2013 • mixed media and collage on board • 31 x 31 cm

4. The Green, Outwood Common Estate, Billericay

Mick Catmull

I hated it. My friends were back in Walthamstow, 20 miles away. That's quite a distance when you're 12 years old and the only direct route is a bus that seems to take forever.

In the late '50s Walthamstow Council built two overspill estates in Essex. One was on Canvey Island but my parents chose Outwood Common in Billericay. It meant nothing to me that our estate had won awards for a design that avoided the drab uniformity of much post-war council housing. At its heart the planners built a parade of shops, next to the rent office. Across the road they laid out a playing field complete with goalposts. Everyone called it The Green. A stream straddled by mature trees ran down one side, left over from when the estate had been meadows. After six weeks of moping I loved it. I'd made a bunch of new friends and when we weren't exploring the fields and woods that surrounded our new homes we'd simply hang out on the green.

I became a '60s teenager on that green. Most evenings I'd rush through my tea and homework so I could get down there. If there were just a couple of us we'd climb trees and swing across the stream. More than half a dozen and we'd kick a ball about. Football was a constant. Pretty soon we were able to put a team into the Basildon Football League, playing on a proper pitch up the road. We lost our first game 15-nil and all our games that first season. The following year we were runners-up. We got lots of practice on the green. When darkness fell we'd cross the road and hang around outside the shops, learning to talk to girls and swapping filthy stories we'd heard from older boys. Life was pretty good. In 1963 my economics teacher told us we were living through a golden age but I think he was talking about a bigger picture.

Outwood Common was conceived and built by idealists from a bygone era. We danced happily to their tune for 20 years. Then Mrs Thatcher offered us the chance to buy our homes for knockdown prices. We bit her hand off. With Essex Man in her vanguard Thatcherite self-interest rampaged across Britain, demolishing municipal socialism and demoralising the collective spirit.

The houses on Outwood Common have been individually improved, separated off from that original creative blueprint, front gardens paved over. Roads are broken for want of repair. The stream is buried, out of harm's way. The empty green stands as the reminder of a vision of community that has all but disappeared from the surrounding estate. The goalposts have been moved.

Mick Catmull *grew up in London and Essex. Starting out as a photographer with the Amber Collective in Newcastle, Mick documented the impact of industrial change upon communities in Newcastle and Sunderland. As a founder member of A19 Film & Video he went on to produce feature length documentaries. In 1995 Mick moved to Cornwall, then Plymouth. He set up A38 Films to produce and direct documentaries for TV, winning an RTS award for his 2005 'Portrait of Cornwall' collaboration with Kurt Jackson. From 2007–14, Mick worked on the Inside Out programme for BBC South West, specialising in fishing and mining. He has now returned to independent film making.*

11. **The goal on The Green, Outwood Common Estate, late afternoon**
September 2013 • acrylic on board • 16 x 25 cm

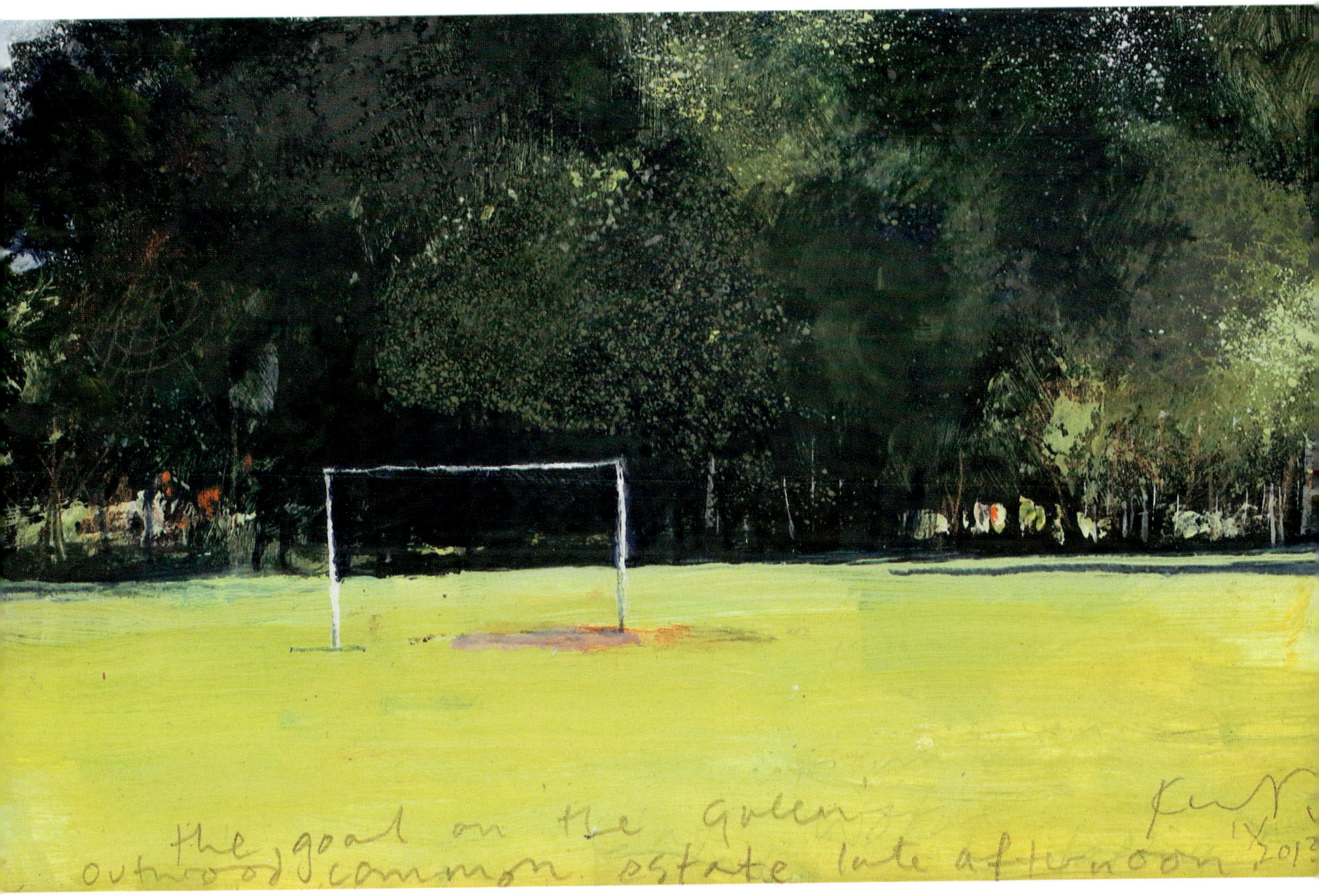
the goal on the green
outwood common estate late afternoon
IX 2013

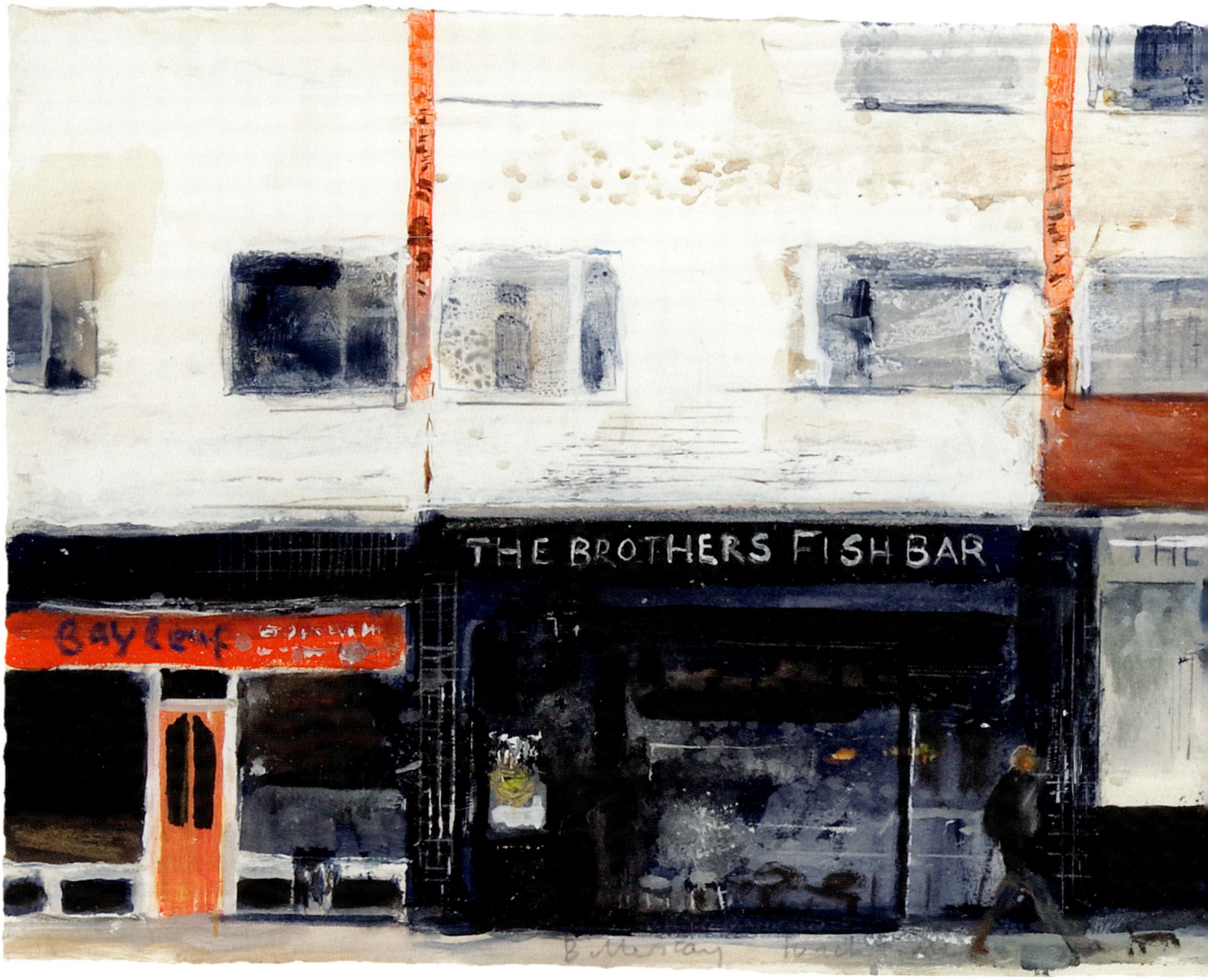

12. **Outwood Common Road – The Parade**
December 2013 • mixed media on paper • 28 x 77 cm

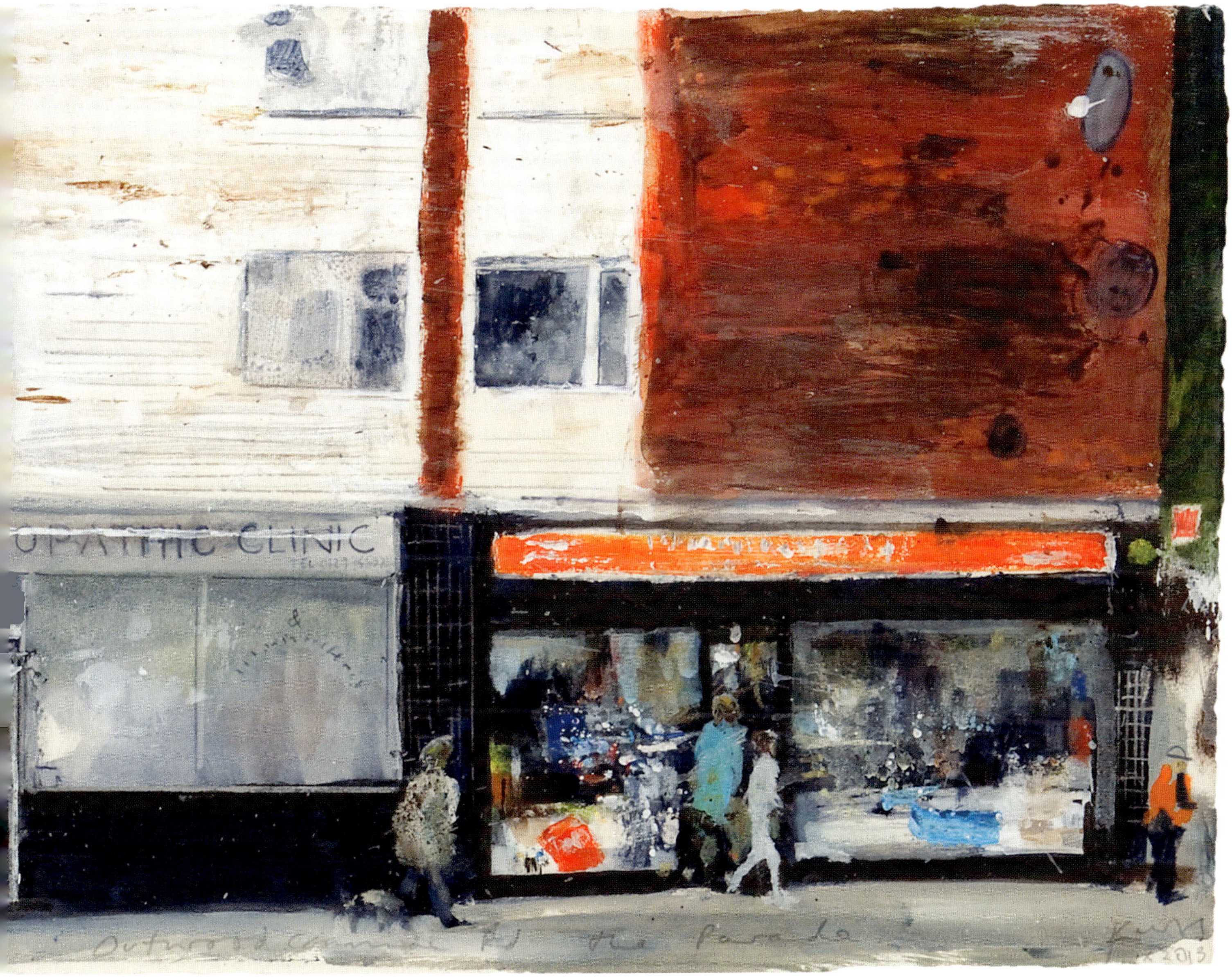
OPATHIC CLINIC

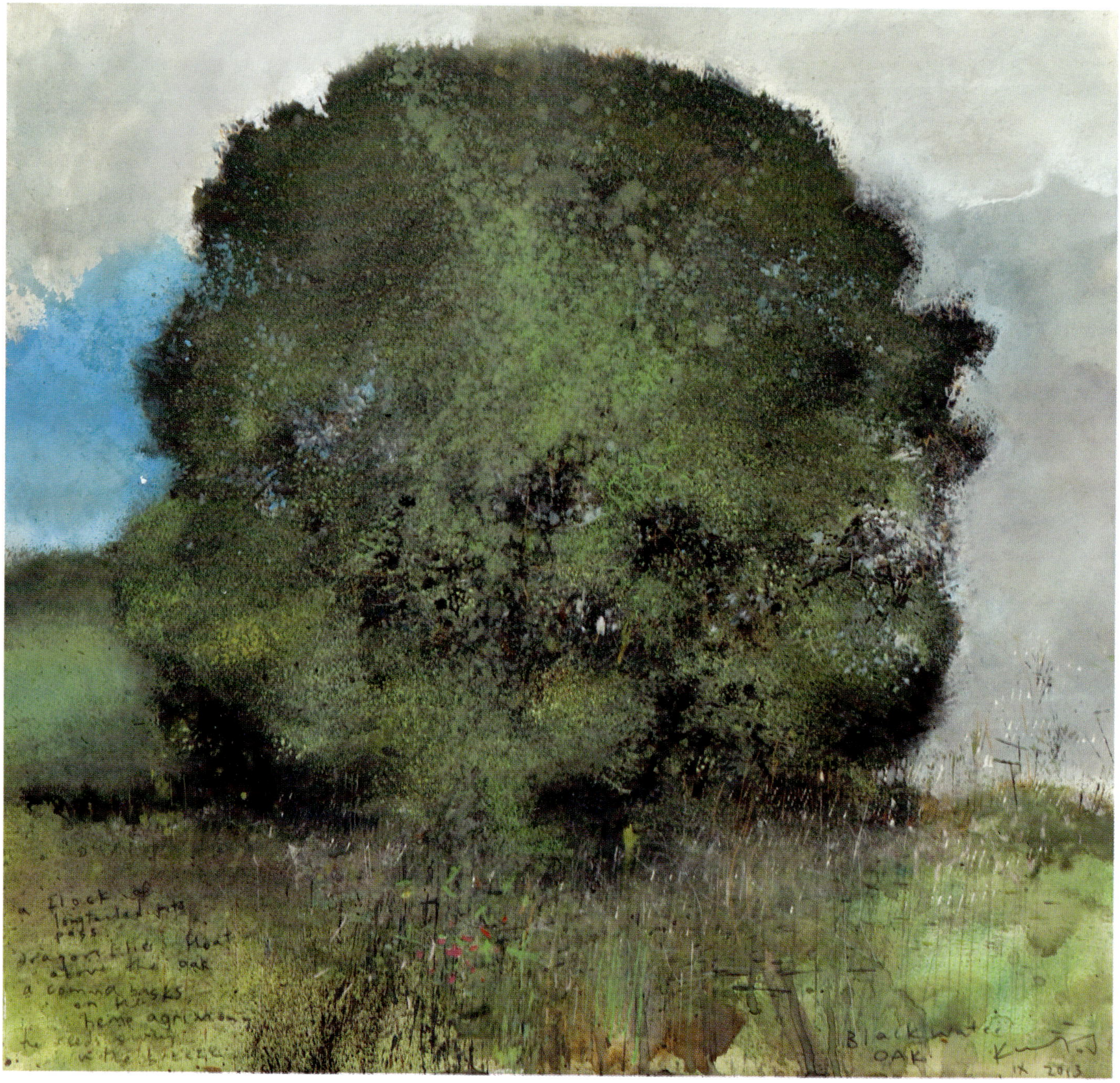

13. **A flock of long-tailed tits pass, dragonflies float above the oak, a comma basks on the hemp agrimony, the reeds sway in the breeze. Blackwater Wood, Norfolk**
September 2013 • mixed media on paper • 57 x 62 cm

5. My oak, Blackwater Carr

Mark Cocker

In the great animal cemetery at Tuna al-Gebel the ancient Egyptians buried hundreds of thousands of mummified ibis. For centuries they carried the preserved bundles down the underground tunnels and slotted them into allotted cut-stone niches. For me it is not just the psychological otherness or the overarching grandeur of such archaeological sites that I find so moving. It is the incidental detail and the casual moment which somehow bring it all to life so powerfully.

On the stairs down into that archive of life and death and memory and human hope the Egyptian priests occasionally carried mummified creatures that were still dripping with the sweet-smelling unguents they had applied to preserve the ibis bodies in the afterlife. We know this because the dark stains where the oils dripped on the stone steps are still there more than 2000 years later.

In nature it is also the detail that can be most affecting. At Blackwater Carr I have a single centurion multi-limbed oak that is skeletal and awkward and upturned-octopus–like in winter. Yet by summer it is an almost spherical solid-seeming fort of green. It has no oak neighbours. The nearest are hundreds of metres away and I cherish the idea of its origins.

Around about the time that motor-cars started to appear on local roads and when the horses and workers in the neighbouring fields were replaced by agricultural machines, a jay flew from the Postwick woods. It landed in the marsh that I now own and regurgitated an acorn from its bucchal pouch. To the incidental sounds of robins or blue tits in the autumnal bushes, the jay pushed that acorn into the peat. Off it went with that slow-winged and strangely faltering action of jays in flight. By spring – who knows why? – it failed to retrieve its nut larder and a sapling sprouted and grew. This is my oak.

This tree is that oil stain on the necropolis stairs. It speaks to us of momentary things – of intimate detail and of unfolding chance events. Yet it also sits within its own vast architectural context. Plants like my oak constitute 90 per cent of the planet's biomass and are so versatile that they embrace environments from Siberia (with winter temperatures of -56°c) to the furnace of the Saharan summer (40°c). The chlorophyll that makes my oak so green now, even in November, and which allows it to convert light to carbohydrates was an 'invention' of algae three billion years ago. The xylem and phloem networks that connect all parts of the tree to its nutritive supplies and then the lignin cladding that defends those living tissues – and which gives the organism its sprawling many-limbed complexity – are elements that evolved at least 400 million years ago.

In our deepest affairs with nature there is always this fruitful movement between the momentary and the ancient or the very ancient. They are the warp and weft that create the fabric of our encounters in the living world. One, many, all – and always – in a circular dance around our imaginations; but it's also just an oak planted by a bird.

***Mark Cocker** is an author, naturalist and environmental activist. The latest of his ten books is 'Birds and People' (with photographer David Tipling).*

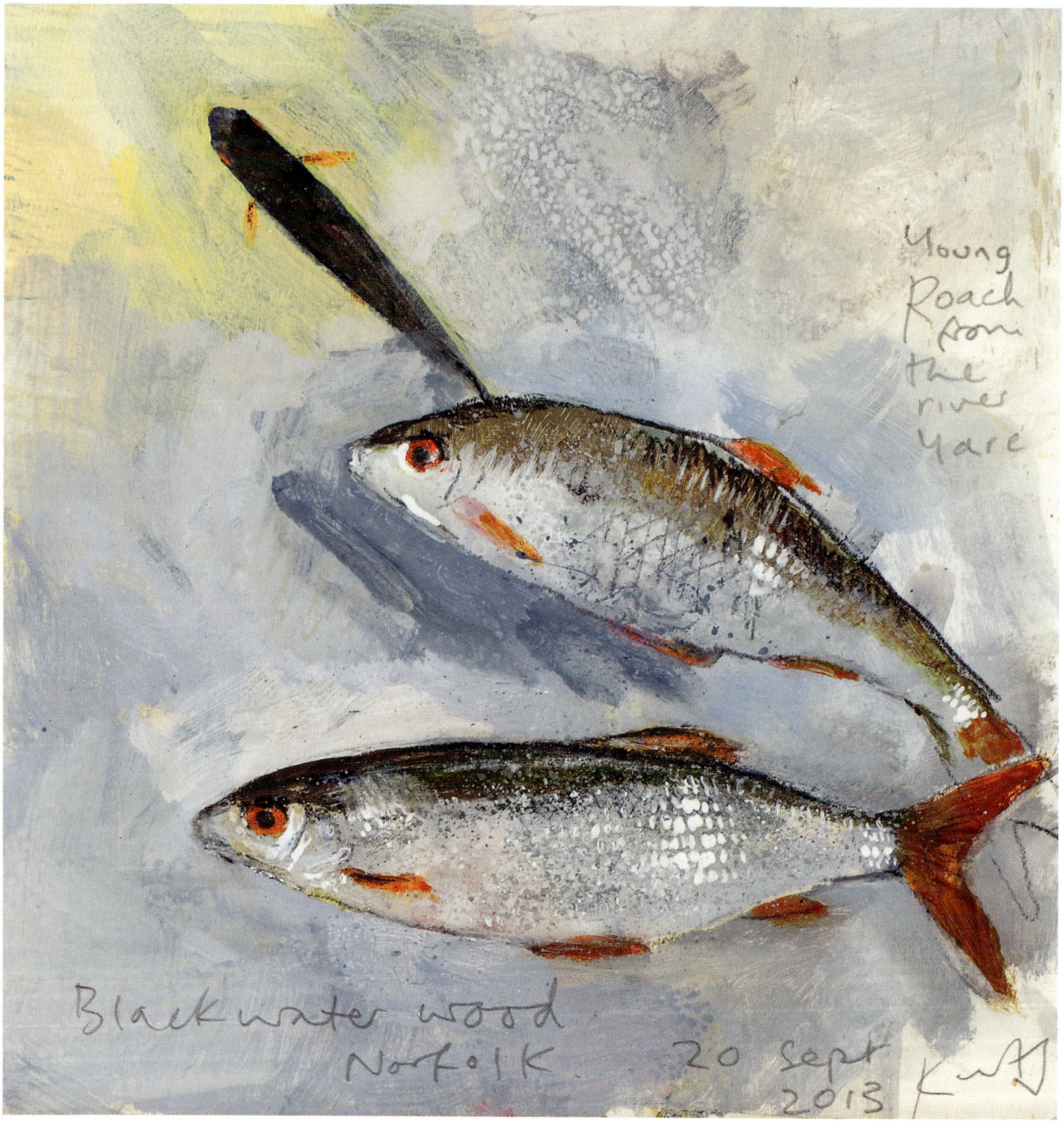

14. **Young roach from the River Yare**
September 2013 • acrylic on board • 20 x 20 cm

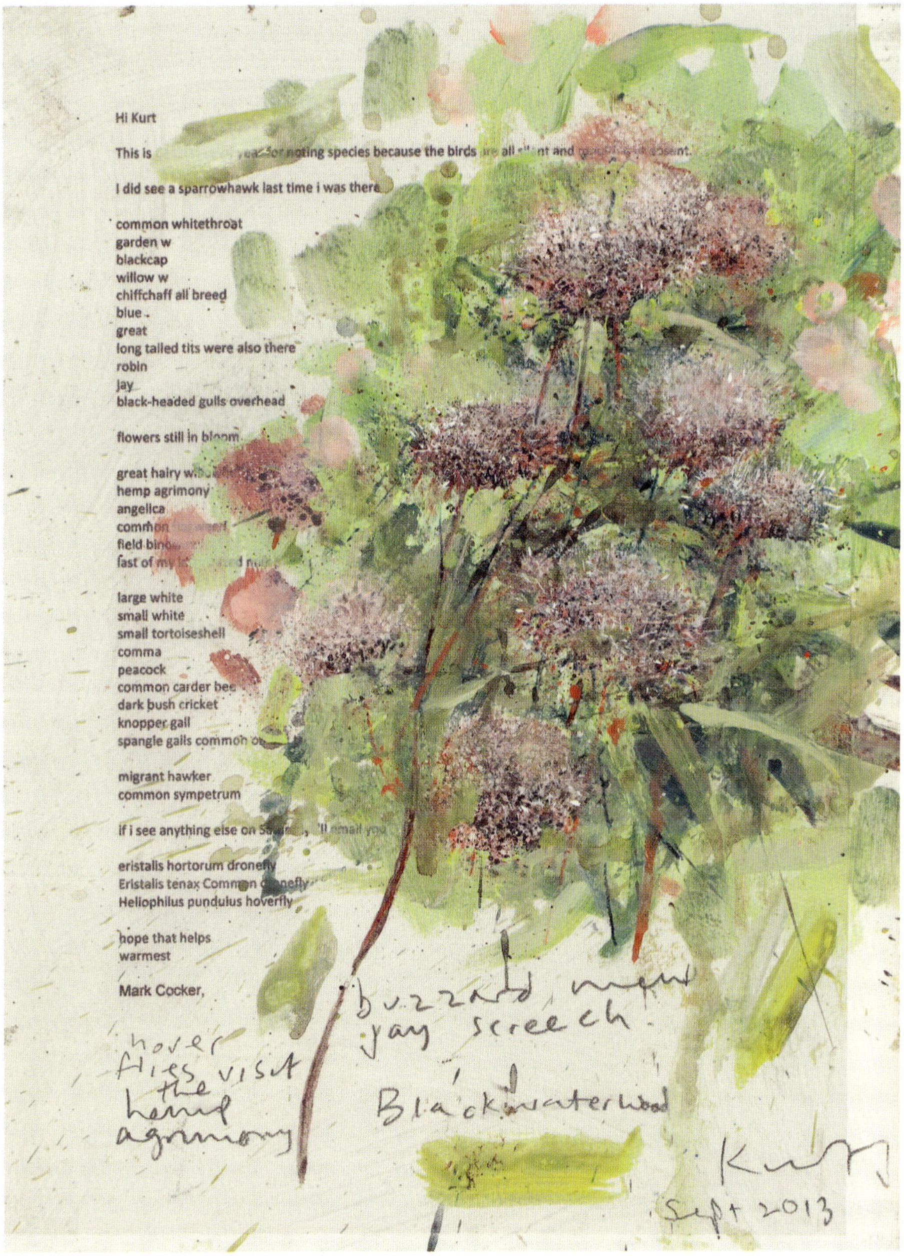

15. **Hoverflies visit the hemp agrimony. Blackwater Wood**
September 2013 • mixed media and collage on board • 31 x 23 cm

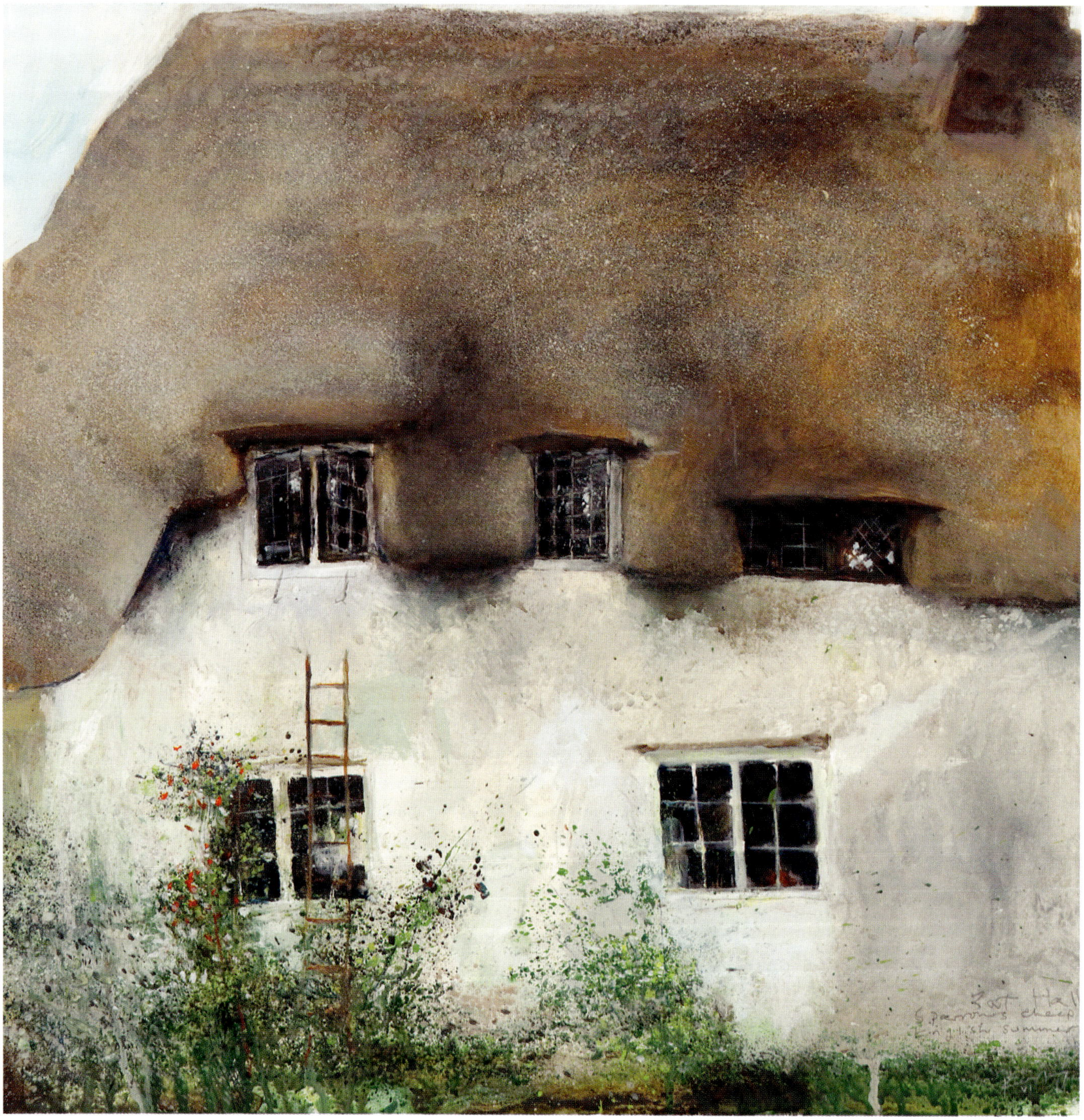

16. **Bat Hall. Sparrows cheep on a very English summer's day**
June 2013 • mixed media on board • 54 x 54 cm

6. Bat Hall, Dorset

Ian Collins

I met the painter John Craxton early in 2000, at the London wake for Prunella Clough. For me it was love at first sight, though I had loved his work since spying it by chance when a teenager, studying the wrong subject in the wrong place and waiting for my rightful life to begin. His pictures seemed pointers on a personal path from exile, via a succession of safe houses, to a proper sense of home.

Our near-ten-year friendship lasted until his death and propelled me on an ongoing journey – starting on that first intoxicating day when we ended in the French Pub in Soho, where my companion had first drunk as a youthful prodigy, aged 18, in 1941, in the wild company of the Two Roberts, Colquhoun and MacBryde. It would take me to Wales, the Scilly Isles and Paris – stepping stones to the liberated life in the south Craxton had sought from the outset before being trapped by war. Ultimately it would lead me to Crete, which he had discovered in 1947 and made his home from 1960.

And, very memorably, the Craxton trail also took me to Dorset where an artistic boy somewhat at odds with a large musical family in London, and escaping from a succession of bad boarding schools, had found an early refuge in an ancient cottage owned by an aunt and uncle, both of them painters. Many old walls have absorbed something of the spirit of former occupants, but here the sense of ongoing habitation is dramatic. So little has changed down the decades – or the centuries. When sets were sought for the 1986 film *Comrades*, retelling the saga of the Tolpuddle Martyrs, this was deemed to be the perfect location. It needed no period dressing.

Dorset is a place apart – you feel it at once driving over the border from Wiltshire or Hampshire. And this tract of a hamlet near Farnham remains caught in a time warp if not a spell of enchantment. Backing on to stream and lane, Bat Hall is one of a pair of cob and thatch cottages in a merged garden rampaging into a nature reserve. Once rather commonplace, this simple but noble building is now so very precious for having been spared the curse of ruination by modernisation.

Romance also rests on an element of retained mystery, and here lies a legend of a dwelling arising for a monk or two around the time of the dissolution of the monasteries. Almost certainly the mullion-windowed structure is pre-Elizabethan Tudor. And Christian and pagan rites mingle here. That space behind the fireplace might have become a priest's hole. An indelible stain on plaster is a grave marker for a walled-up dog or sheep. Recent rethatching revealed the carefully placed forelegs of a deer. John Craxton's sheep-farmer cousin keeps the place alive in the old way, but now as a wildlife refuge. Bats are indeed welcome. Hedgehogs and refugee chickens winter in the porch. Rescue cats sleep cushioned on deep windowsills amid a filigree of geraniums and a wood fire crackles through chill months until the return of the nightingale.

Ian Collins *is a writer and curator whose books include the best-selling monograph on John Craxton. He is curating a Craxton retrospective exhibition at the Dorset County Museum in Dorchester in the spring and summer of 2015.*

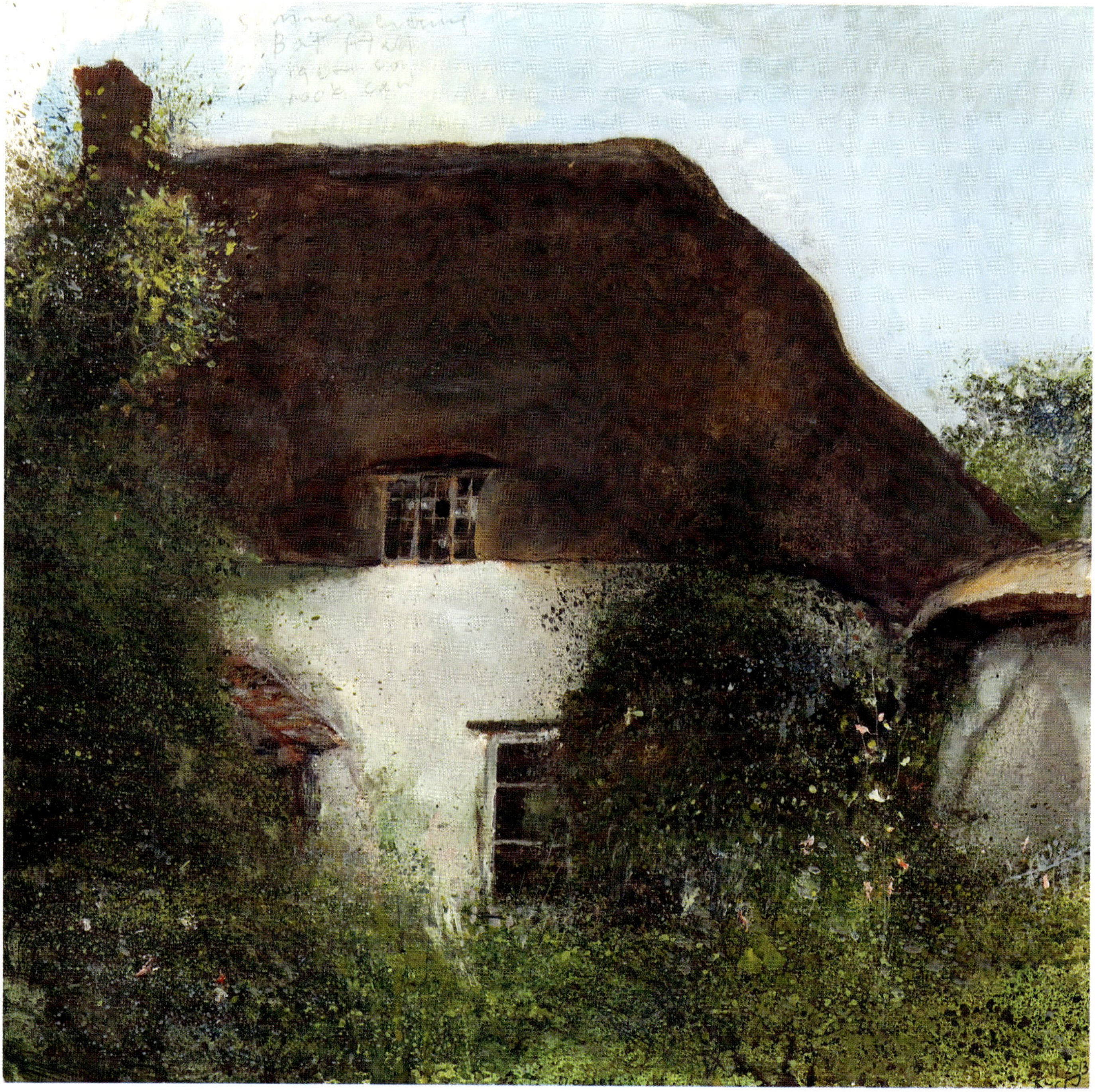

17. **Summer's evening, Bat Hall, pigeon coo, rook caw**
June 2013 • mixed media on board • 51 x 53 cm

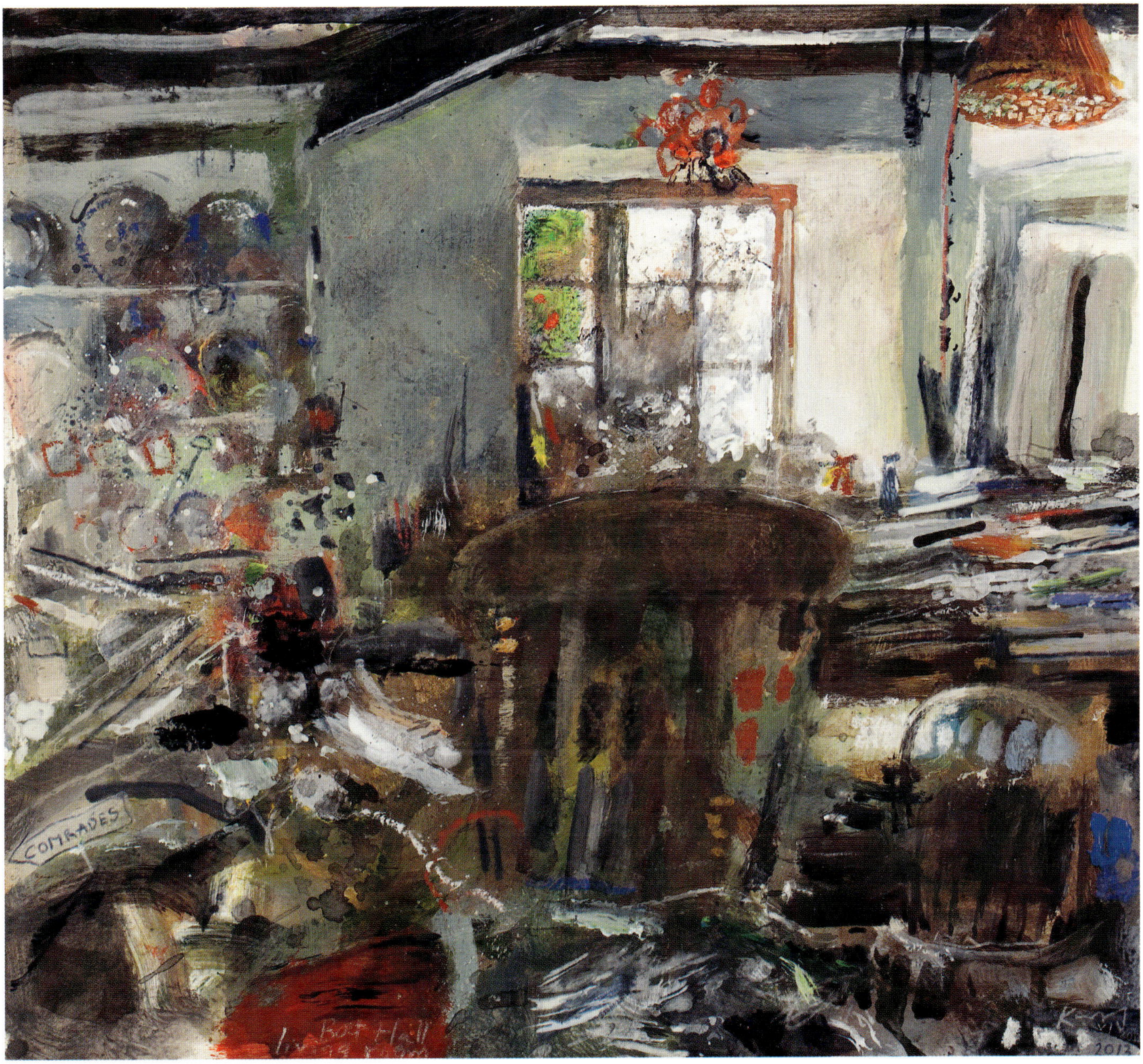

18. **The living room, Bat Hall. Cats and stuff**
June 2013 • mixed media on board • 25 x 28 cm

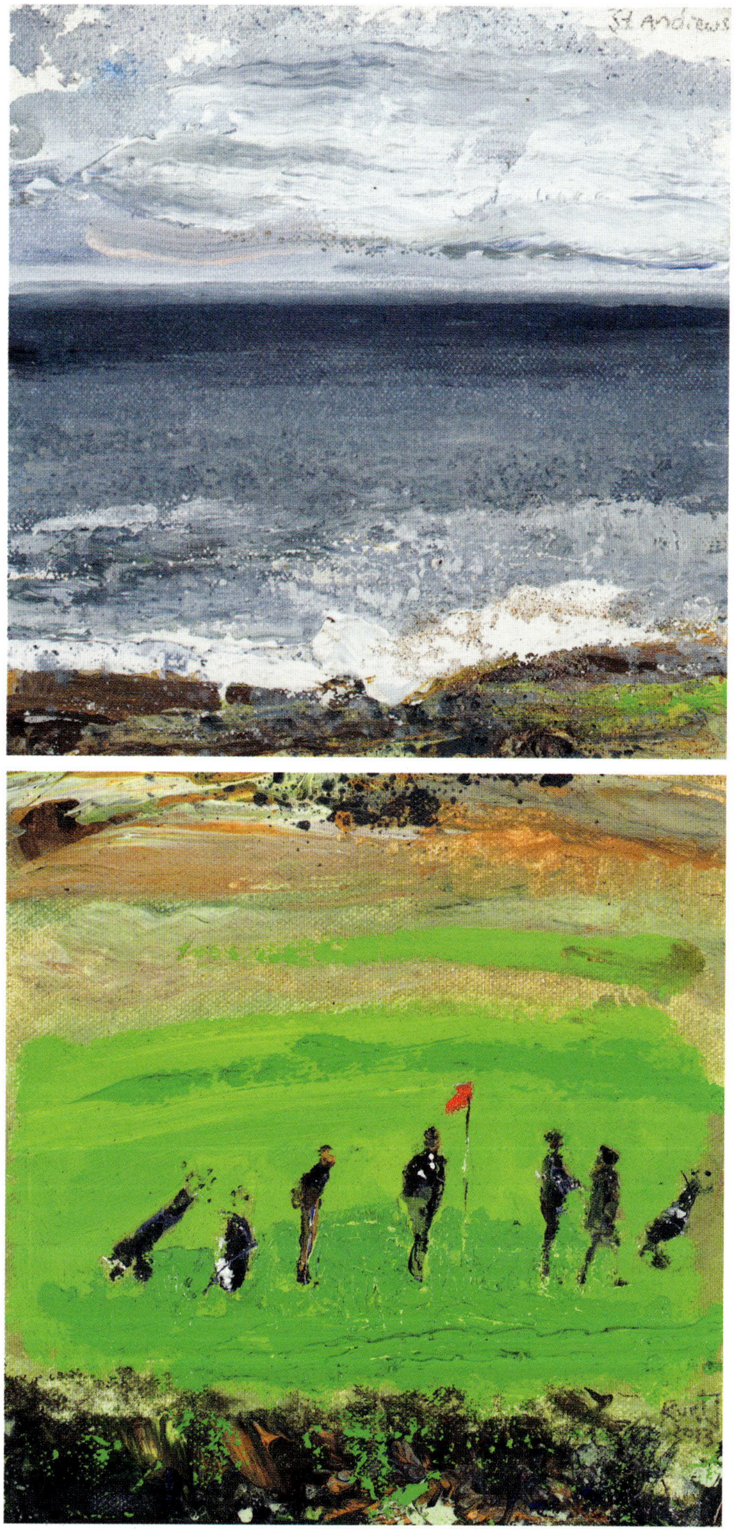

19. **St Andrew's golf diptych**
2013 • oil on canvas • 30 x 15 cm

7. 15th hole, Kingsbarns Golf Links, Fife

Gina Cox

When Kurt asked me to write about my favourite place my thoughts turned to summer: warmth, birds singing, family … but which special place would be my first choice? Sailing up the Dart river, dropping the anchor and having a picnic on board; gathering mussels off the rocks at New Polzeath before cooking them with wine and garlic; walking on Dartmoor or in the Lake District with an inviting pub beckoning at the end of a long day? I soon realised that choosing my favourite place would be more complicated than my first thoughts suggested. So I decided to coalesce all my favourites into one.

Walking makes me happy, playing golf stimulates me and St Andrews in the Kingdom of Fife is my favourite town. Here the people are friendly, interested in finding out what I am doing so far from the southwest of England, and the climate is challenging, making me feel alive. St Andrews, the 'Home of Golf' saw in 1457 King James II banning golf by an Act of Parliament because his archers were neglecting archery practice in favour of playing the game. Golf is addictive, and should you have a competitive nature, then it's inevitable that once started striving to lower your handicap will become a matter of honour!

And so we combine these three ingredients and arrive at the 15th hole at Kingsbarns Golf Links Club. The greens are immaculate even in spring when the east wind, frozen in the air, hits the rocks off the bay beside Kingsbarns. The sea is up, crashing against the land, throwing white spray majestically upwards. Puffins fly low just above the water; from their feeding grounds miles out they commute to the Isle of May. The air is filled with sounds of the calls of oystercatchers and redshanks. Walkers and their dogs jog along the nearby beach at low tide defying the weather, and still the greens remain immaculate, untouched by all that nature is throwing in their direction.

The 15th hole is nearest to the sea, a stark contrast between professional taming by man versus havoc whipped up by the Gods. The red flag sometimes gently flutters, while at other times it strains to stay upright. But the 15th hole is calling, challenging – an oasis of tantalising calm against a backdrop of untamed nature.

Gina Cox MA was the curator of fine art at the University of Exeter for 14 years until 2012. Notable exhibitions on campus which Gina has curated include Lucian Freud, Bridget Riley, Wilhelmina Barns-Graham, Terry Frost and Kurt Jackson.

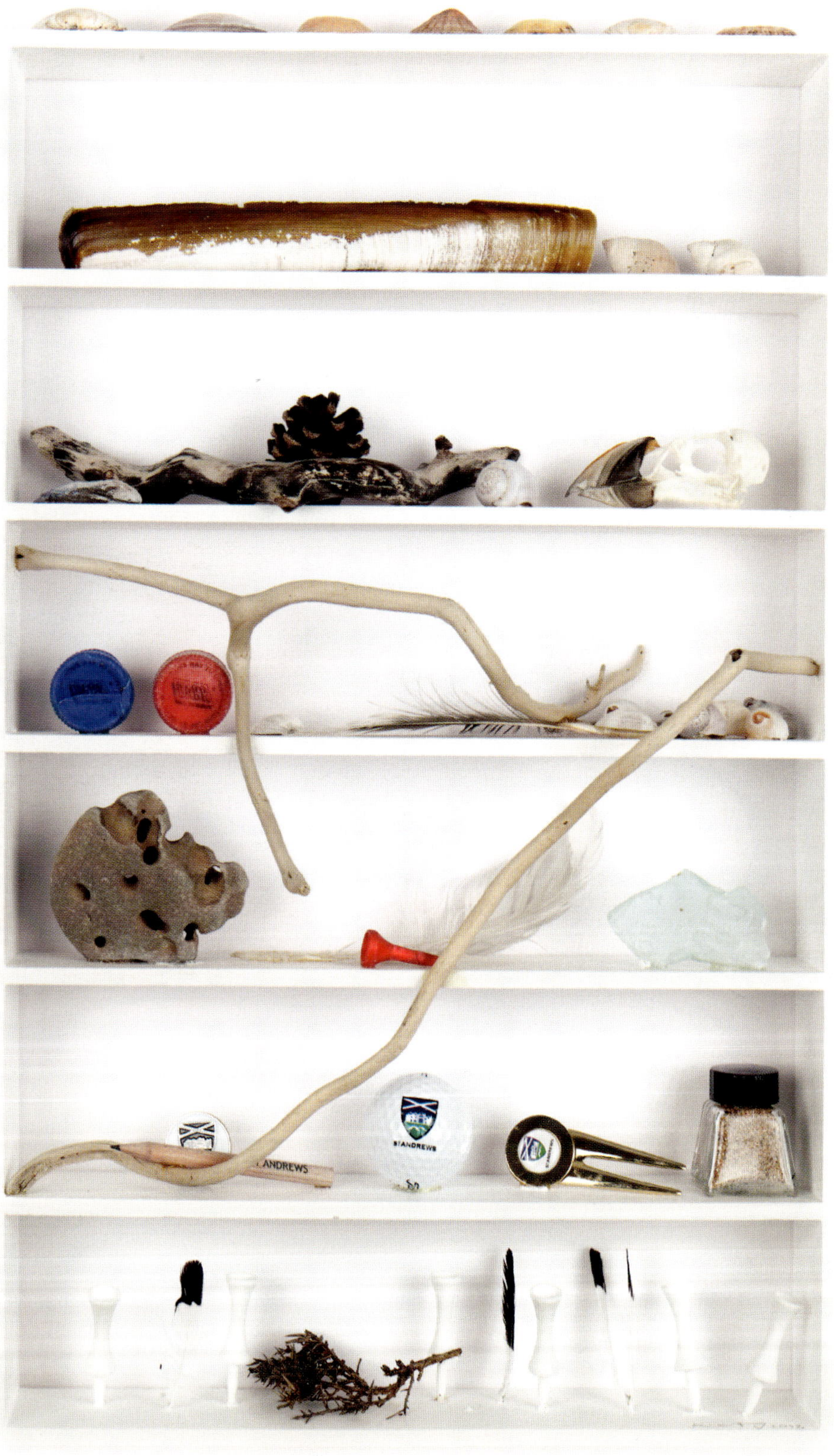

20. **St Andrew's Cabinet**
2013 • found objects construction • 49 x 35 x 7 cm

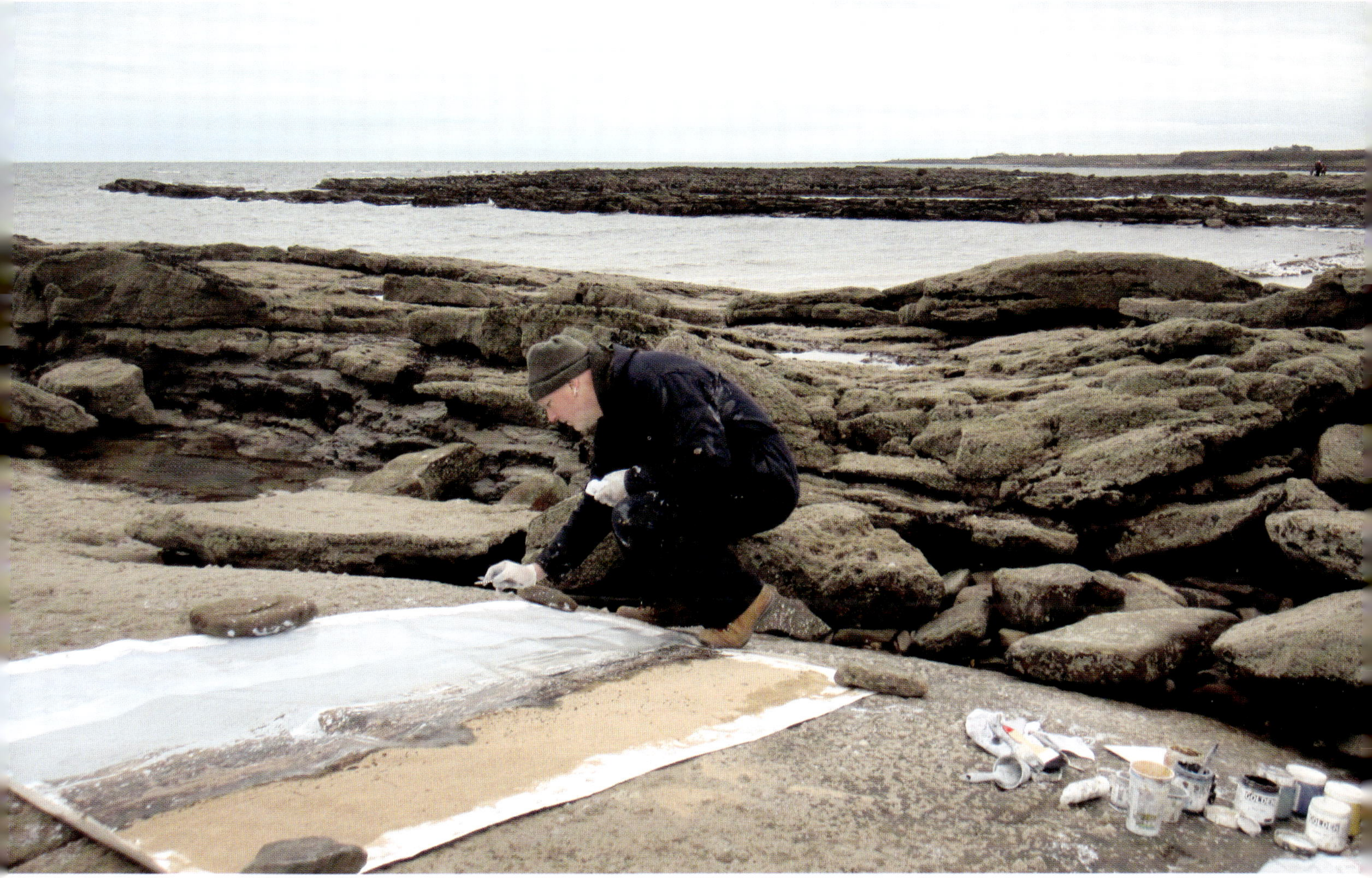

overleaf

21. **Chased by the tide. St Andrews**
2013 • mixed media and sand on linen • 120 x 198 cm

between the golf + the sea

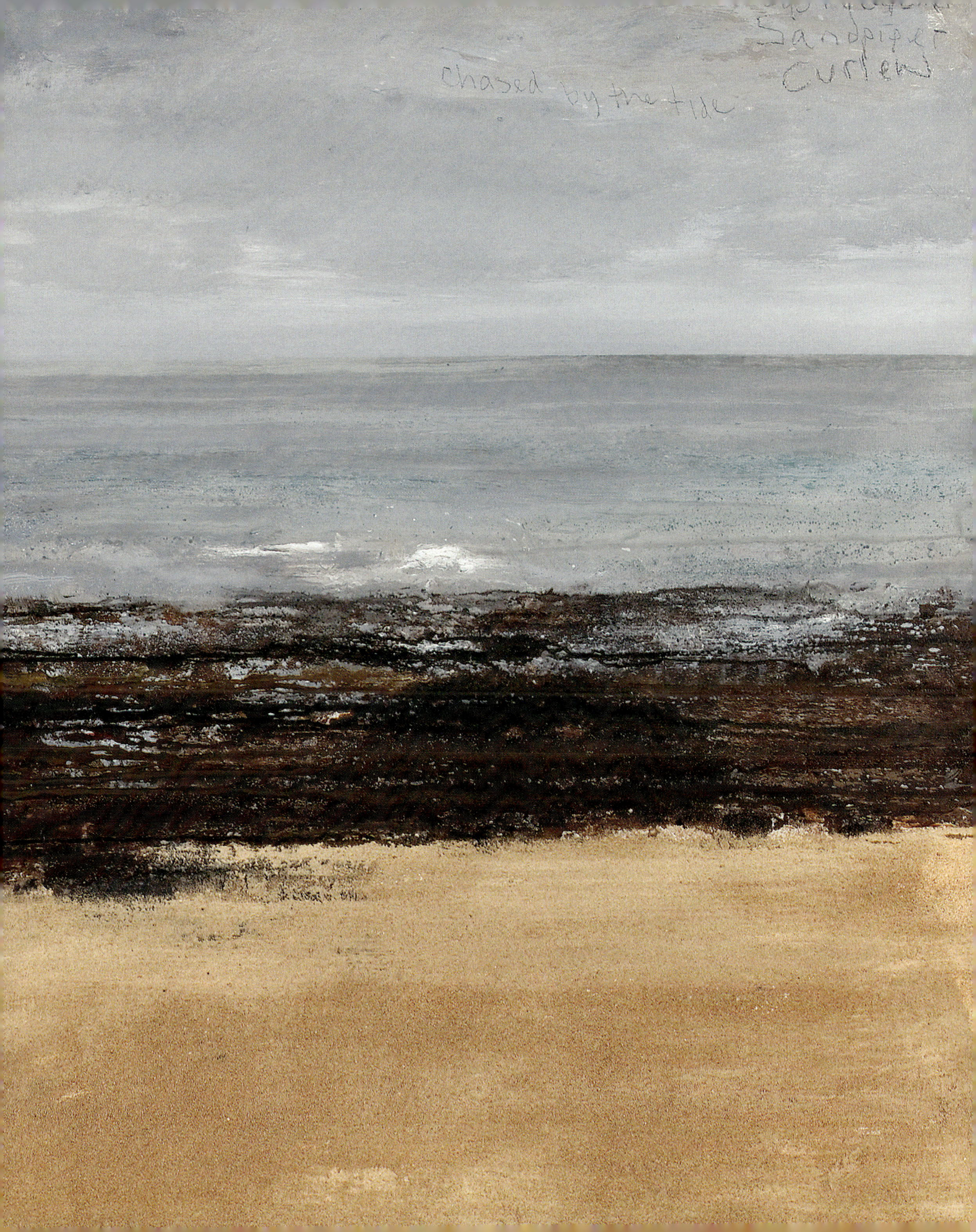
Sandpiper
Curlew
Chased by the tide

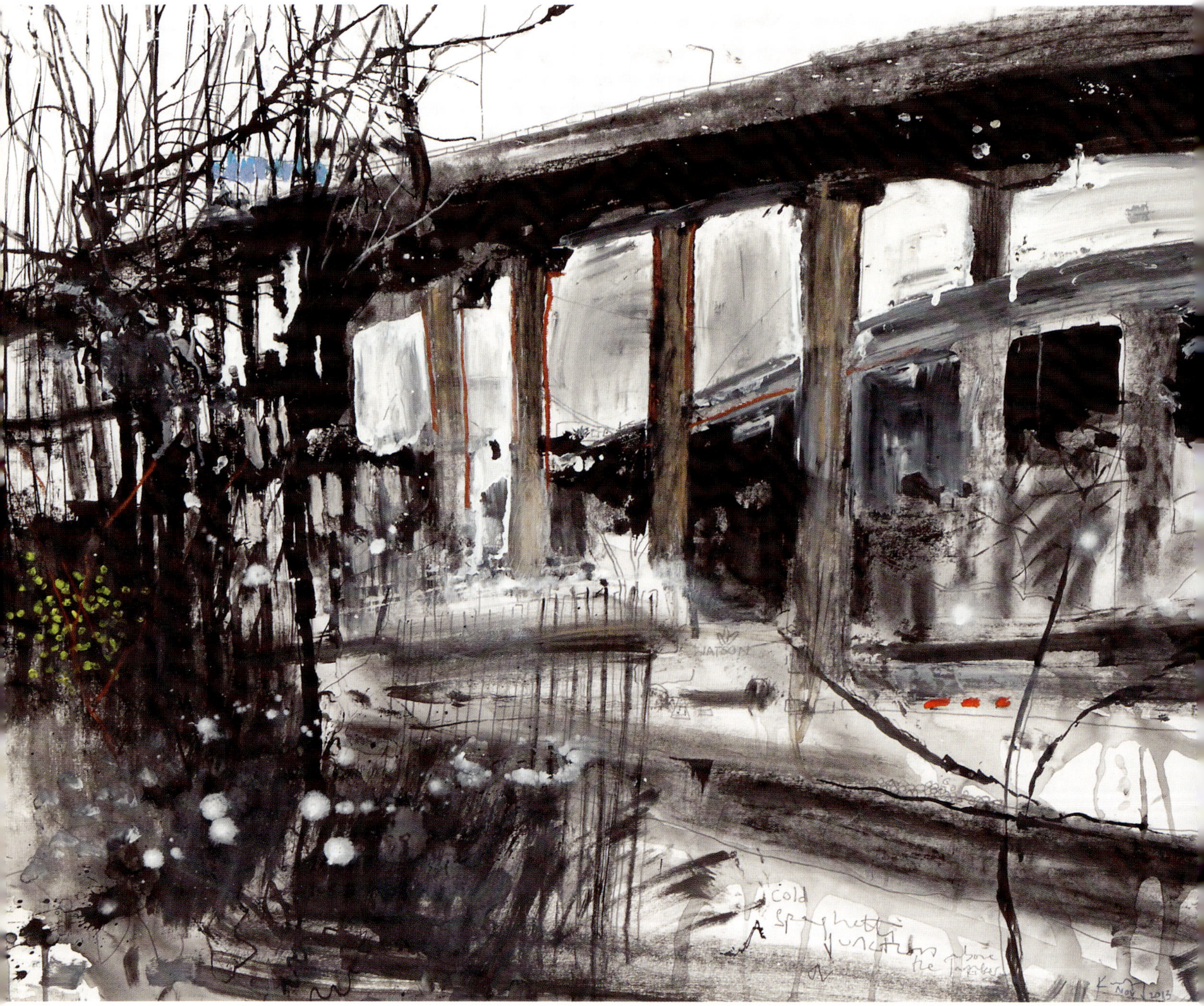

22. **Cold Spaghetti Junction above the Tame River**
November 2013 • ink, charcoal, pastel, pencil on paper • 50 x 65 cm

8. Spaghetti Junction

Jim Crace

No-one dignifies the Gravelly Hill Interchange by using its proper title. It is Spaghetti Junction to the world. Its nickname and its reputation declare it to be an unsightly and perplexing knot of roads which does its damnest to test and bewilder any driver ill-advised enough to leave the M6 motorway at Britain's second city. But this is my home town and I am fond of it – the city and the junction both. We have to make the best of what we have in Birmingham.

Of course, if I plan to linger there, I do not try to reach the Interchange by car. It is a gratifying paradox that driving to the undercarriage of our most notorious traffic system is practically impossible. No, I always am on foot and follow the towpath northwards from the city centre basins along the Birmingham and Fazeley Canal and its rosary of more than 20 locks to the point where the junction's 600 concrete columns come into view and where the boom of traffic on the M6, its summits 80 feet above the ground, is at its most deafening and defeating.

This is not a pretty sight and anyone with any sense would turn tail. Warwickshire, a few miles to the south, has a thousand greater joys than here. But just as the natural world cannot comprise only rainbows, daffodils and nightingales but also asks us to engage with dung and viruses and nettles (I have to tell myself), so it is with city scapes. It is no challenge to enjoy the castellations and the spires of more historic towns but this high and noisy engineering feat, needing to be more functional than elegant, takes effort to admire.

Yet, it is easy from a walking distance to take pleasure in the giddy playfulness of so many vehicles gyrating like over-powered toys on this stack of carriageways. And once the concrete catacombs and vaults directly underneath the pasta of intersecting routes are reached, it is also easy – though a little grandiose – to be reminded of cathedral aisles, the Coliseum and Stonehenge. This is a place of space and columns, after all. Its concrete girders are its sarsen beams. Its shapes and shadows can seem as deep and satisfying as any found in ancient crypts. Of course, it is hard to find a blind eye for the litter and the building debris on the tow path or the scum and dross in the canal, or to ignore the blisters and the lesions on the concrete surfaces (where salt and grit have weakened the joints) and their combative taggings of graffiti. It is not a pleasure to breathe deeply on the dust-laden air. The mighty junction itself does not seem so mighty or so permanent when the spalling flakes of it are gritting up your eyes. This place is brutal and industrial.

And for me there is usually a sense of danger, too, especially when I'm on my own, walking past the signs which tell parents to 'warn their children of the dangers and consequences of playing on this site,' and heading into the loitering darkness of its many tunnels, into the din and clutter. I am fearing everything from minotaurs to muggers. The traffic up above is so thunderous that nobody will hear my screams.

Yet here's the point where, despite the evidence of sight and sound, walkers should hold their nerve. After all, the noise is no greater than a storm or weir. The place has a second proper title other than the Gravelly Hill Interchange, remember. This is the ancient Valley of the Tame. There's been running water here for many thousands of years and no amount of traffic can put a stop to that or entirely drown out the cheerful rilling of the main river where it meets up with the puny Rea. On a higher level, 15 feet or so above the Tame, three canals connect and narrow boats, limited to a stately 5 mph, can find open routes to anywhere from Cumbria to Kent. A further level is for trains between Staffordshire and Birmingham. And high above the less than stately M6 motorway, where there is either gridlock or a hurtling rush, passenger jets are stooping on their flight paths and closing in on BHX. The history of human transportation is here displayed in tiers.

It is at foot level, though, where the satisfactions multiply and flourish. The junction is as deeply wooded as any suburban park with vigorous stands of cherry, ash, elder, silver birch and goat willow. This is not a birder's paradise, despite (today) a pair of wagtails, a single grebe and some goldfinches but, fittingly, there are determined populations here of Canada geese, magpies, gulls, and coots, nature's indiscriminating and ruthless survivors, its ruffians and rogues. And the foliage on the banks and berms includes as rich a mix of wayside plants as you would find in any Midland lane; there are the usual charlocks, willow herbs and cow parsley but feral plants as well, domestic escapees such as columbine, honesty and brick-loving buddleia – plus a haze of lupins which in June produce a blue display fit for any garden show.

I find myself mischievously pleased to discover flourishing patches of that outlaw immigrant from Japan, the knotweed, renowned for its muscle and destructiveness. It can crack and splinter concrete and it will, I'm sure, given time and opportunity (for nature always has the final say, left to its own devices) begin to tear apart The Gravelly Hill Interchange and return it to The Valley of the Tame. I am not sure if that's a happy prospect, but I am certain that once in a while the tussle here between the natural and the built is pleasing to witness and to wonder at. Yes, this is more a thought-provoking spot than one of beauty, but coming here is always worth the walk, and worth the risk, and worth the challenges it makes. Such are the unexpected solaces of forbidding and unsightly places.

__Jim Crace__ is the multi prize-winning author of eleven novels including 'Quarantine' and 'Harvest', both short-listed for the Man Booker Prize, and 'Being Dead', winner of the Book Critics Circle Award. He has lived close to Birmingham for more than 40 years.

23. **Under Spaghetti Junction**
autumn 2013 • acrylic on board • 21 x 22 cm

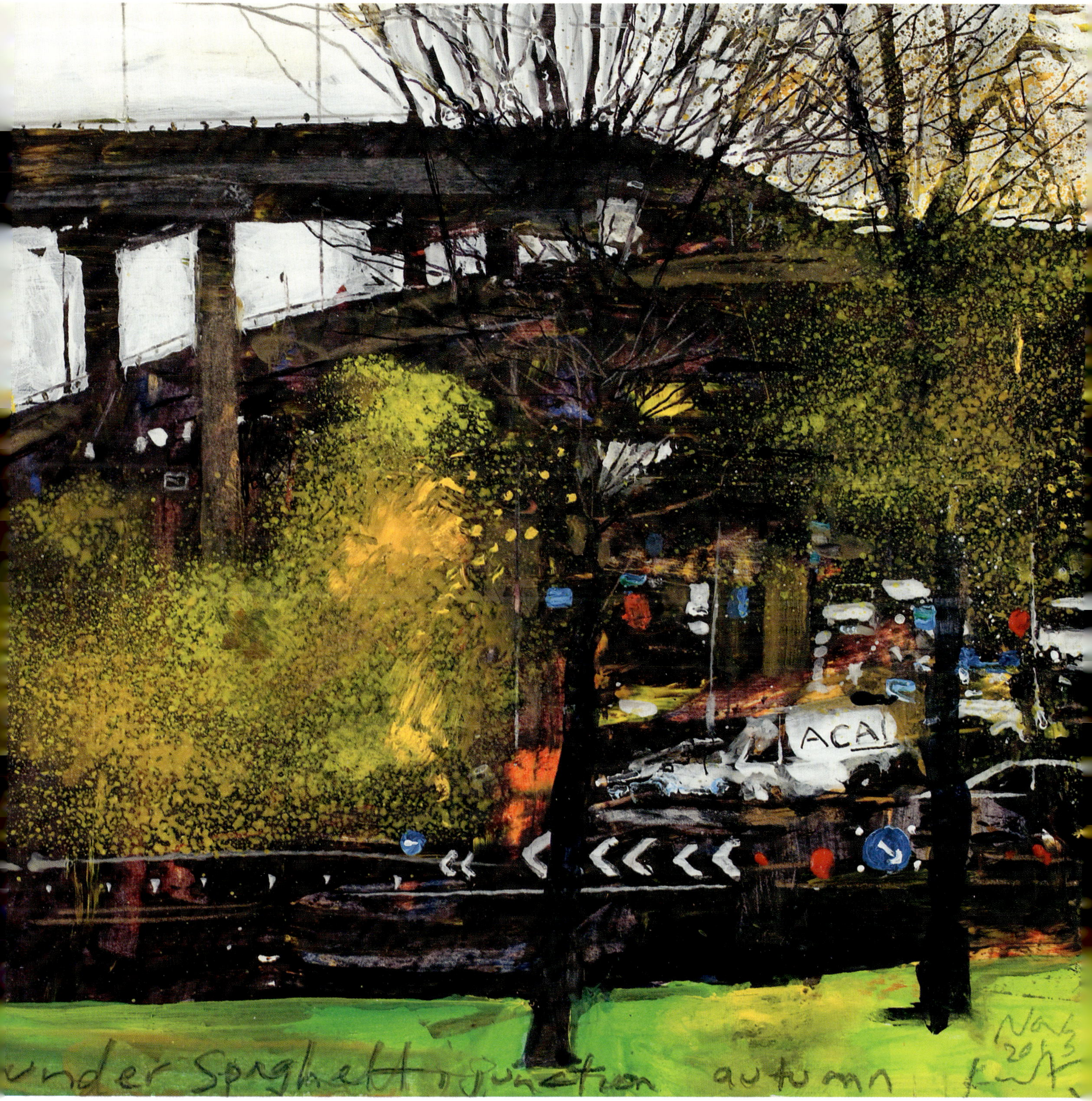
ACAI
under Spaghetti junction autumn

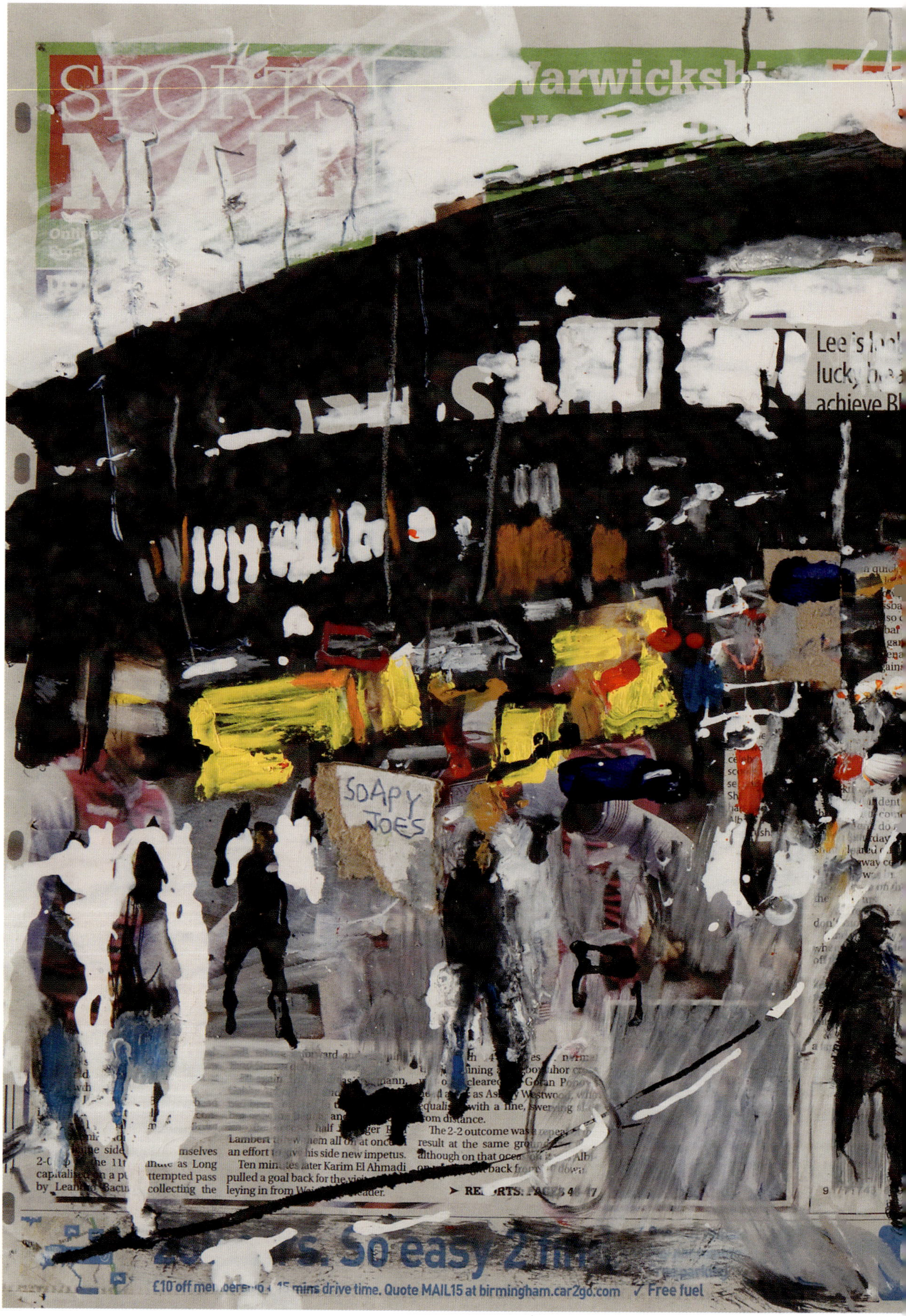

24. **Busy Spaghetti Junction**
November 2013
mixed media and collage
on board • 36 x 59 cm

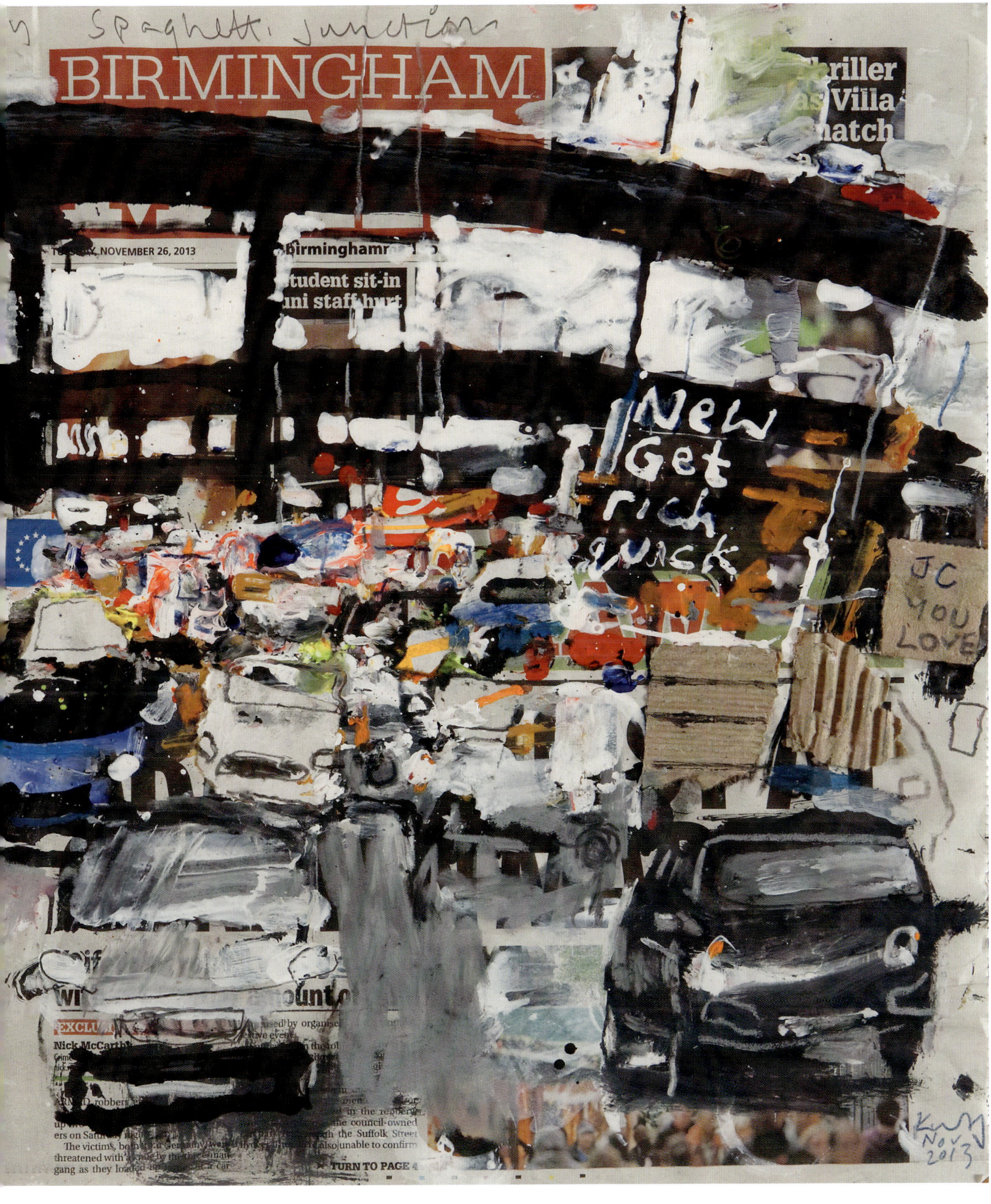
Spaghetti Junction
BIRMINGHAM
NOVEMBER 26, 2013
New
Get
rich
quick
JC
YOU
LOVE
TURN TO PAGE 4
Nov
2013

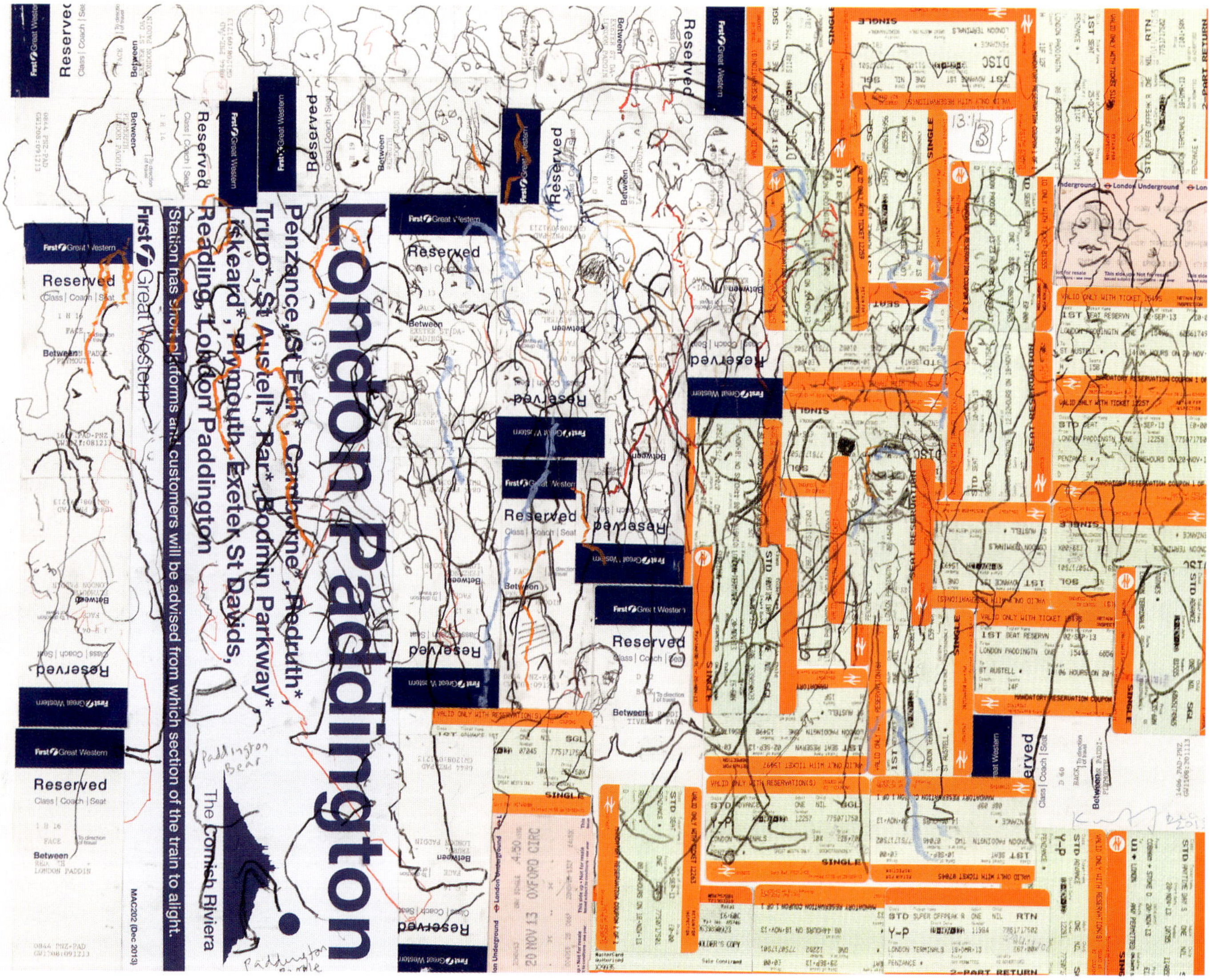

25. **Paddington people**
December 2013 • crayon, pencil and collage on paper • 50 x 65 cm

9. Paddington Station

Helen Dunmore

Halfway down platform one on Paddington Station, the bronze soldier reads his letter from home. His scarf is tied loosely around his neck. His tin hat is slightly askew. His unbuttoned greatcoat is thrown around his shoulders like a cape.

Light from the vaulted glass roof gleams on helmet, nose, cheekbones and the knuckles of the hands that hold the letter. His face is utterly absorbed. He doesn't hear the engines, or the echo of announcements around the station's interior. Millions of footsteps have gone past him since this memorial was dedicated in 1922, and he has cared for none of them. He is so intent that the station appears like a dream beside him. Inside the plinth on which he stands there is a casket, and in that casket there is a vellum roll bearing the names of the war dead who were employed by the Great Western Railway.

The soldier stands, while the station moves around him. Skirts shorten; hats are taken off; porters disappear. There are no more ladies' compartments or non-smokers' compartments. Steam gives way to diesel, and the 'lawn' becomes a concourse full of shops, cafés and fast-food outlets. If you could map the swirl of passengers, perhaps not so much has changed. The same crowds pour off the incoming trains. These meetings and partings, these kisses, these toddlers lifted onto shoulders, these sunbursts of recognition: all these outposts of private worlds in the most public of spaces belong to any time and none.

Streams of light pour down just as they did in Bert Hardy's 1942 photograph of a young woman at Paddington turning away in tears from a departing train. There are no more suitcases of stitched leather and canvas, or tin trunks waiting for a porter's trolleys, but the same holiday hopes are packed into expandable roller-cases.

Your Station Back Home, said the old HTV advertisement over the platform exits, promising that after every sojourn in crammed, elbows-out London we'd be allowed the journey westward again. The air would taste of green fields, and later of salt. The landscape would grow wilder and the people fewer. But Paddington also promises that its dazzlingly engineered spans and arches will echo all the way down to Penzance, with God's Wonderful Railway connecting the West to the wealth of the metropolis.

The connection still holds. A writer friend finds himself at a London meeting with sand from Porthmeor beach in his trouser pocket. The world of publishers and agents, national writers' societies, libraries and archives is overwhelmingly concentrated in London, and so we come and go for meetings, research sessions, lunches, launches. But always, at the back of the mind, there's the thought of the journey home. The skedaddle from the Tube and the race to the platform. After Reading, the packed carriages ease a little. The train picks up speed, racketing through the night. And at Paddington, rapt in his dream of home, the bronze soldier stands.

Helen Dunmore *is a poet, novelist, short-story and children's writer, whose work is translated into more than 30 languages. She was the inaugural winner of the Orange Prize for Fiction, and is a Fellow of the Royal Society of Literature.*

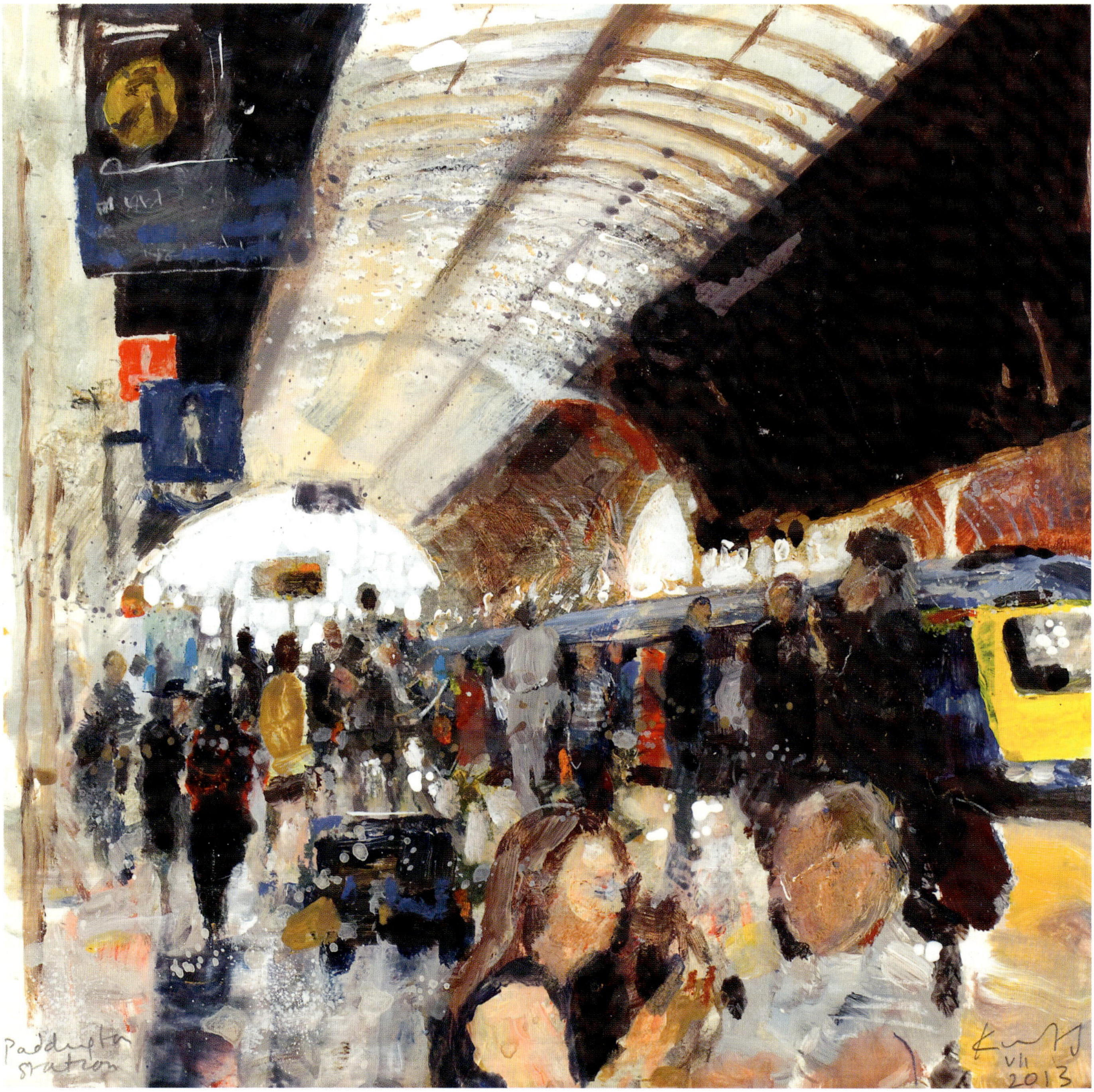

26. **Paddington Station**
July 2013 • mixed media on board • 23 x 23.5 cm

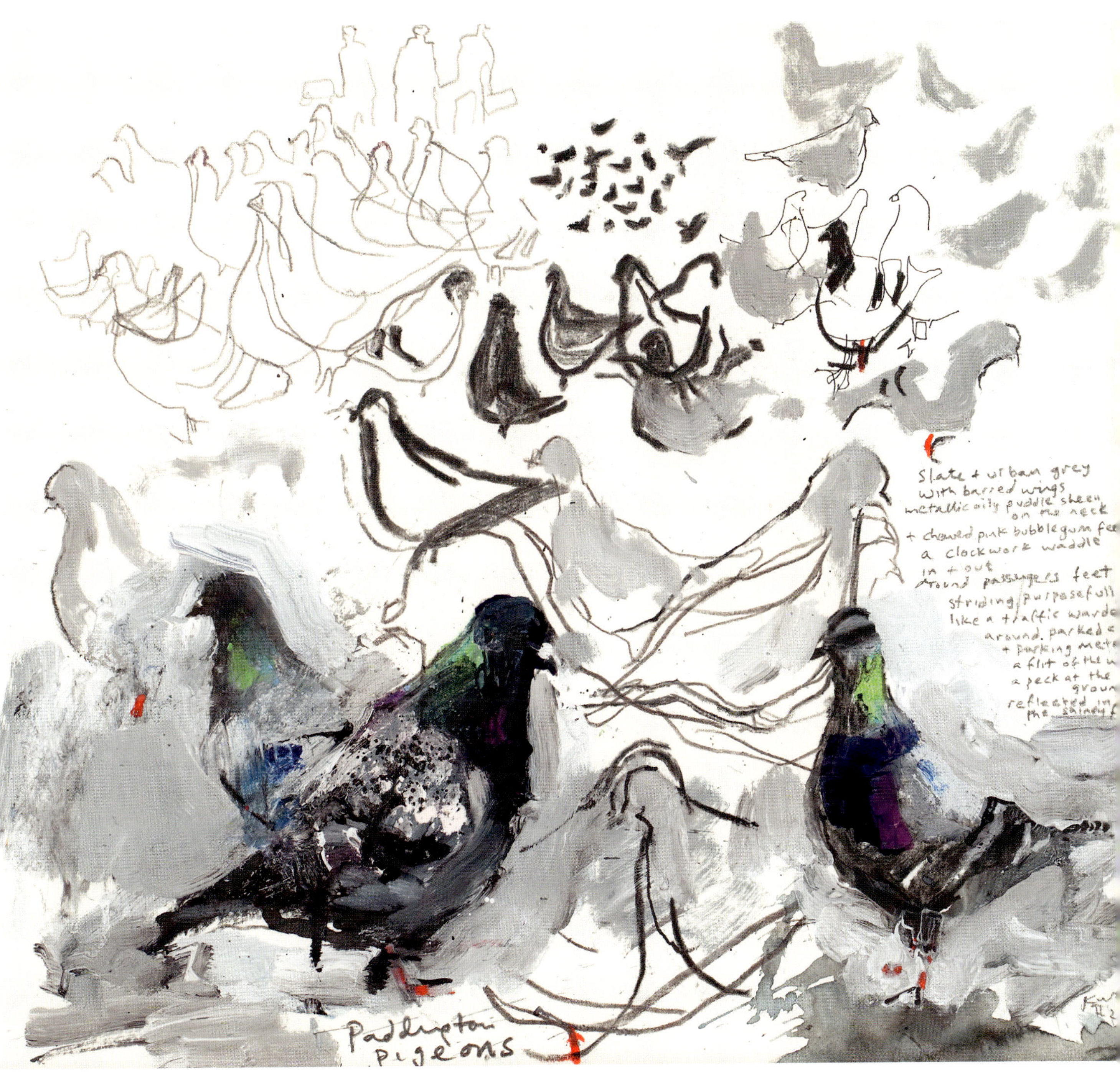

27. **Paddington pigeons**
February 2013 • mixed media on board • 32 x 35 cm

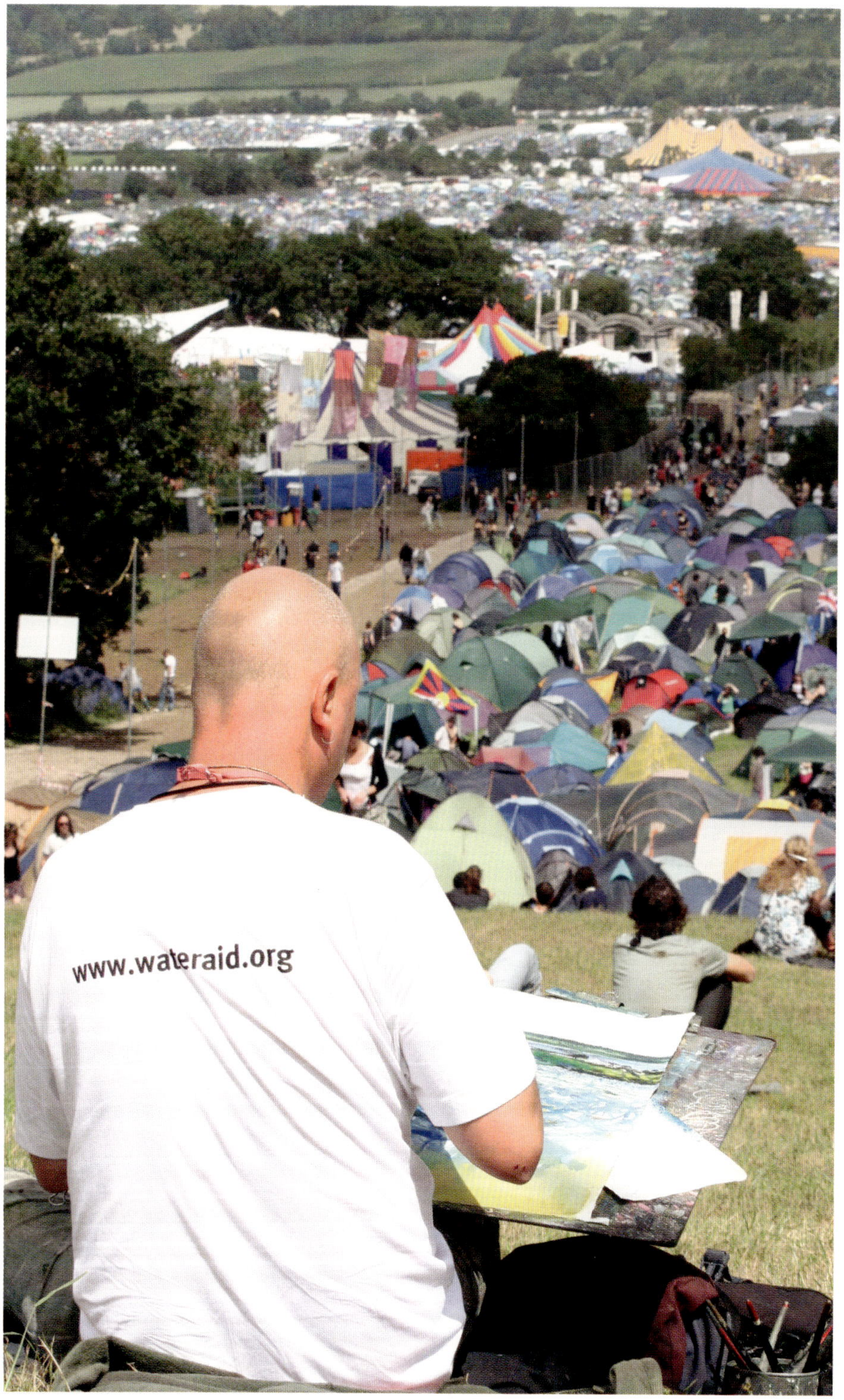
www.wateraid.org

10. Worthy View, Worthy Farm, Somerset

Michael Eavis in conversation with Kurt Jackson

[KJ] ***Where is the place you are suggesting I paint?***
[ME] The thing is I need the perfect view, very high on the hill overlooking the whole farm, the whole of Avalon, the whole valley. It will be a fantastic place to paint from.

When we were kids we used to run up on the hill, chasing the foxes and doing everything we shouldn't have been doing, you know, we used to build camps up in the woods, rival camps with the next door neighbours in which we used to fight them off, with medieval gadgets and that sort of thing. I'm not really that old, but we used to pretend to be Julius Caesar and they were the rubbishy gangs in the village next door.

So we used to play up there a lot when we were kids.

Was the land farmed back then?
It was farmed forever really, but it isn't really the best quality land up there, as it is so steep. The cows graze in the meadows at the bottom of the hill; the lower land where there is more fertile grass. The land is plush further down, which is where the festival is held.

We have taken all the grass off by that time – made it into silage or hay and the cows would have grazed in the spring, so when that is finished with then the festival comes on and 200,000 people squat or run or hop, skip and jump or whatever they do here.

So that has become the tradition for the 43 years that we have been running the show for. It is a long time, isn't it?

My family have been farming here for 150 years or so with cows. My great-grandfather came here from Dorset with a herd of cows, travelling with the cows, which he had to milk and sell the milk on the way. We have been here ever since.

And has the chosen viewpoint always been in your family's farm?
The hillside actually belongs to Somerset Nature, they actually own the woodland here and they are very good to us, it is for us to use and we have used it for years.

So you are calling it Worthy View?
Yes, as Worthy Farm is the land below, Worthy View is just what I call this particular place.

But everyone calls it that now?
Yes I christened it; that was just my name for it, we use that name now as we have a campsite up there on the farm we rent from our neighbours during the festival, although it is a steep climb up there.

You have put a new road up through there this year?
Yes, a new road and 39 brilliant steps. My pride and joy this year, I oversaw it and it worked really well, no broken legs and always nice and busy and very good exercise.

So 8000 people stayed on top of the hill in all our coloured tents, that are made in England by the way, in Bradford in British factories with the best tented material from Holland, which won't rot and can breath and of course can be reused again. We chose a number of colours so that people can find where they were staying, so I have ordered another 1000 tents now.

Did people spend much time up there?
We had a big café on top of Worthy View, they did really well, people just sat there looking at the view of the festival.

That whole thing was a new situation for the festival, it's always been there for us since we were kids, but that is why I wanted you to paint from that position.

So it is about looking across the whole festival, but also to your farm in the distance?
Yes it is very idyllic, the farm in the distance, the meadows in the bottom – of course the fields don't look so good during the festival with people there, but in the springtime it is really beautiful, absolutely beautiful, sitting up there looking down there, you know. You see the weather; you see the rain, the storms on their way, the thunder and lightning. No, it is a beautiful place to be.

I think Tennyson probably wrote 'Morte d'Arthur' (death of Arthur) from this point –he must have done!

I am going a long way – to the Island valley of Avilion where falls not hail or rain or any snow nor ever wind blows loudly: but it lies deep meadowed, happy fair with orchard lawns and bowery hollows crowned with summer sun.

***Michael Eavis** was born in Pilton, where he still lives, in 1935 the first child of five from a farming family who have been at Worthy Farm for over 100 years. He was weaned in the Methodist non-conformist tradition. This may seem surprising to some, but probably because of this he was always encouraged to question the status quo, and fight for change and justice.*

'I was always crazy on pop music from the Bill Haley/Elvis days, and when smuggling a transistor under my pillow at boarding school was chastised and beaten for listening to the top 20 on Radio Luxemburg late into the night. Funnily enough it didn't put me off music!'

In the late 1960s the new phenomenon of outdoor music festivals began to catch on and after a casual visit to the Bath Blues festival with his girlfriend Jean he was totally caught up with the effect of the flower power craze at that time.

'I kicked off my own show the same year at Worthy Farm, and although stunned and shaken, I wanted to carry on regardless. The rest is history!'

28. **Hot Saturday, midday from Worthy View.**
Birdsong and drifting music and voices through and over the trees
June 2013 • mixed media on paper • 57 x 61 cm

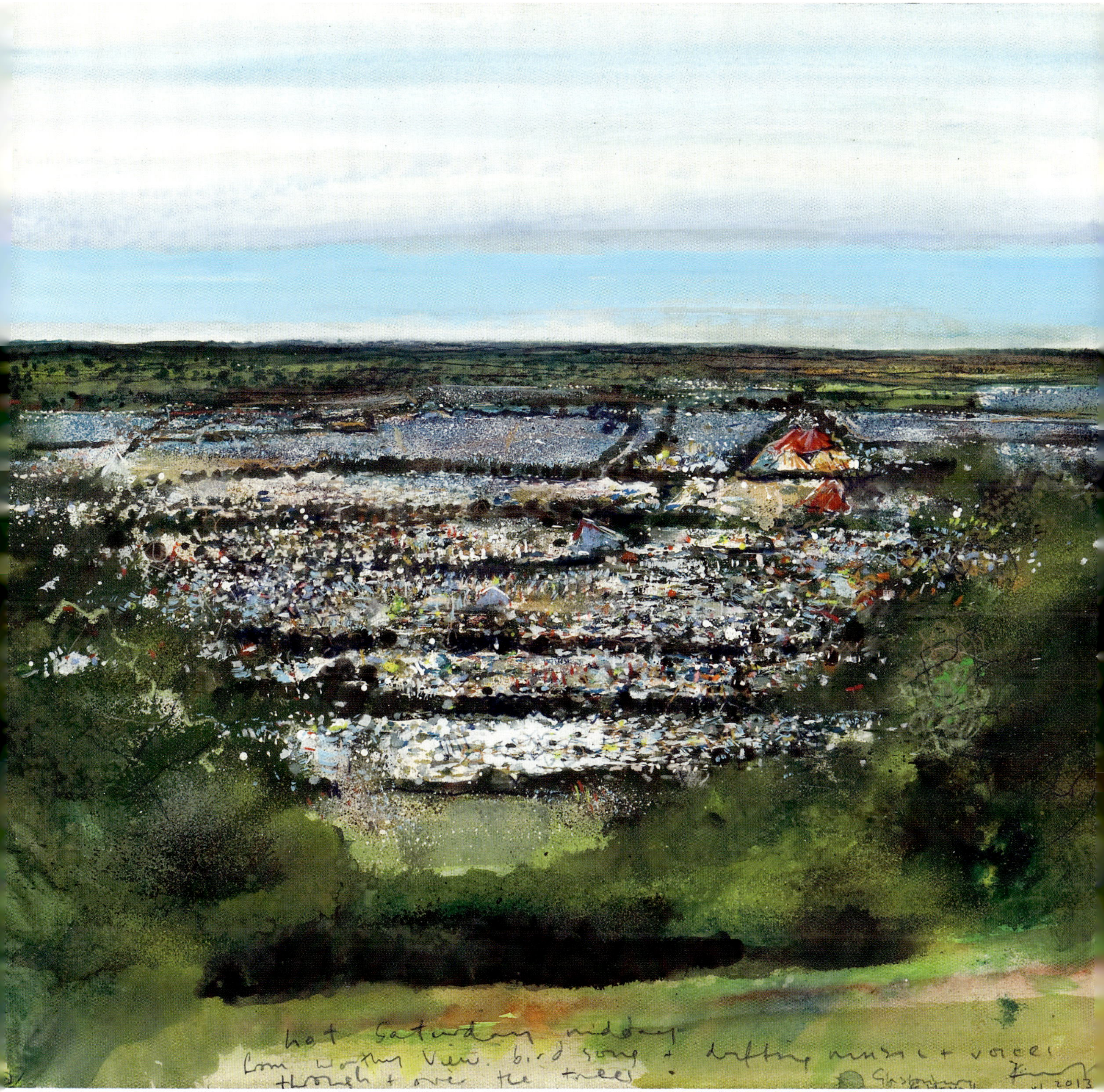
hot Saturday midday
from worthy View. bird song + drifting music + voices
through + over the trees

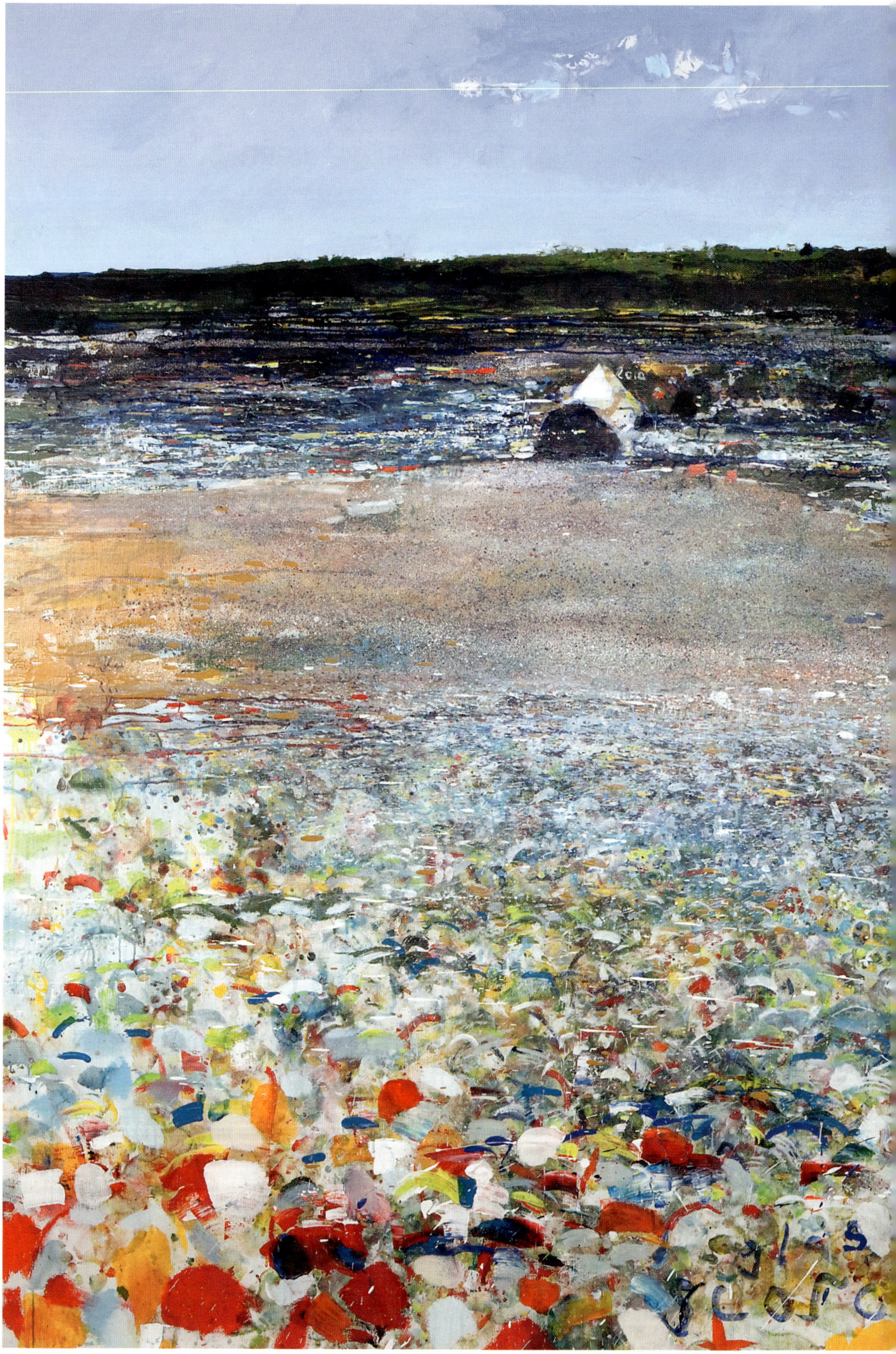

29. **Scorcher, Femi Kuti on the Pyramid stage, Glastonbury**
2010 • mixed media on linen
200 x 320 cm

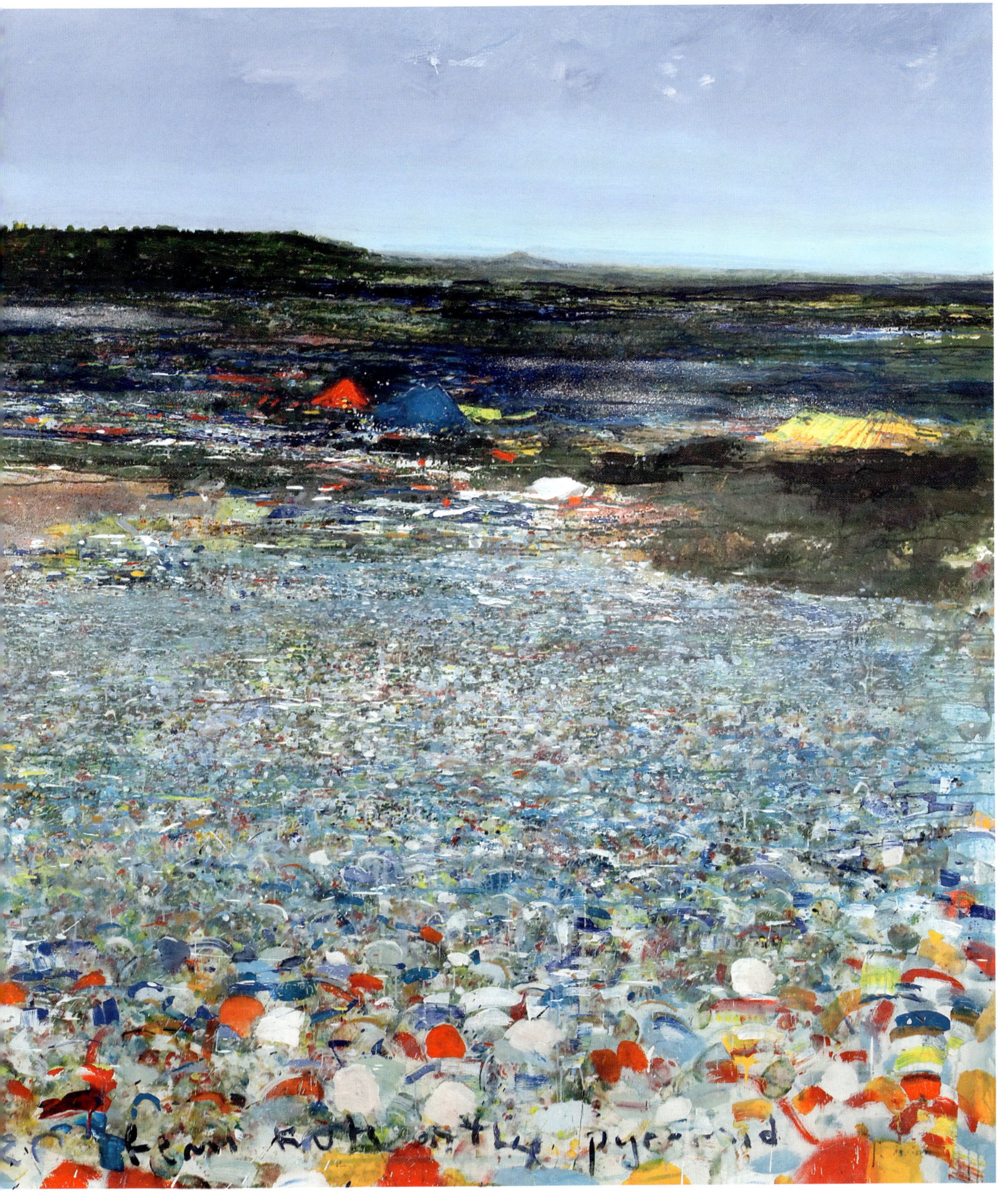

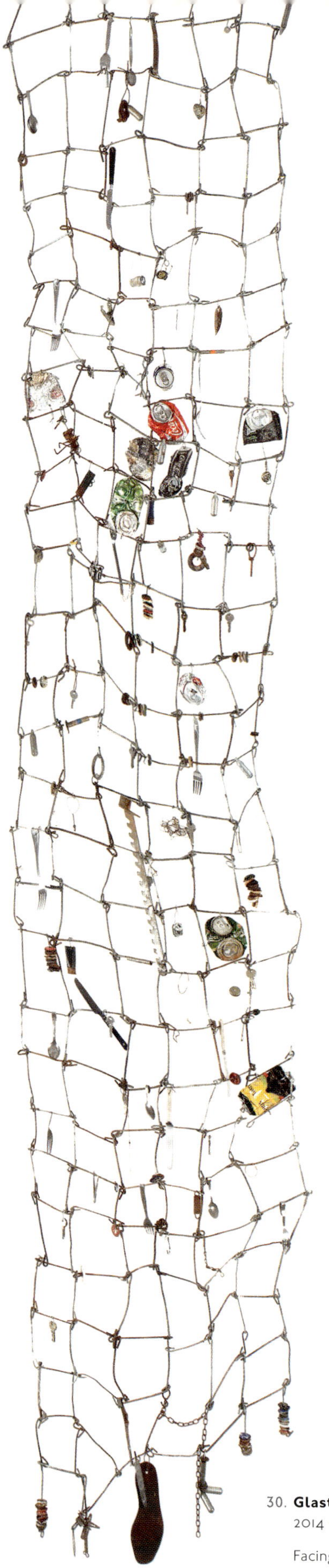

30. **Glastonbury Festival fence**
2014 • reclaimed tent pegs and other metal objects • 400 x 70 cm

Facing page: detail

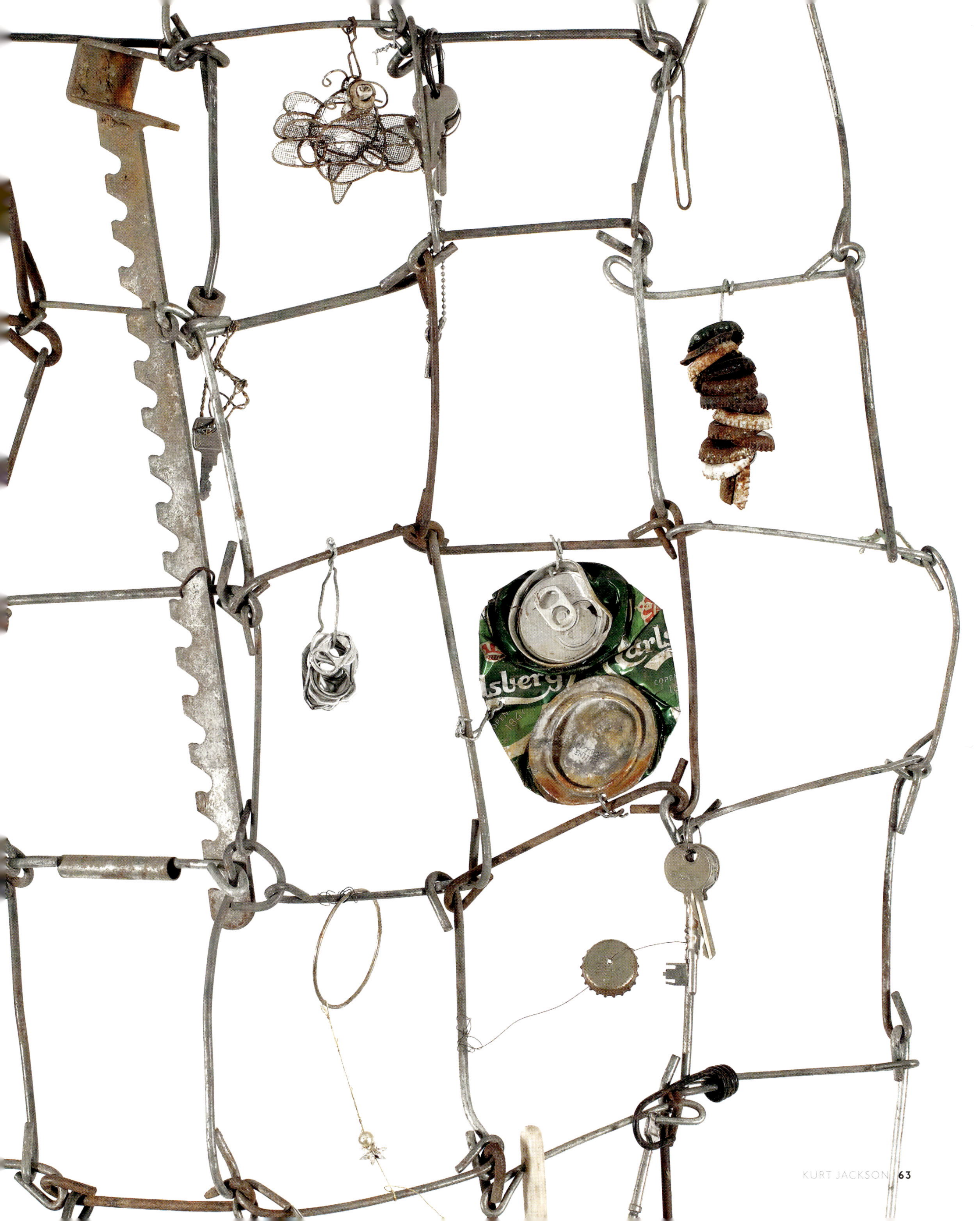

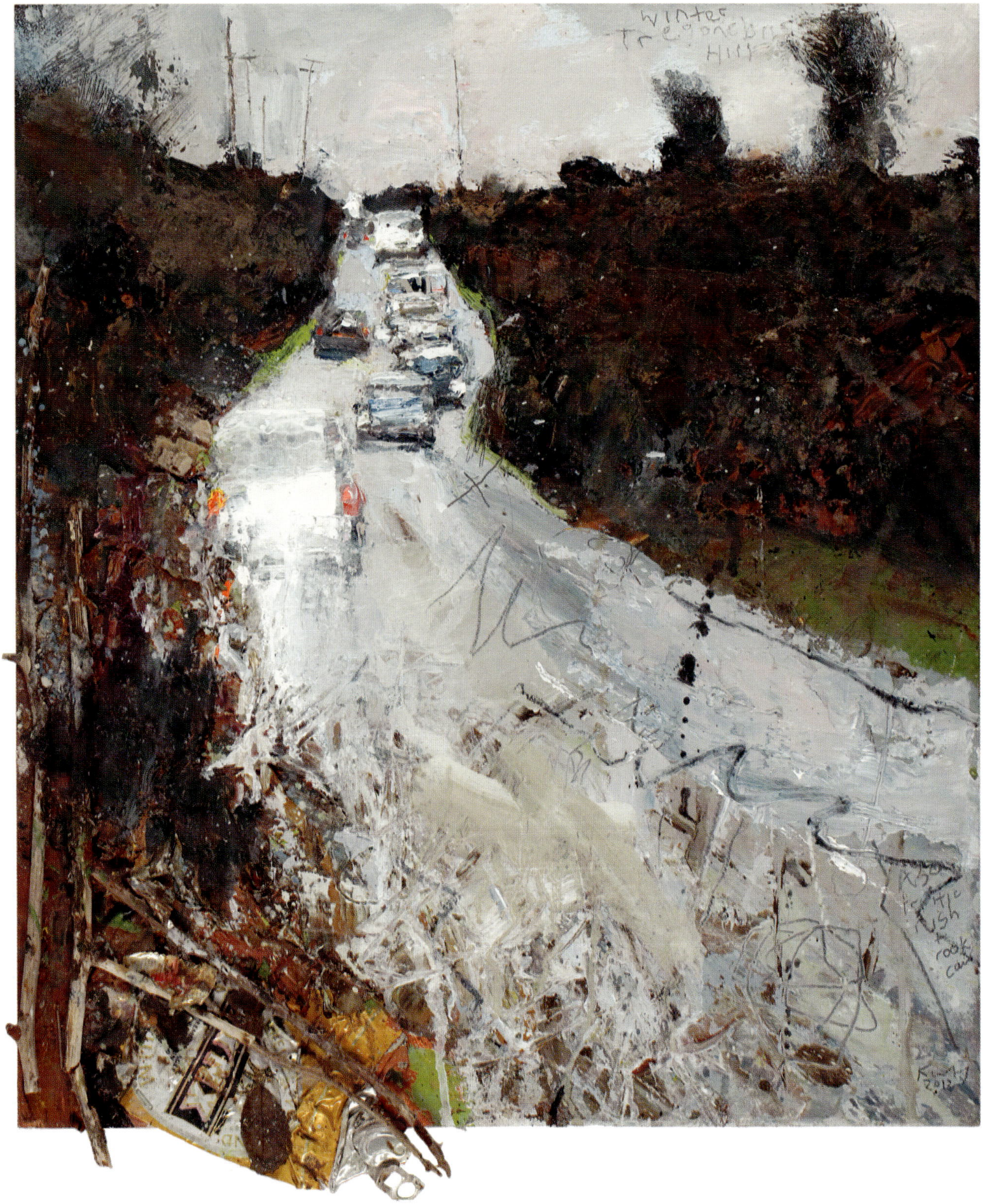

31. **Winter, Tregonebris Hill, A30. Traffic rush and rook caw**
2012 • oil and collage on board • 50 x 44 cm

11. Tregonebris Hill, West Cornwall

Patrick Gale

I'm a firm believer that the subtlest beauties in a landscape are often the man-made ones or the ones where man and nature have interacted.

I've always had a bit of a thing about telegraph poles and wires and having them in a view has never bothered me at all. When I lived in Camelford I had a great maypole of wires directly outside my sitting room window, which my mother always complained about but which gave me endless quiet pleasure.

I think it goes back to boyhood and lying on my temporary bed in the back of our Volkswagen dormobile letting myself be mesmerized by the way the wires seemed to dance up and down to the regular 'beat' of the passing poles as we moved. Holiday weeks spent on the Isle of Wight around the same time woke me up to a tantalizing association between telegraph poles and remote beaches and beauty spots. One of the games my mother invented to keep warfare at bay on long drives was to have us each look for houses we could claim as 'ours'. I wasn't especially bothered by the architecture of my dream house, I realized; what mattered was that it must lie at the end of a lane with grass growing in the middle (to signify minimum traffic) and with its approach marked by a single telegraph line, dipping and rising along a line of weather-beaten poles, to signify few, if any, neighbours.

The other game was to see who on a trip could spot the sea first. Living at the far end of the Cornish sock makes one a creature of habit, deeply familiar with every twist, turn and likely sticking point on the A30. My heart always gives a little, holiday lift at the first glimpse of Mounts Bay from near Crowlas. But it's at this point, on Tregonebris Hill, as the westward A30 climbs steeply up from Catchall, where one is all too often stuck behind a gaggle of labouring end-to-ender cyclists, where I know the first glimpse of proper ocean is near at hand and start to feel that I'm almost home. The pleasing anticipation of home-coming has somehow always blended with my pleasure at the shifting configuration of poles and wires alongside and over the road here.

No passenger to whom I've enthused has ever seen the charms I'm describing, but I don't care: this is a private pleasure!

Patrick Gale *lives near Land's End and has written 14 novels, including 'Notes From an Exhibition', 'Rough Music' and 'A Perfectly Good Man'. He bought his first (tiny!) Kurt Jackson painting shortly after moving to Cornwall in 1988.*

32. **Walking into dusk, Tregonebris Hill, A30. Traffic rush and rook caw**
2012 • oil on canvas • 9 x 7 cm (x 9)

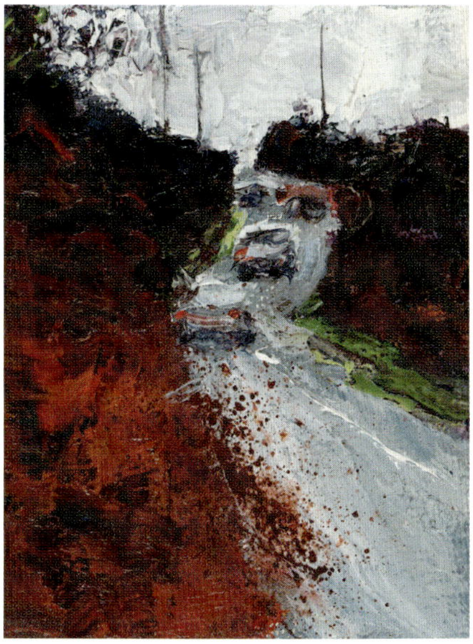
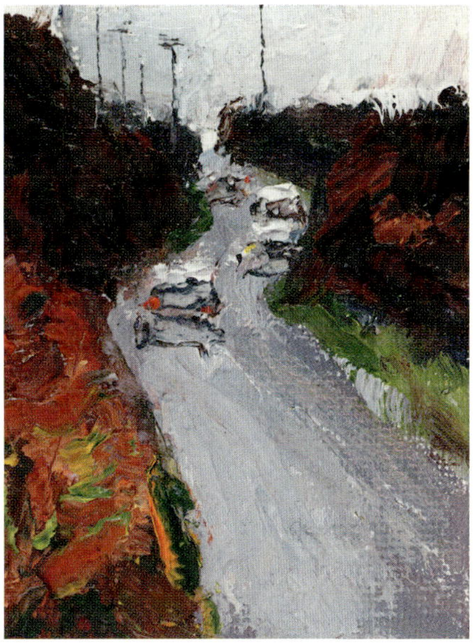
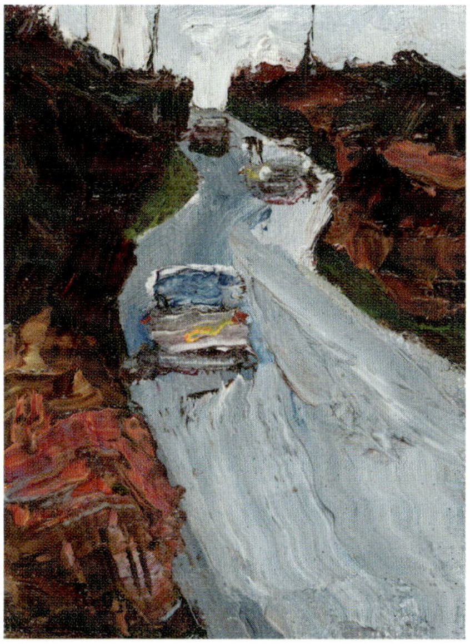
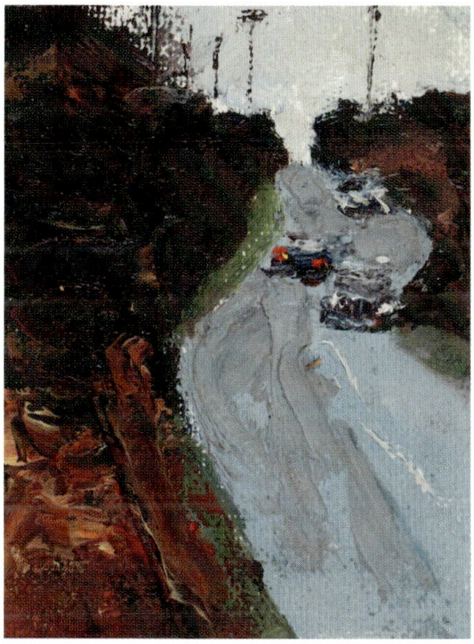
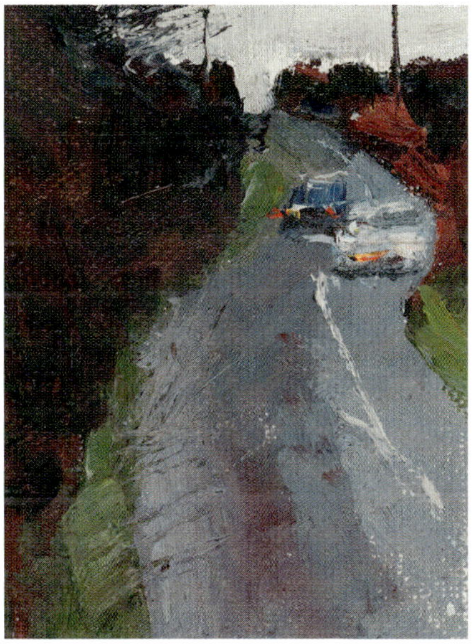
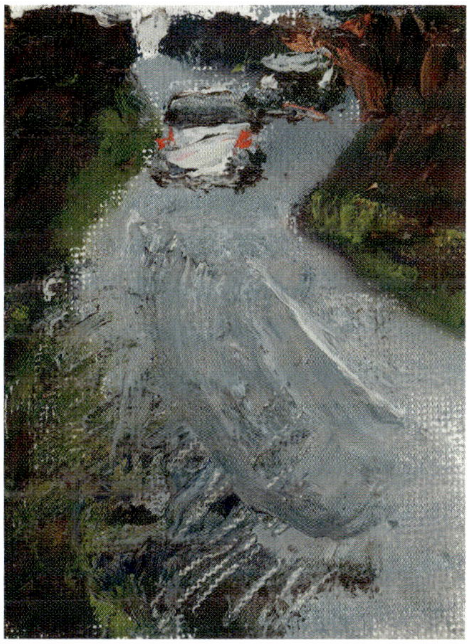
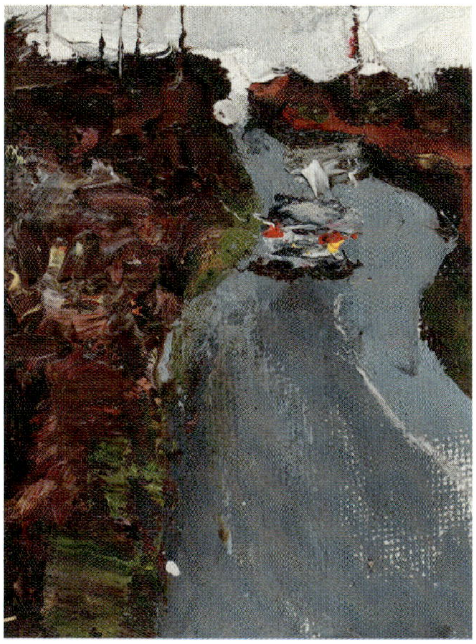
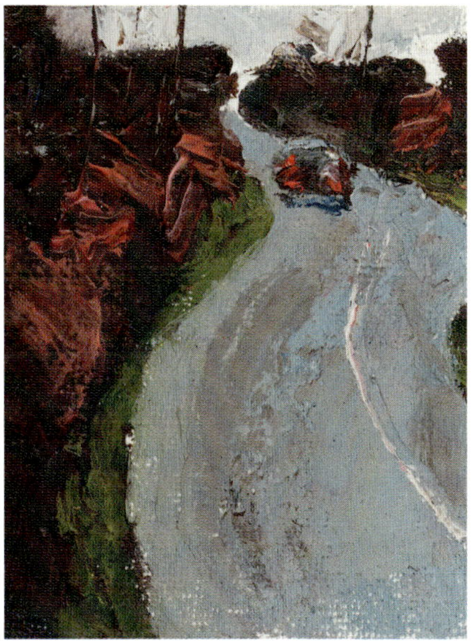
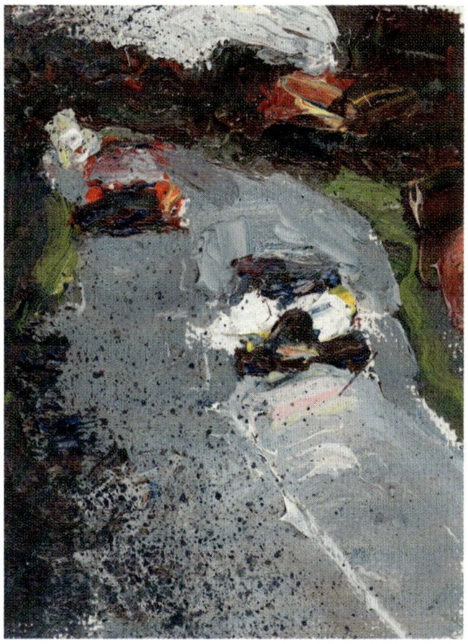

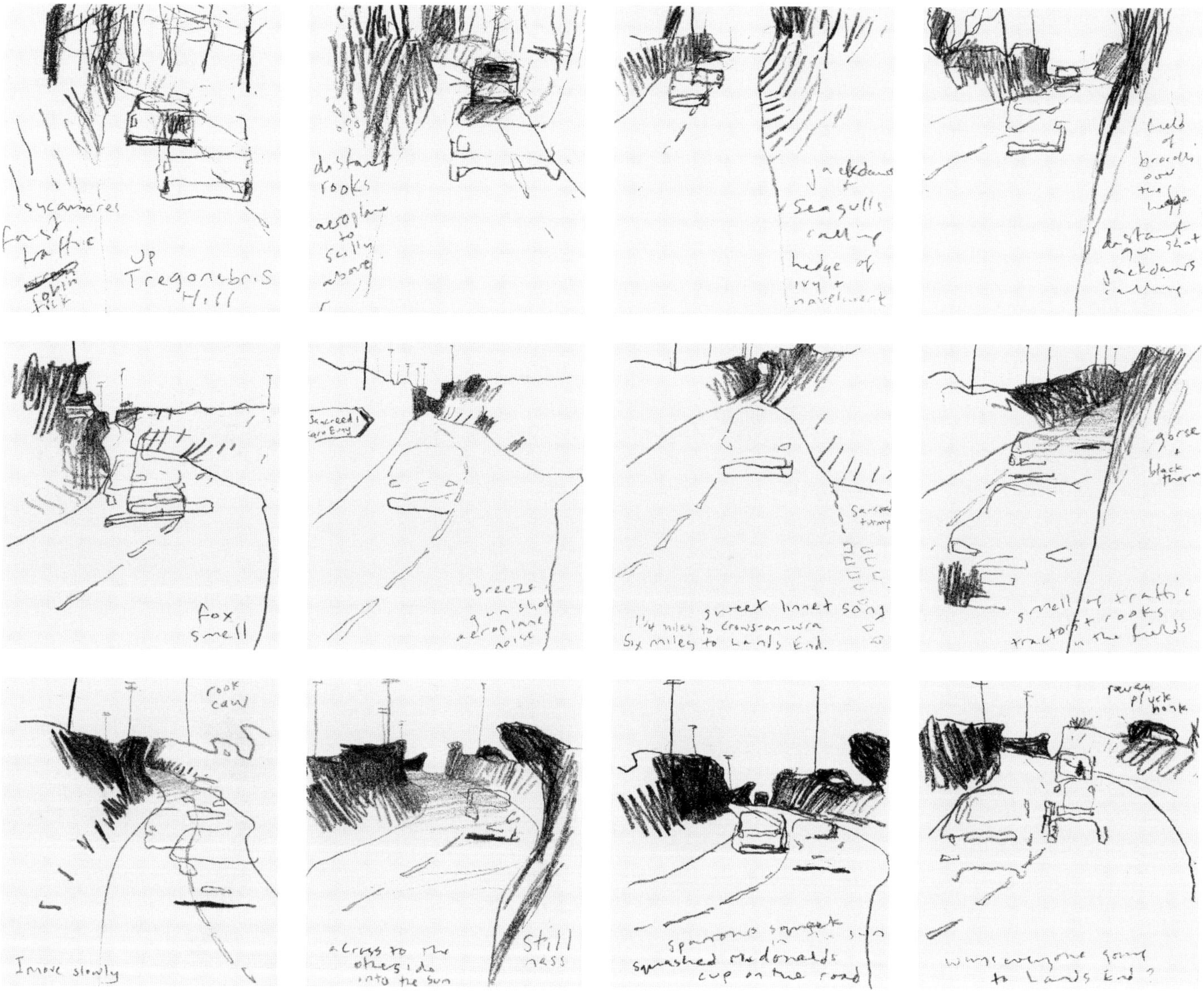

33. **Walking up Tregonebris Hill**
winter 2012 • pencil • 15.5 x 14 cm (x 25)

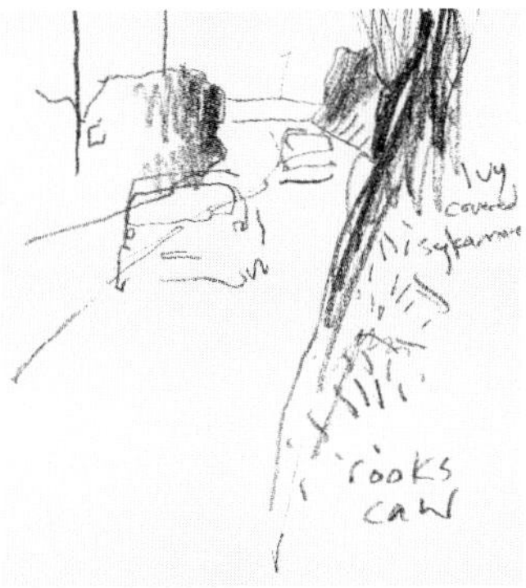
ivy covered sycamore
rooks caw

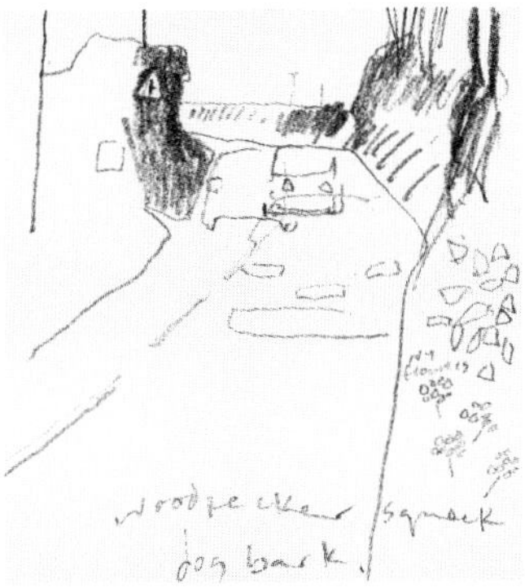
woodpecker squeak
dog bark.

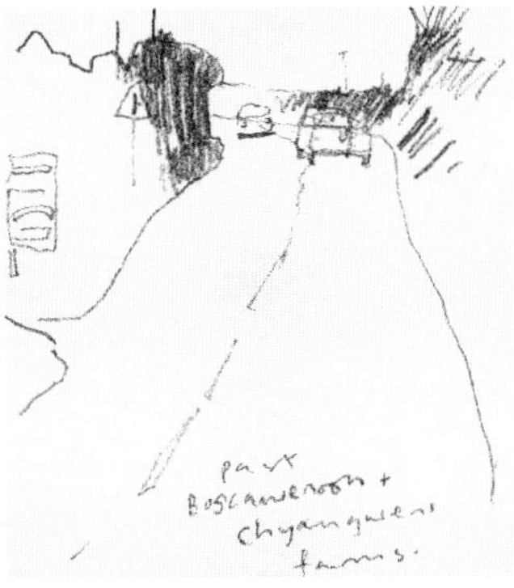
farms.

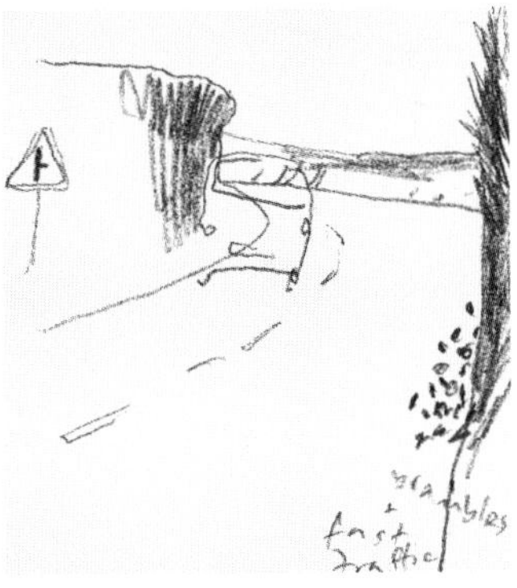
fast traffic

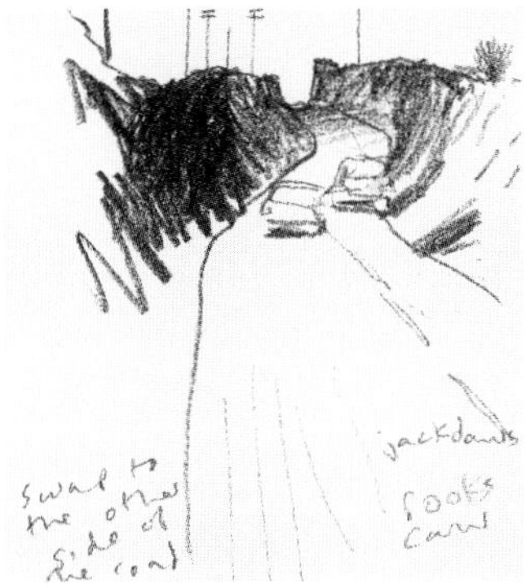
swap to the other side of the road
jackdaws
rooks caw

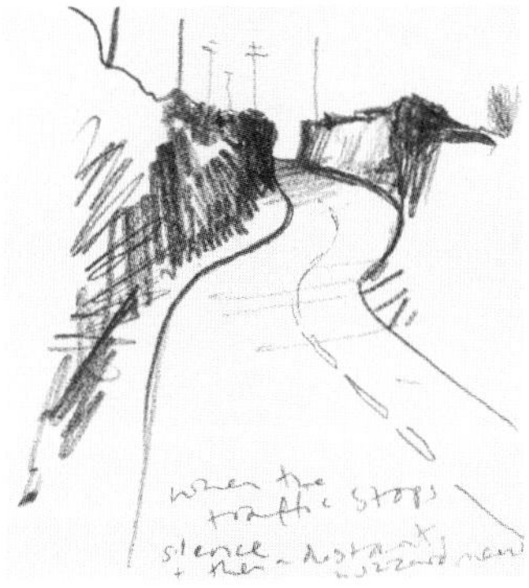
when the traffic stops

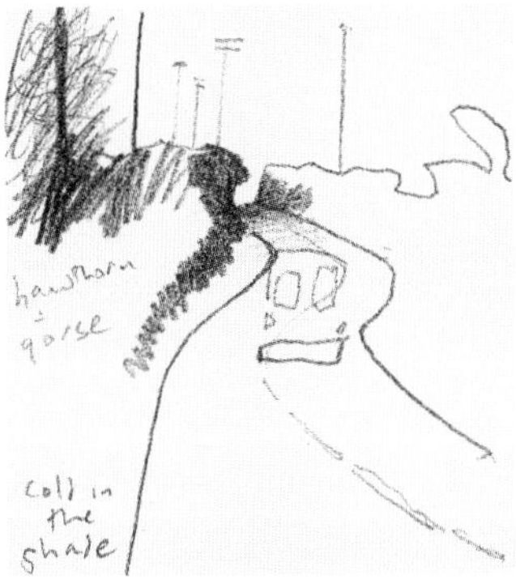
hawthorn + gorse
cold in the shade

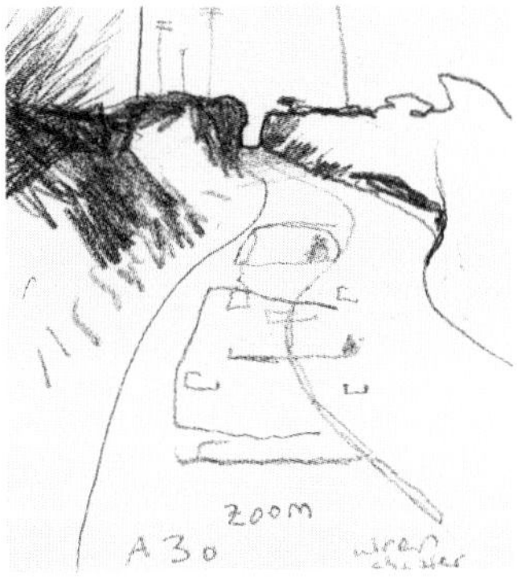
A30
zoom

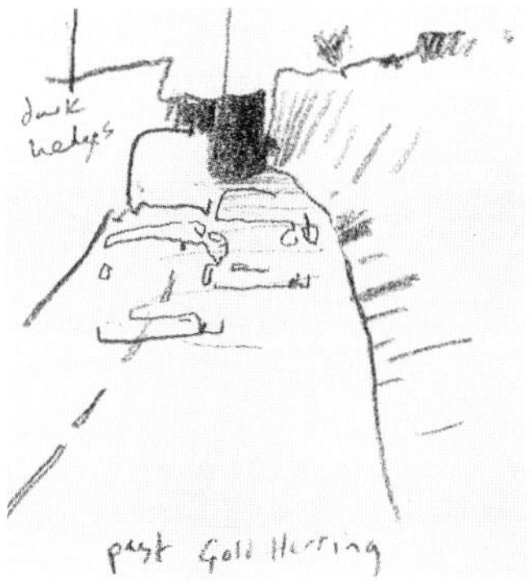
dark hedges

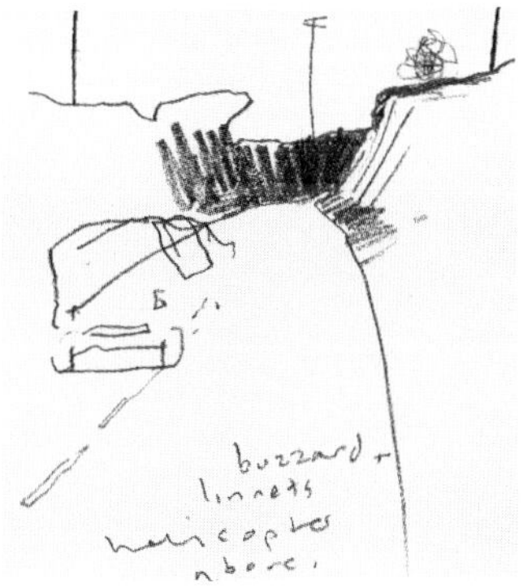
buzzard + linnets
helicopter above.

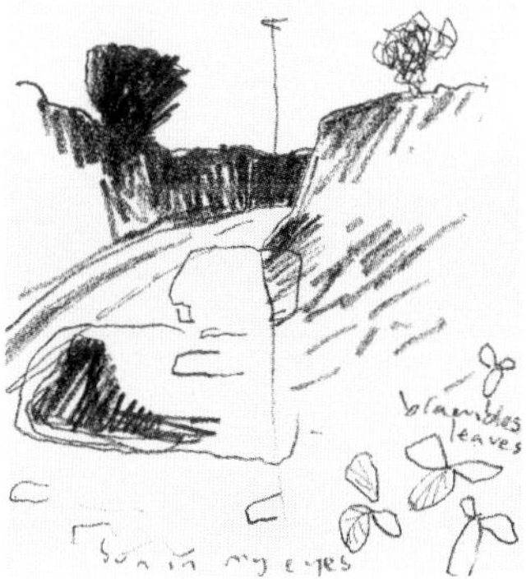
brambles leaves
sun in my eyes

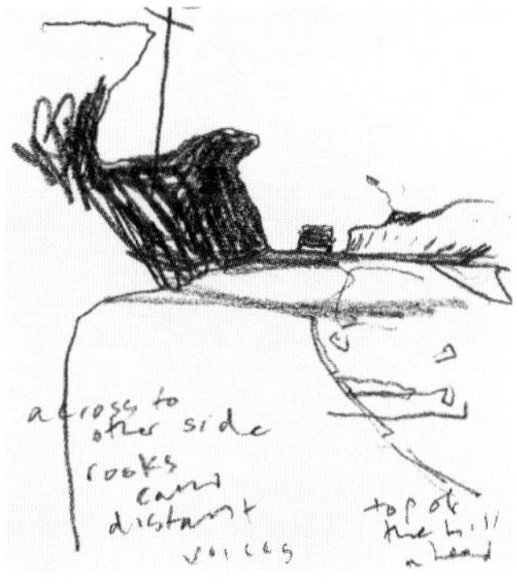
across to other side
rooks caw
distant voices

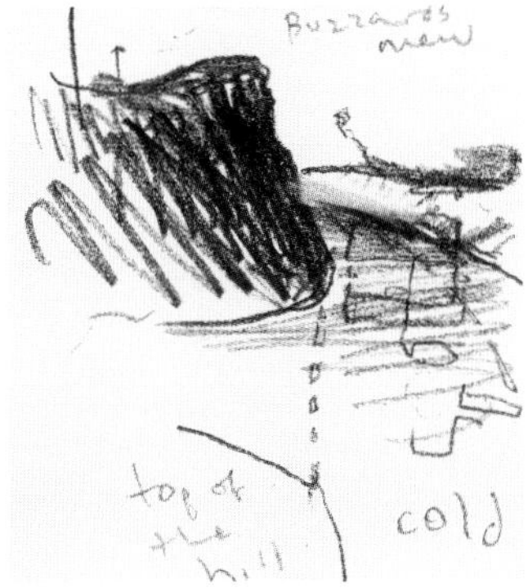
top of the hill
cold

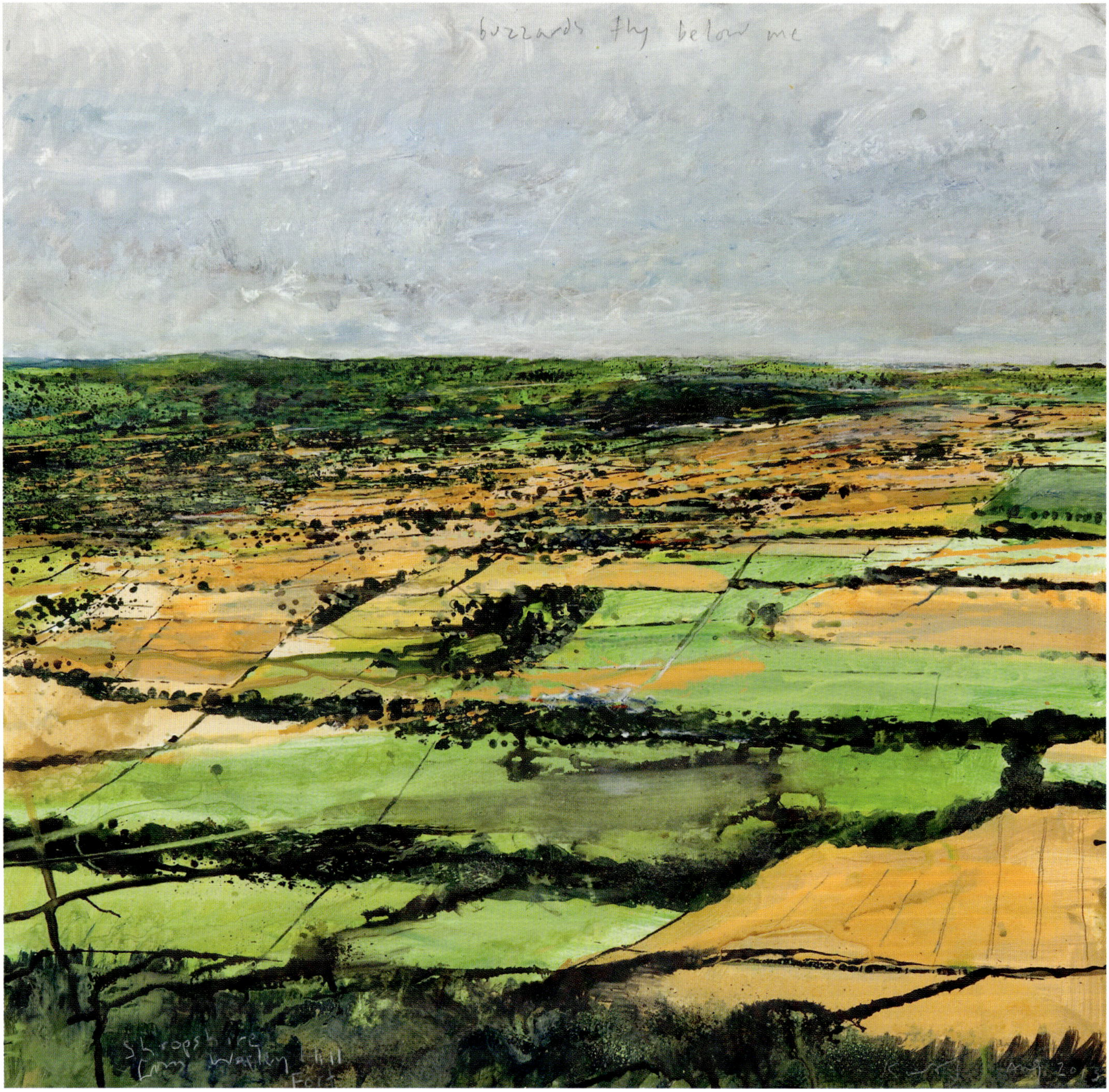

34. **Buzzards fly below me. Shropshire from Wapley Hill Fort**
August 2013 • mixed media on board • 60 x 63 cm

12. Wapley Hill, Herefordshire

Jimi Goodwin

Wapley Hill
I'm Smoking Homegrown Weed
I'm Fourteen
I'm Listening to Donald Fagen's The Nightfly on the ubiquitous Walkman
On the flip is Level 42's Level 42
When they were good.
I wonder all over the hill.
Pushing back the grass with a cautious toe
An Adder lying there.
Pied Flycatcher's
The Dunnock run ragged by the Cuckoo imposter.
Miles, he once had a Puma called Khan
Now he's got gorgeous young American girlfriend Sue
I try not watching her take a tin bath.
Muntjac Deer in the garden at night
I watch them with Freddie the Tawny Owl.
A Beer barrel half moon Nestbox either side of an Oak
In one a Kestrel with 3 young
In the other a Mallard duck with 14 chicks ...
Thirty feet up, Duck!
Either side of the oak
Strange bedfellows.
I'm Smoking Homegrown Weed
I'm Fourteen
I'm Lis ...
On Wapley Hill
Life will never be the same.

Jimi Goodwin is the lead singer and bass player in Doves. He is currently working on a solo project. His debut solo album 'Odludek' came out in March 2014.

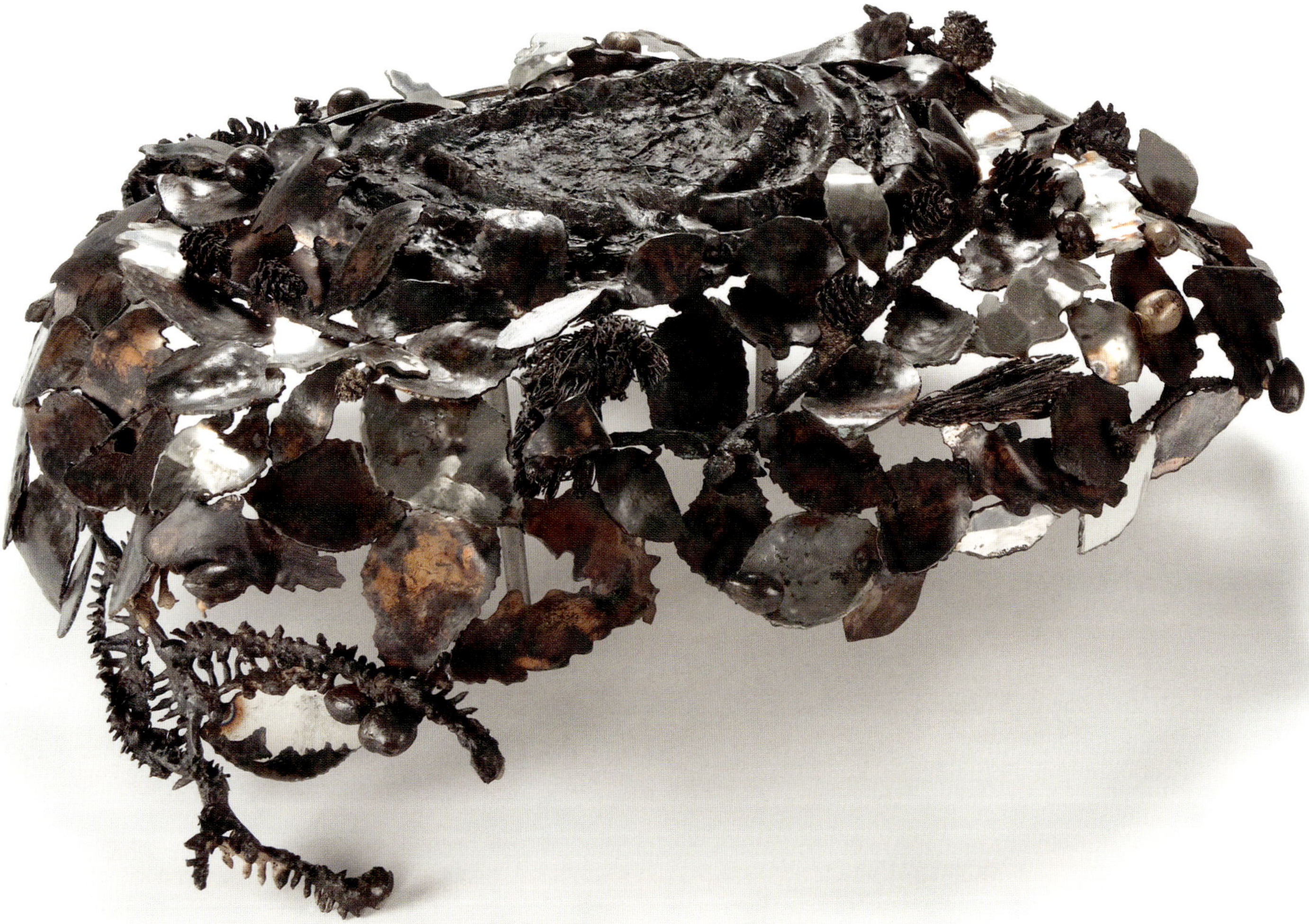

35. **Wapley Hill Fort**
2013 • bronze and stainless steel • 18 x 55 x 40 cm

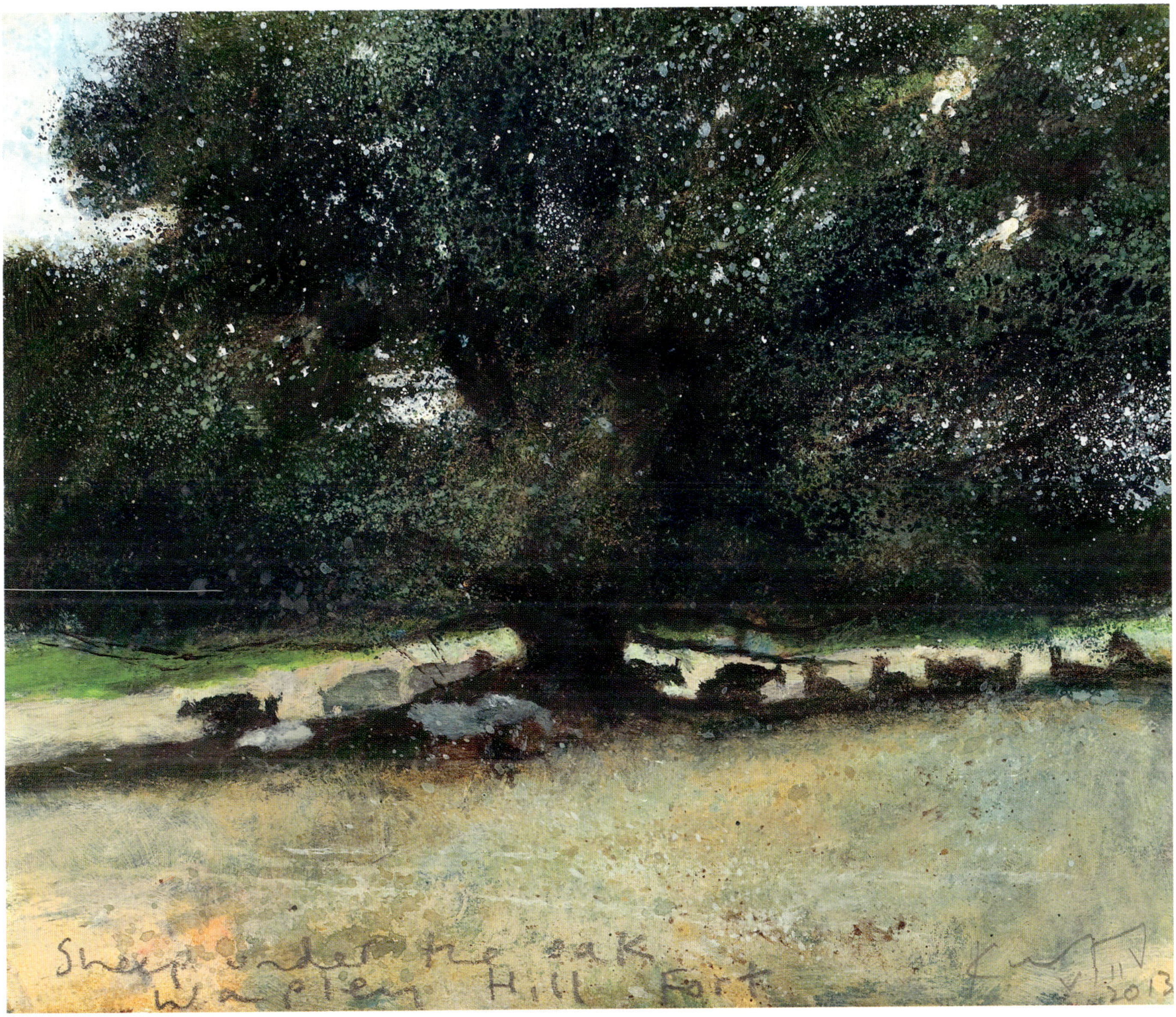

36. **Sheep under the oak in Wapley Hill Fort**
July 2013 • acrylic on board • 17 x 20 cm

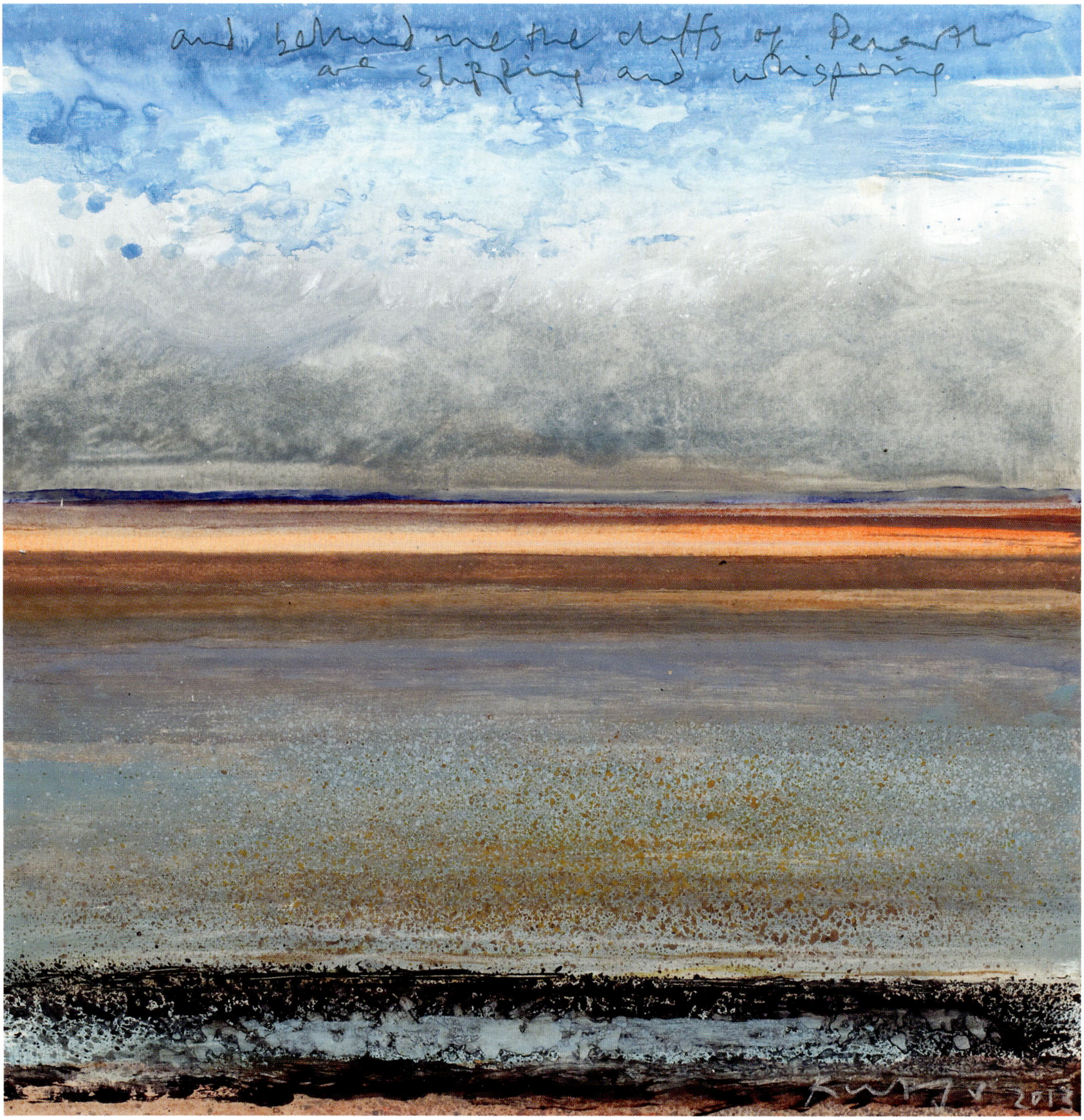

37. **And behind me the cliffs of Penarth are slipping and whispering**
May 2013 • mixed media on board • 21.5 x 21.5 cm

13. Penarth Head

Philip Gross

These are the crumbliest cliffs I've ever shared my life with. Just a slight breeze is enough to set them whispering – prickling grains of dried mudstone turning into sand. You want to come up close to listen, and you want to back away carefully. There can be spectacular slumps. One day we are walking round beneath the Head, round to the barrage that contains the high property prices of the man-made Cardiff Bay … and we don't recognise the profile of our cliff. An 80-foot-high slab has sunk to its knees on the shingle. The collapse might look leisurely, almost graceful in a gently drunken kind of way, but look closer: those are chisel-sharp edges where whole blocks have sheared. The broken surfaces are clean and crisp for a few weeks, then soften and darken. A few months on, it all looks normal. Only the houses at the cliff top are a metre or two closer to the brink of their insurance premiums. The dinky belvederes and gazebos at the bottom of their gardens are wooden ones, prefabricated, movable.

You can see the remnants of an earlier generation, built to last; they're hanging half way down the cliff. There is a broken flight of concrete steps, steel sinews showing. So these cliffs are like a book, or a long parchment, opening a slightly new text every day. Walk slowly, you can almost read it. Or figure them as a crude recording, somewhere between a wax cylinder and reel-to-reel tape. Along it, undulating lines of ochre and green mudstone … A centimetre band could be a century, a swerve of a prehistoric river emptying into a shallow lake, swishing back and forth and back, its vacillations turned to stone. Then again, crisp-looking nubs of gypsum, pinky-brown-white, the texture of old Kendal Mint Cake or coconut ice … As I bend to pick one up, the wind lifts, and that whisper spreads across the cliff face, grain to flaky grain. They seem to know something… and they do; I've been here five years, in Penarth; them, 200 million. They are bound to know more.

Philip Gross *is a poet, a writer for children and professor of creative writing at the University of South Wales. His exploration of the Severn estuary in 'The Water Table' won the TS Eliot Prize for poetry in 2009; his latest collection is 'Later' (2013).*

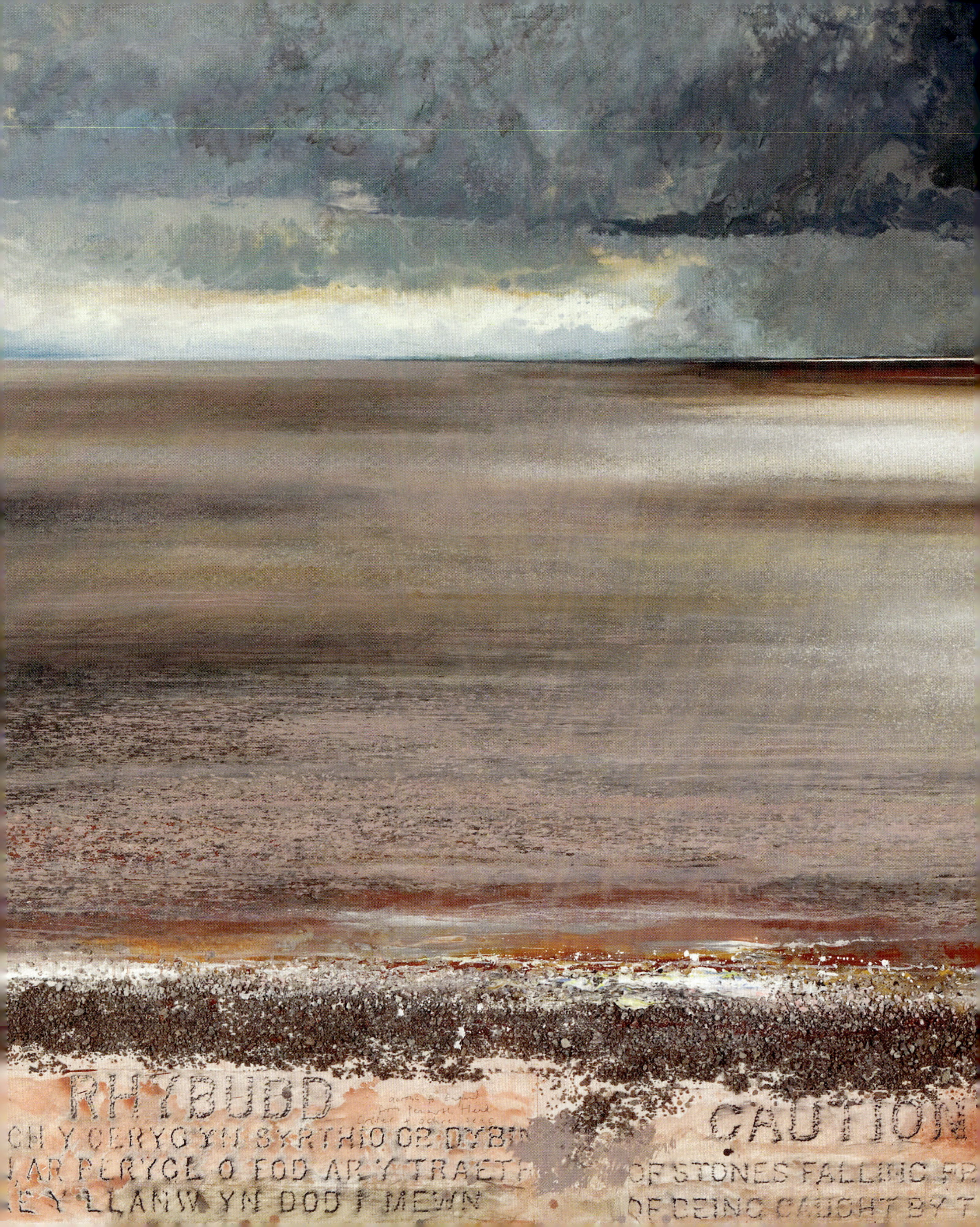
RHYBUDD
CH Y CERYG YN SYRTHIO OR DYBN
AR PERYGL O FOD AR Y TRAETH
EY LLANW YN DOD I MEWN
CAUTION
OF STONES FALLING FR
OF BEING CAUGHT BY T

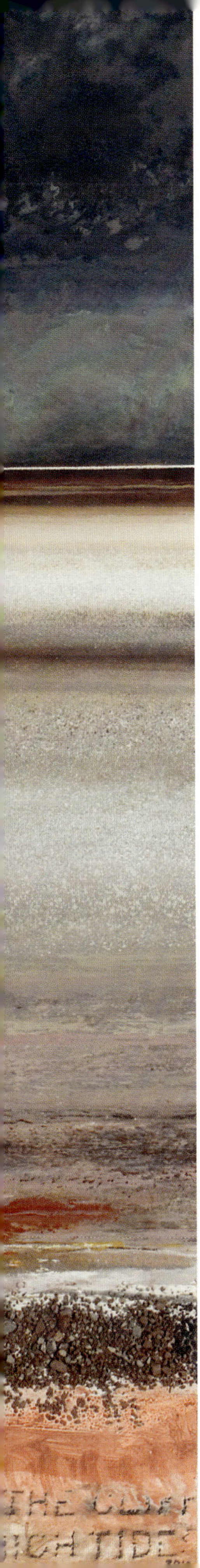

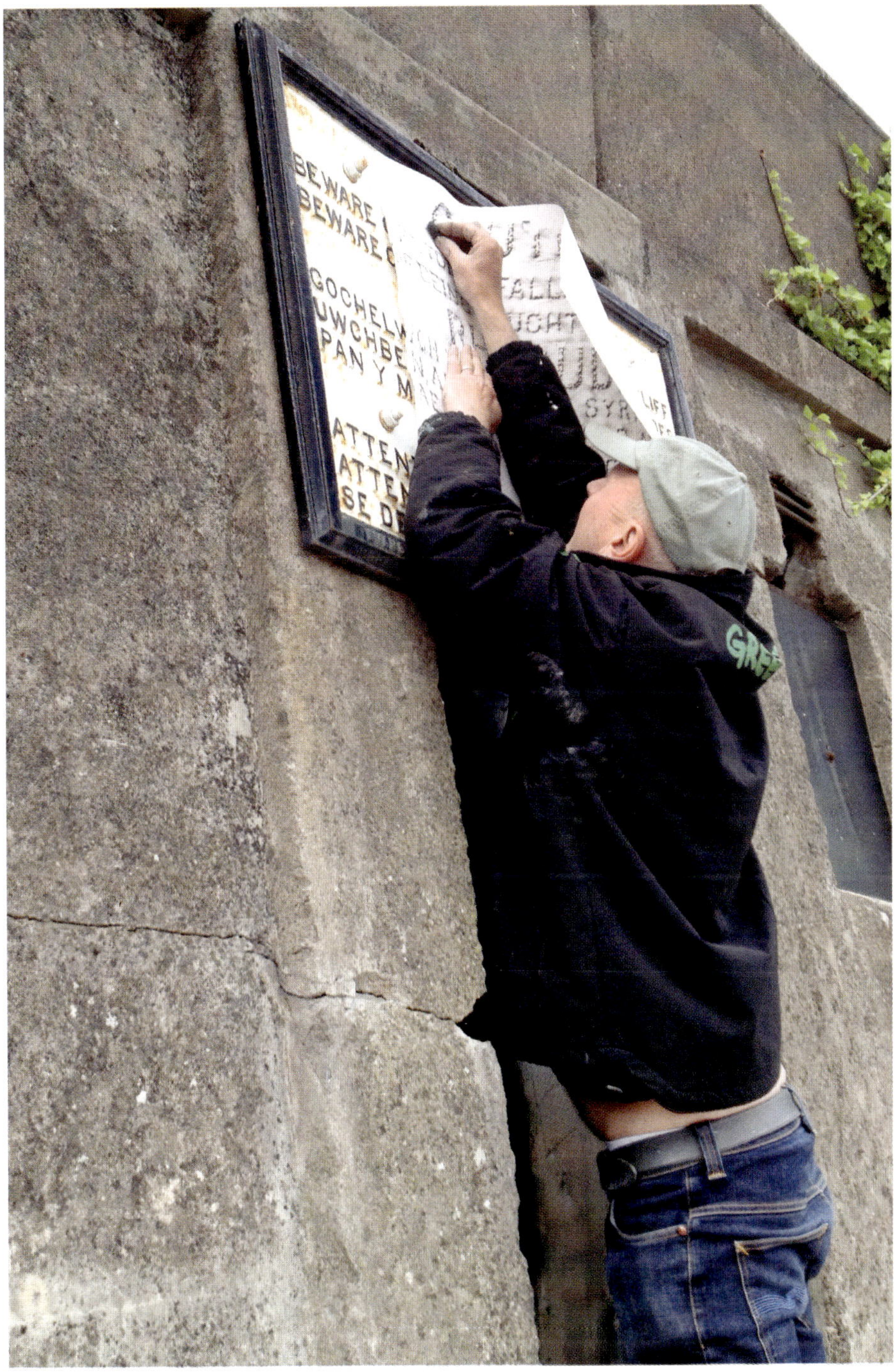

38. **Across to England from Penarth Head. Copper and ochre seas**
2014 • mixed media on canvas • 183 x 183 cm

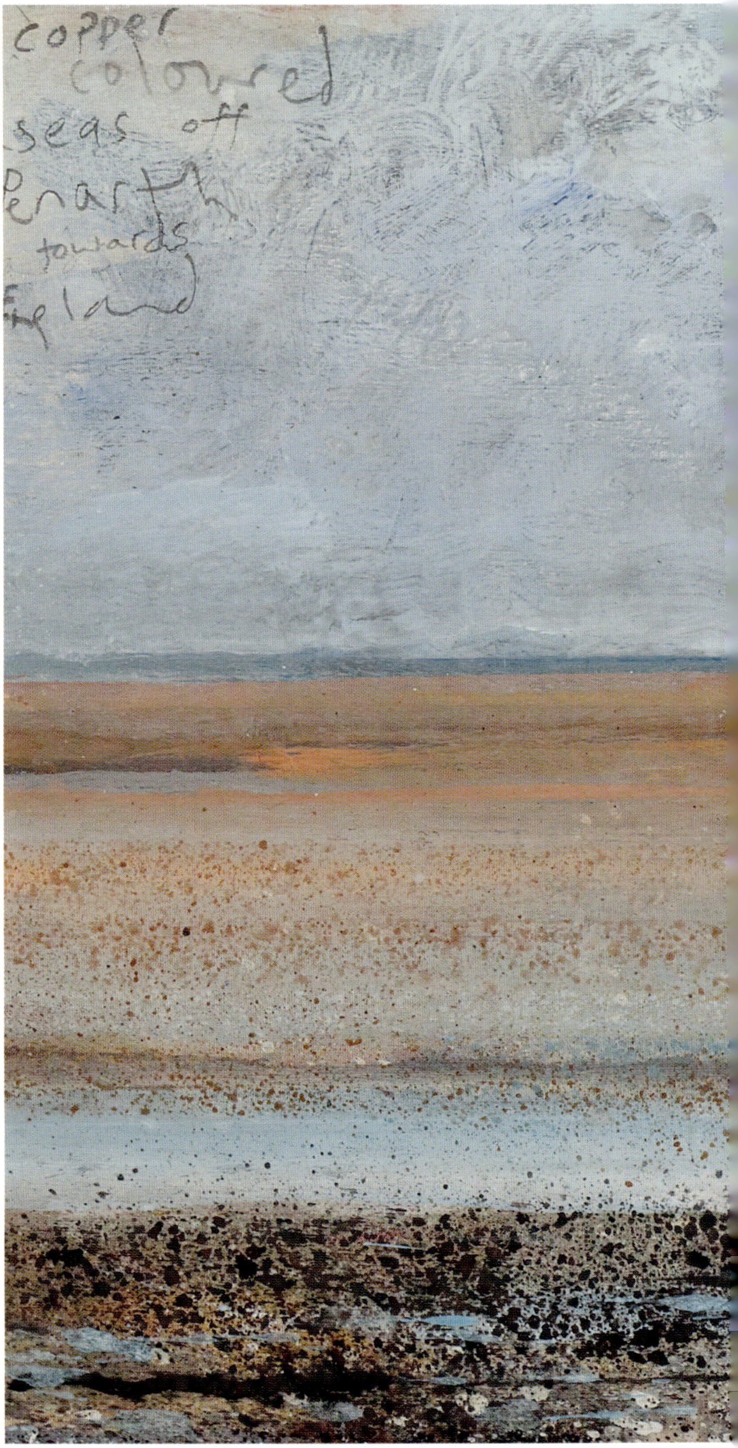

39. **A peregrine screams from the cliff tops behind me. Copper coloured seas off Penarth, towards England**
May 2013 • mixed media on wood panel • 19 x 32 cm

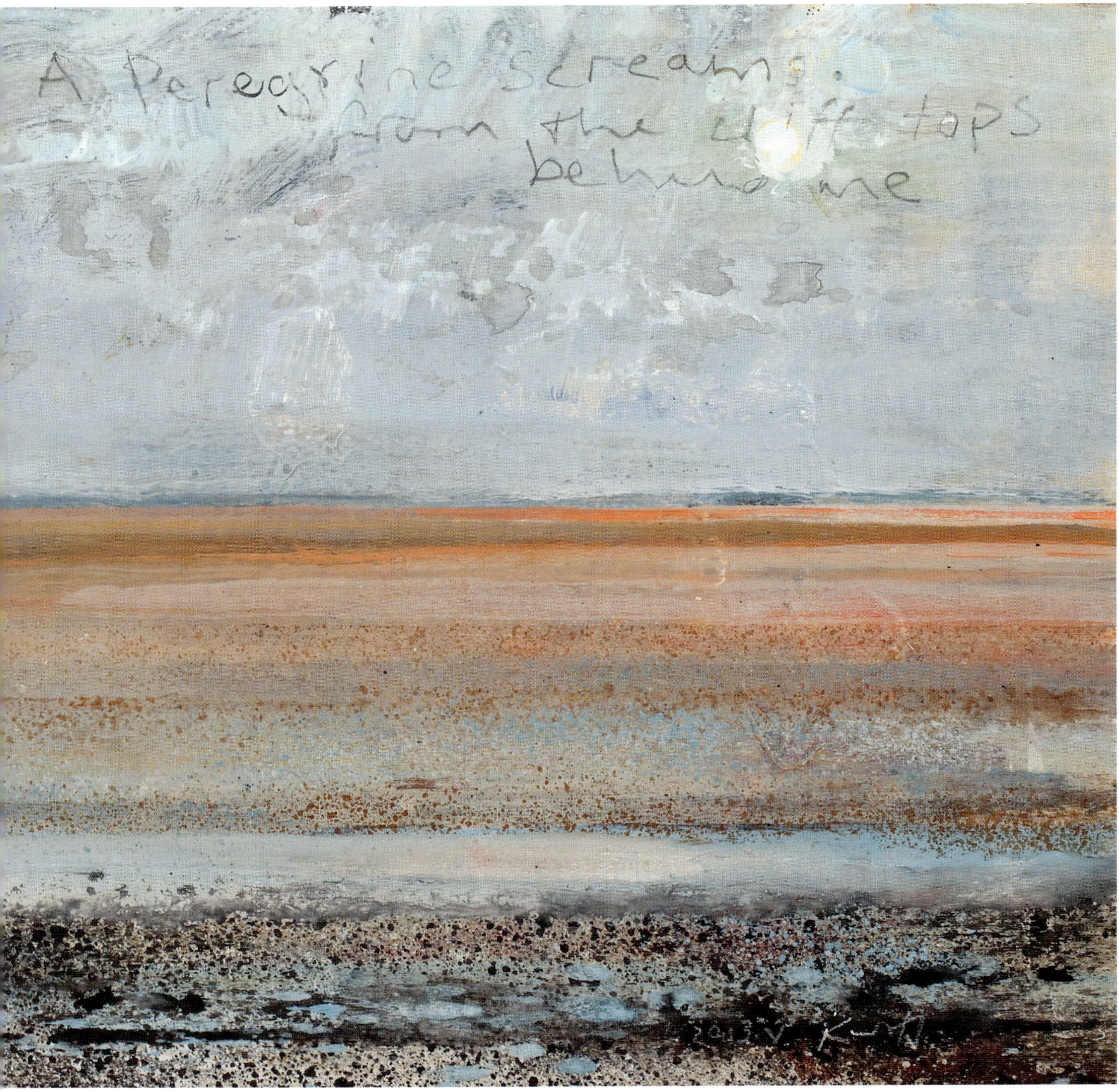
A Peregrine screams.
from the cliff tops
behind me

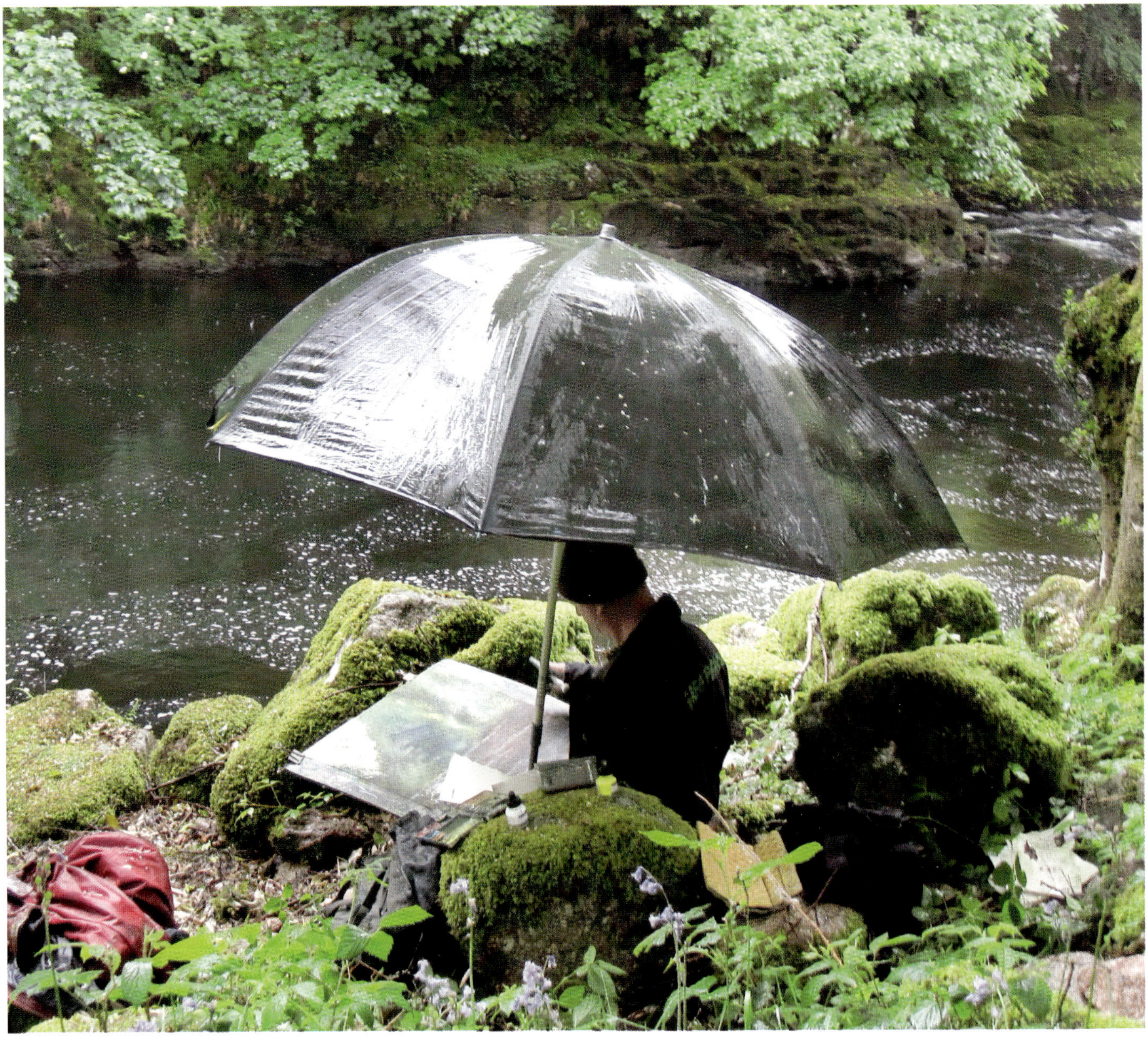

14. **The River Dart, Dartmoor**

Charlotte Gunn

Being asked to choose a place that is both special and personal sounded a real treat and an honour to be given. My mind raced all over Britain, starting with the stunning wildness of Ardnamurchan, then swooping down collecting place names with meaning and attachment all the way back to St Just. It wasn't too long before an avalanche of guilt and indecision crashed over me – slight over-reaction you might think? But my loyalties straddle two counties, one being Cornwall where I grew up until I was 30 and the other being Devon, where I now live.

Indecision is easier to explain because of the many, incredible places which each hold a particular memory or association. Guilt is more difficult to explain but it felt like choosing between my children or comparing one friend to another. This depth of feeling truly shocked me, as on the most simplistic level I was just being asked to choose a parcel of land. But in choosing Mothecombe, Leather Tor, Dewerstone Wood, the rivers Dart, Tamar, Tavy and Erme rather than somewhere in West Penwith, I felt I was literally letting down Avarack, Pendeen Watch, Cape, Church Rocks, Nanquido, Polandese, Scillies and St Just itself.

Therefore, after much thought and soul searching, really the only option of a not so level-headed 50-year-old, was to pull one out of a hat (a woolly one, which I hope has no reflection on the way I think). So, hat overflowing with coastal, moor, valley and river place names needing only a shake and like a raffle I needed only to plunge my hand in and pluck out the 'winning number'! Oh, if only it were so simple, doubt and nerves surged in as I then realised that they are *all* part of me, inseparable. With no other option I tipped the whole lot out on the floor and reread each piece of carefully folded paper, lingering over the places that mapped my life – reluctantly rejecting some and lovingly putting them a note book so that they wouldn't feel too offended.

Replacing the remaining names, a final shake of the hat, butterflies in my stomach – not sure exactly which species, Kurt – I once again began to plunge in, moment-arily hesitating as I do whilst standing on the edge of icy water before diving in, stilled by thought. Eventually I fished out Sharrah Pool which dwells within the River Dart beneath Hockinston Tor on Dartmoor, a wondrous dark and peaty pool , deep with secrets. With a mixture of pleasure and sadness the deed was done.

Now of course, I will have to revisit all the places that were left behind and whisper a secret apology, whilst explaining about the hapless twins of luck and statistics that were involved in them not being chosen. I will let Kurt depict the beauty of 'Sharrah' with the moor rising high and the river achingly cold as it pulls you in.

P.S. Shhh! Don't tell the others but when I close my eyes it's the Brisons which are burnt upon my retinas and I'm sitting anywhere between Nanven and Cape, but to be honest, mostly down at Church or up on high at Carn Gloose.

__Charlotte Gunn__, born in London 1962, was, from 1964, brought up in West Penwith, Cornwall. Followed by Falmouth and Bristol Art Schools, work on farms, lots of travel and a University of Plymouth environmental science degree. She currently works as a learning officer in Plymouth City Museum & Art Gallery. Married with two children and living in Plymouth, Devon, she loves swimming in cold water, walking and talking.

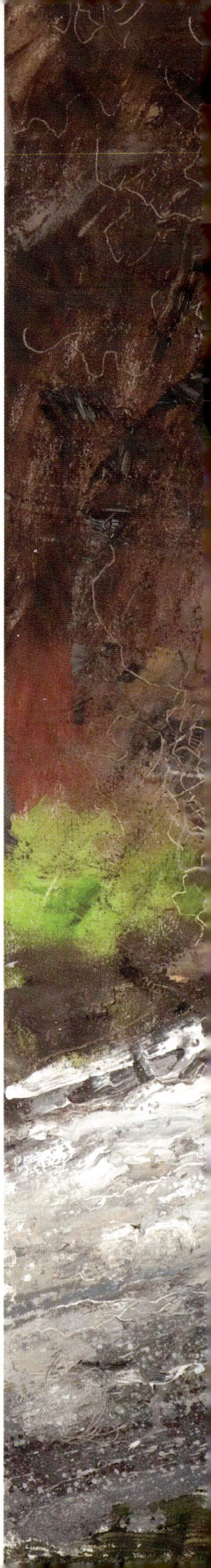

40. **Under Holne bridge, wagtails, Dart**
2009 • oil on canvas • 91.5 x 91.5 cm

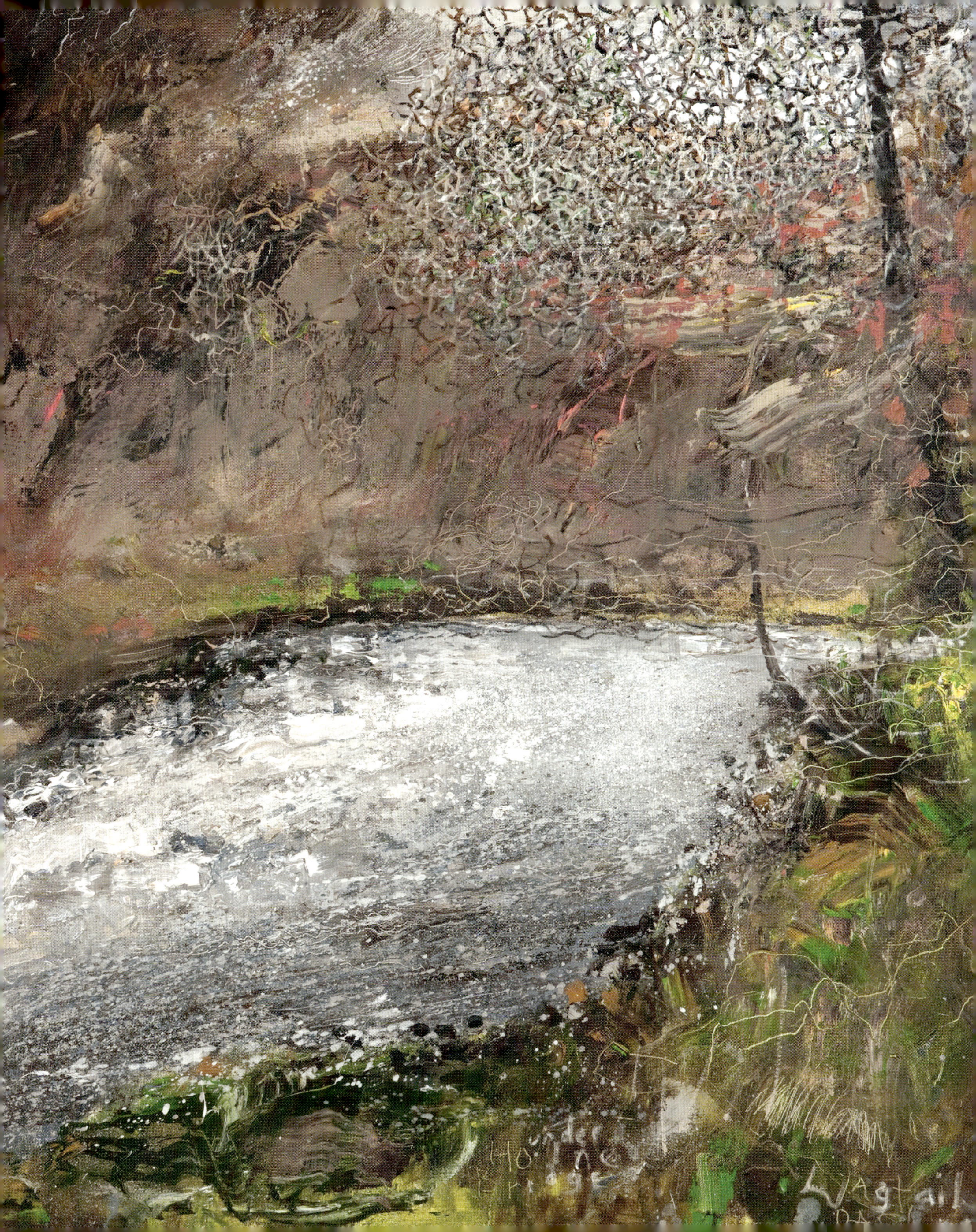
under
Holne
Wagtail

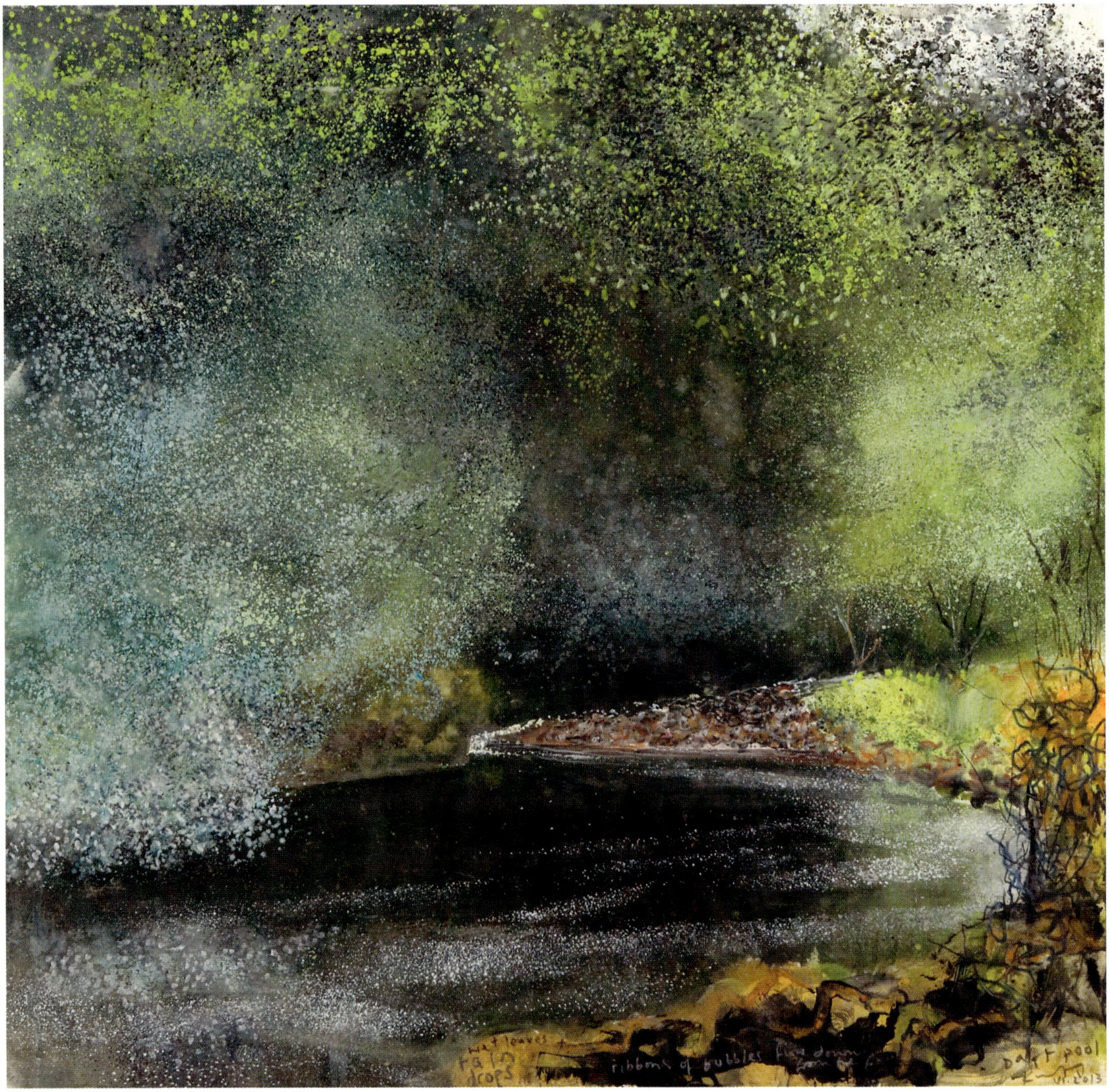

41. **Dart pool. Ribbons of bubbles flow down from the falls. Wet leaves and raindrops**
June 2013 • mixed media on paper • 56 x 60 cm

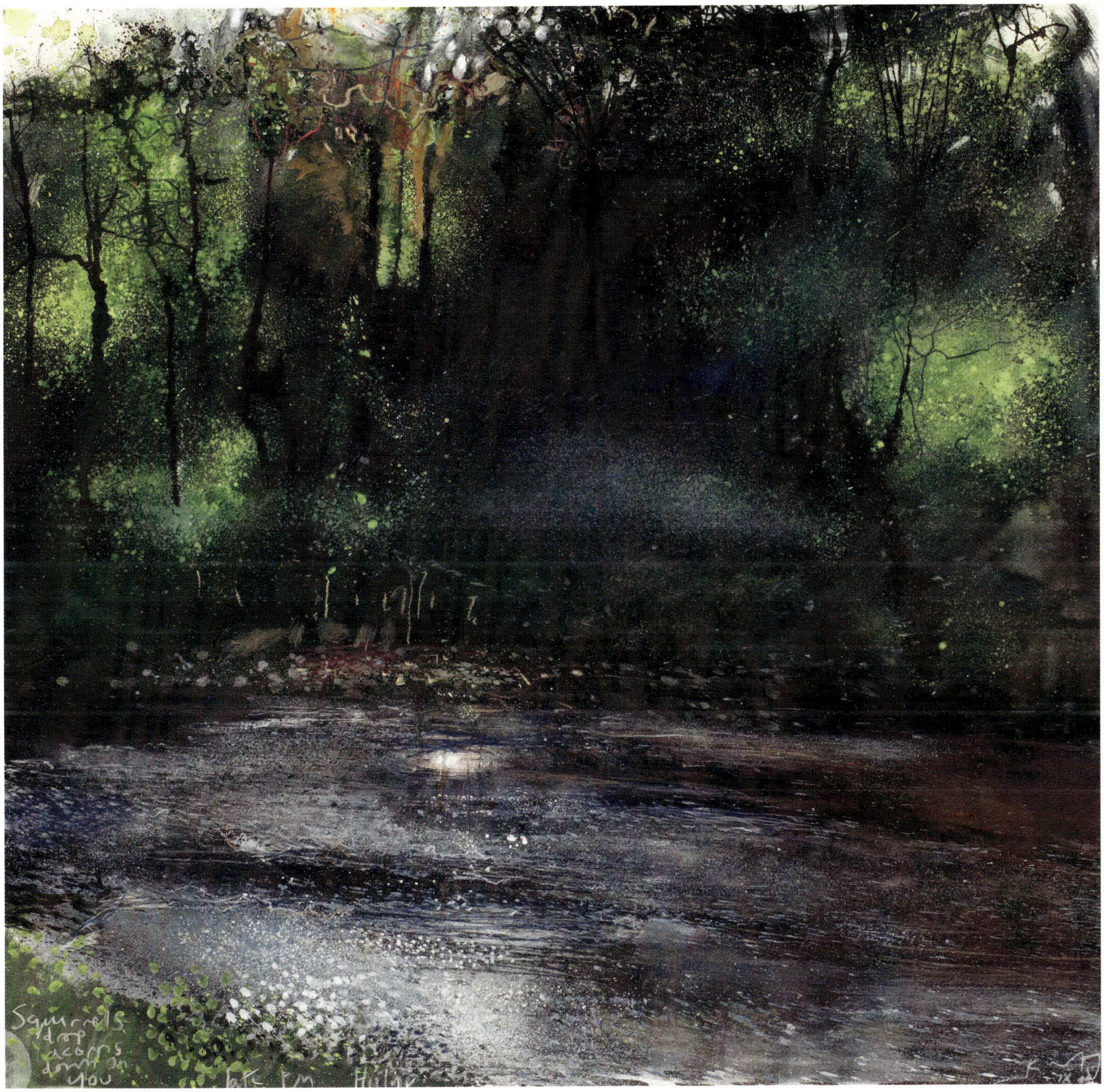

42. **Squirrels drop acorns down on you. Late afternoon, Holne**
September 2009 • mixed media on paper • 56 x 60 cm

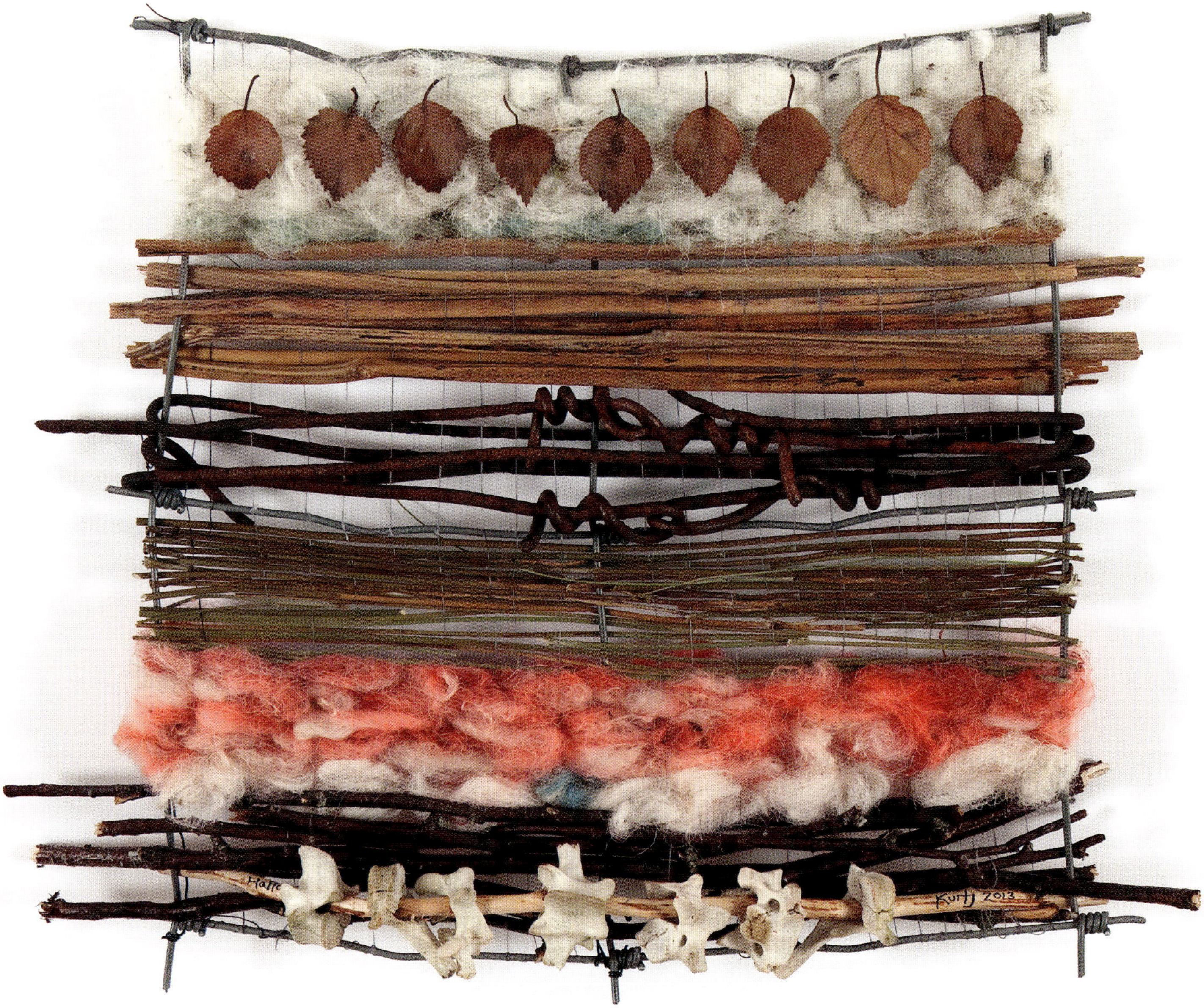

43. **Hallaig**
2013 • found materials • 30 x 43 cm

15. **Hallaig, Raasay, Inner Hebrides**

Stephen Hesselbo

Hallaig is an abandoned settlement on the east coast of the island of Raasay, in the Inner Hebrides. Hallaig was evidently quite a sizable community but disappeared a couple of hundred years ago as a result of the Highland Clearances. Sheep replace people. Hallaig is approached from the south on foot along a track and takes just over an hour to reach. The time of year to go is around Easter.

I need to explain a bit about the geology. This part of Raasay comprises Jurassic sedimentary rocks. Geologically, Raasay is like Dorset – same age and rock type – but the landscape is much more foreboding. On Raasay there are two great flat-lying sandstone formations, each forming cliffs rising up hundreds of metres sheer from the very deep water of the Sound of Raasay. Between the sandstone formations are a few metres thickness of ironstone, the Raasay Ironstone, which results in a bench that runs along the east coast. It is along this bench that the track to Hallaig is sited.

Just before you get to Hallaig the track brings you to a headland overlooking a bay. This is a good spot to appreciate the setting. Hallaig is on the other side of the bay beyond a wood and a stream. There is a poem by Sorley McLean in Gaelic and English on a cairn. The wood is stunningly beautiful in the sunlight of March before the trees leaf out. Old trees that look very young. The ruined buildings ofHallaig are on a narrow grassy plateau. The coast northwards from this point comprises an immense landslide formed when a few thousand years ago the Jurassic rocks slid away catastrophically into the glacially over-deepened Sound.

A freshwater loch is developed in the depression above and behind the landslip and is overshadowed by the towering sandstone cliffs above. The loch is fed by a moss-covered spring. The water is crystal clear and cold, but more often than not there is the carcass of at least one sheep that did not make it through the winter: don't drink the water. Dead sheep are common around here. Below, towards the bouldery shoreline the ruins of the landslipped sandstone form precipices and over-hangs of gothic proportions.

Hallaig is at once both beautiful and intimidating. Brimming with life but filled with ghosts. About as decidedly eastward-facing as anywhere can be on the west-facing Atlantic Ocean margin. Not really a place where you'd want to live.

Stephen Hesselbo is professor of geology at the University of Exeter, Camborne School of Mines, where he recently moved to from Oxford. Through his 30-year academic career he has researched and taught on major environmental change events in deep time with a focus on field-based geological observations.

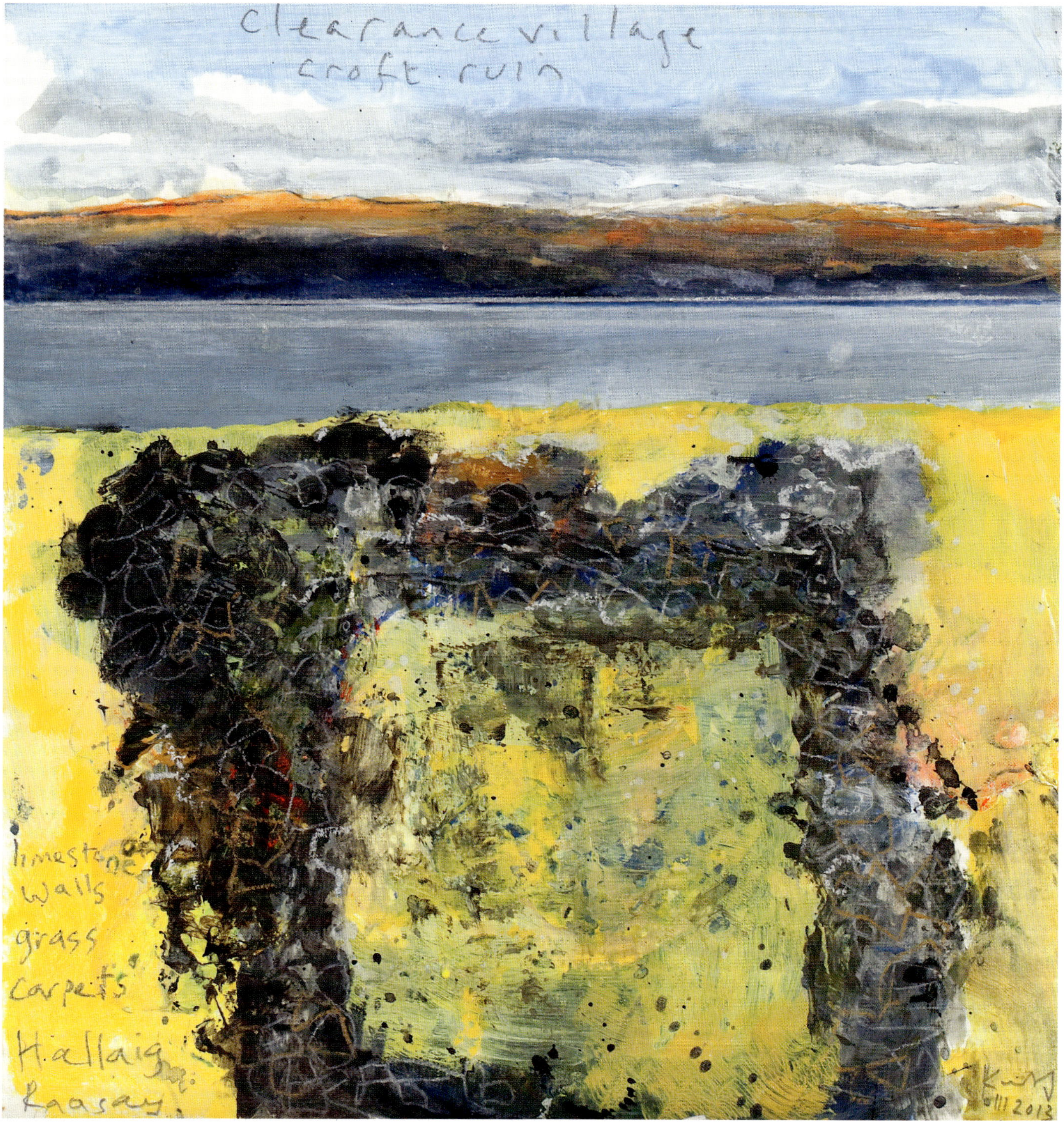

44. **Clearance village, croft ruin. Hallaig, Raasay**
August 2013 • mixed media on board • 21 x 20 cm

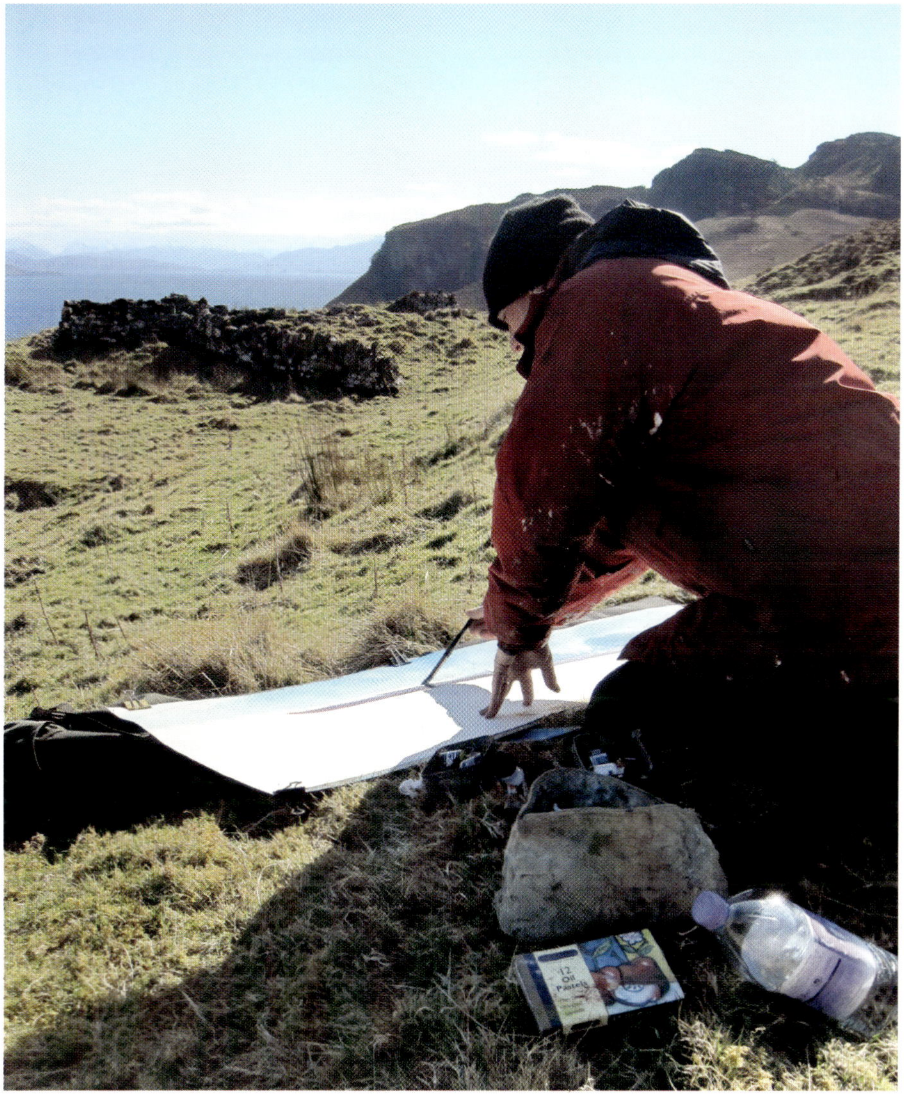

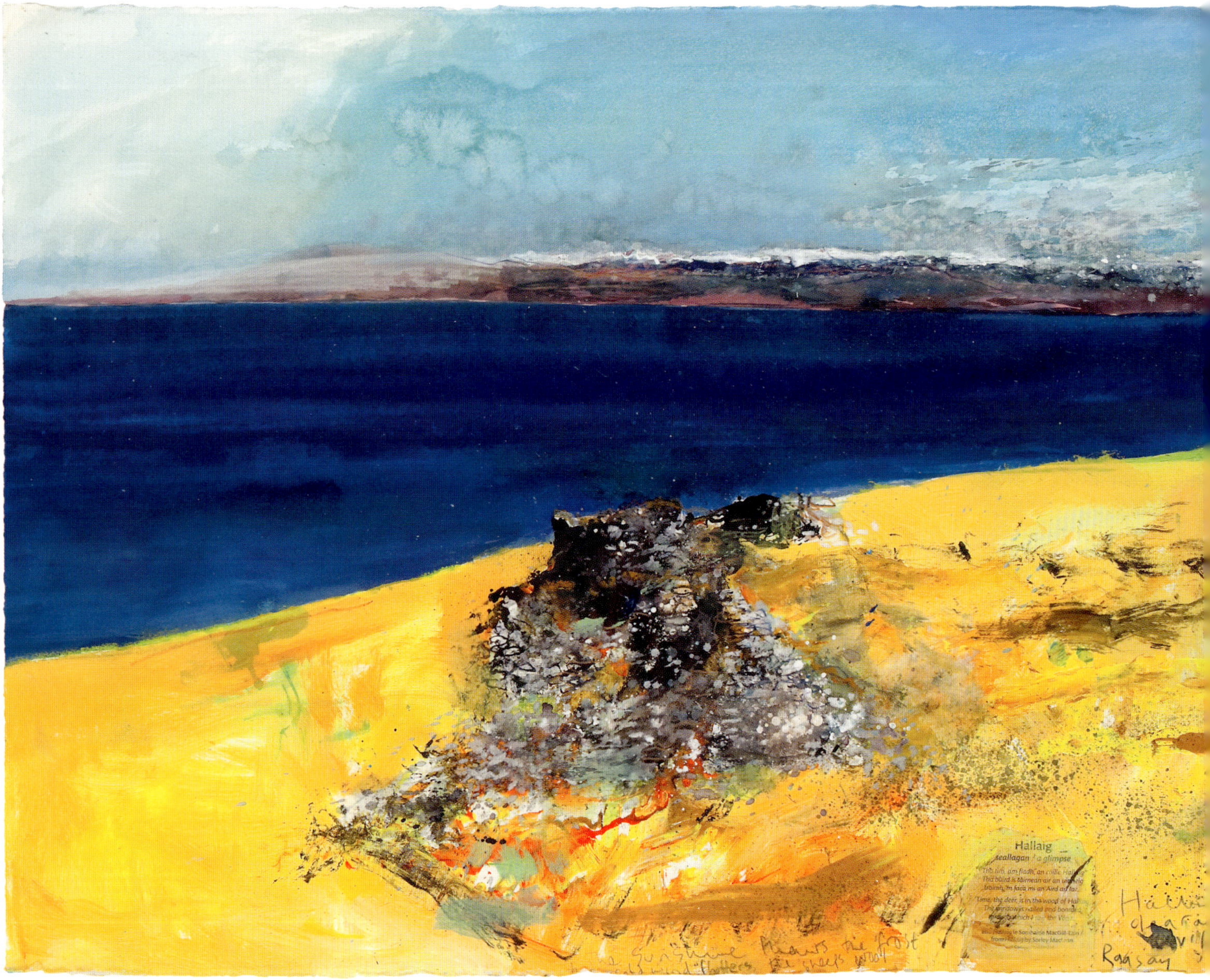

45. **Hallaig clearance village, Raasay.**
The sunshine thaws the frost, the cold wind flutters the sheep's wool
March 2013 • mixed media on paper • 57 x 150 cm

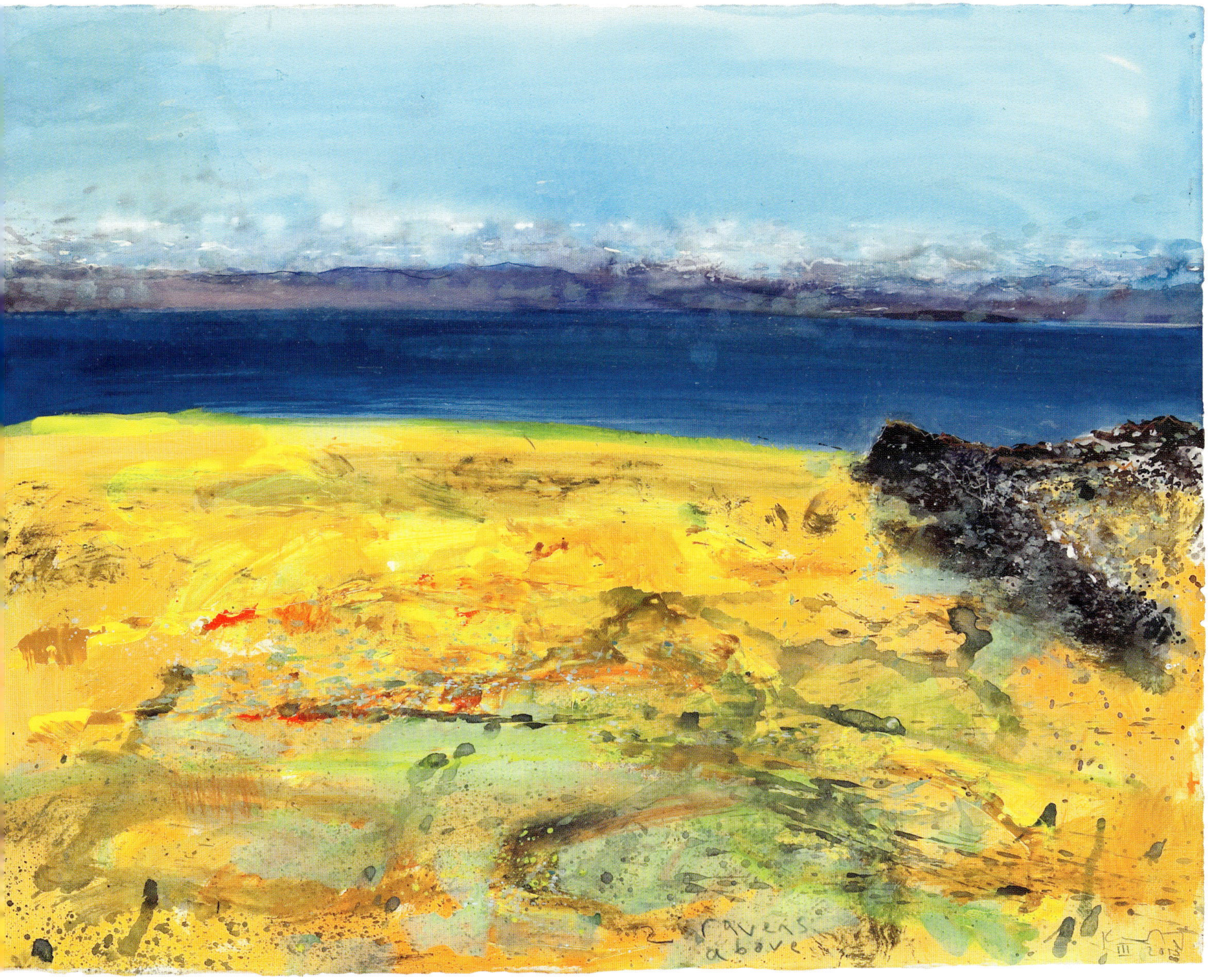
ravens above

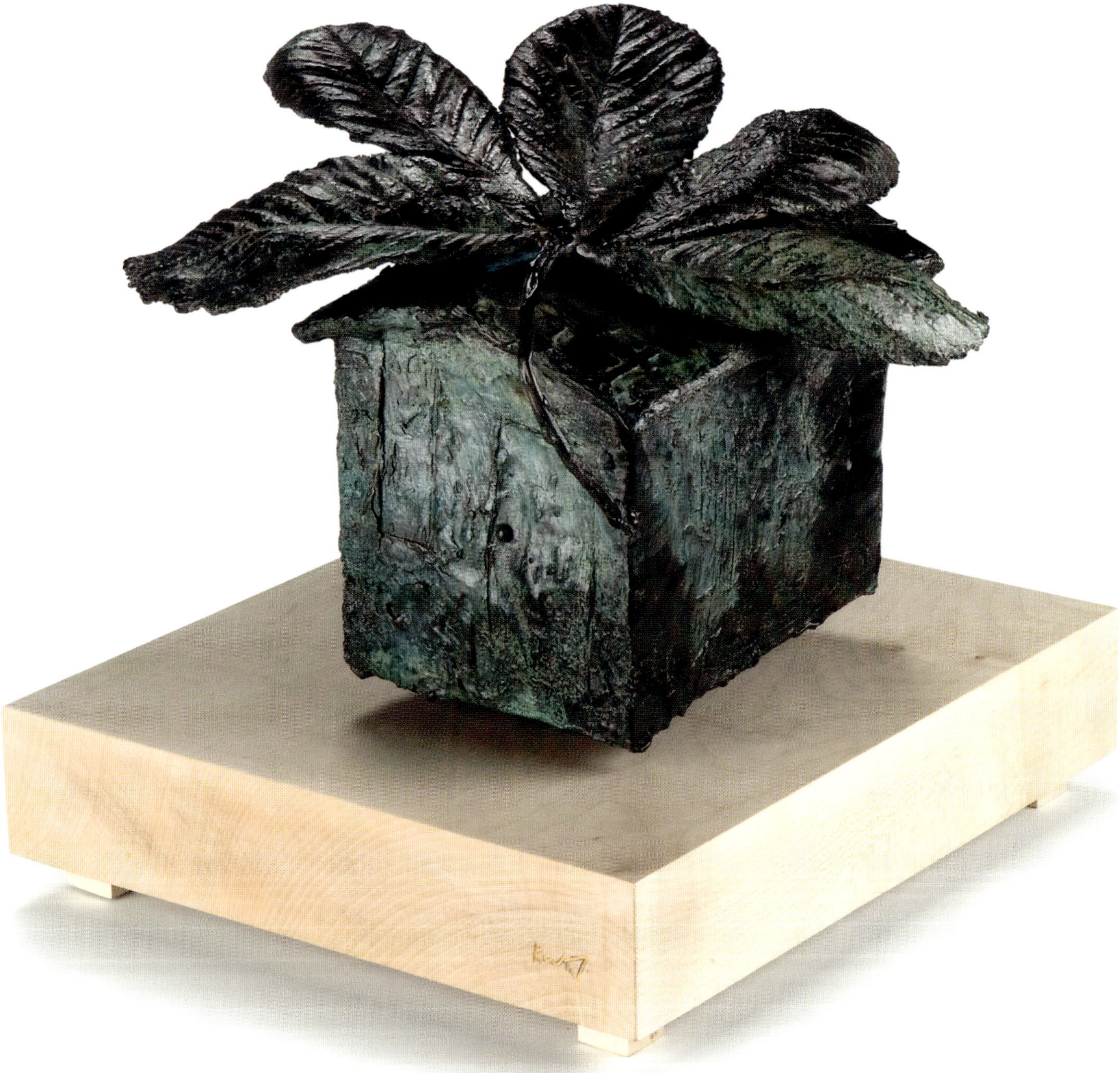

46. **Hut, horse chestnut and poetry**
2013 • bronze unique on sycamore base • 25 x 27 x 35 cm including base

16. Ted's writing hut, Devon

Carol Hughes

'hut'

Carol Orchard and Ted Hughes married in August 1970. After a spell in Paris and Persia in the autumn of 1971 they settled at Court Green where she still lives.

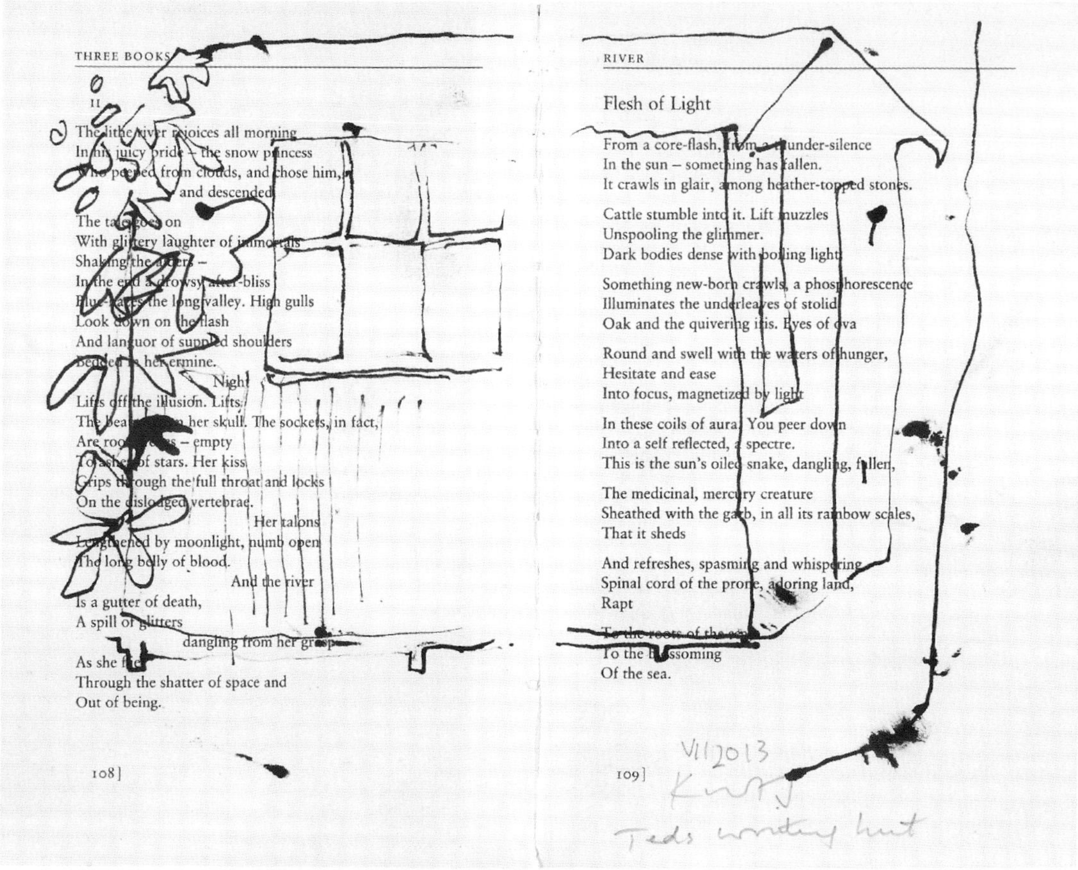

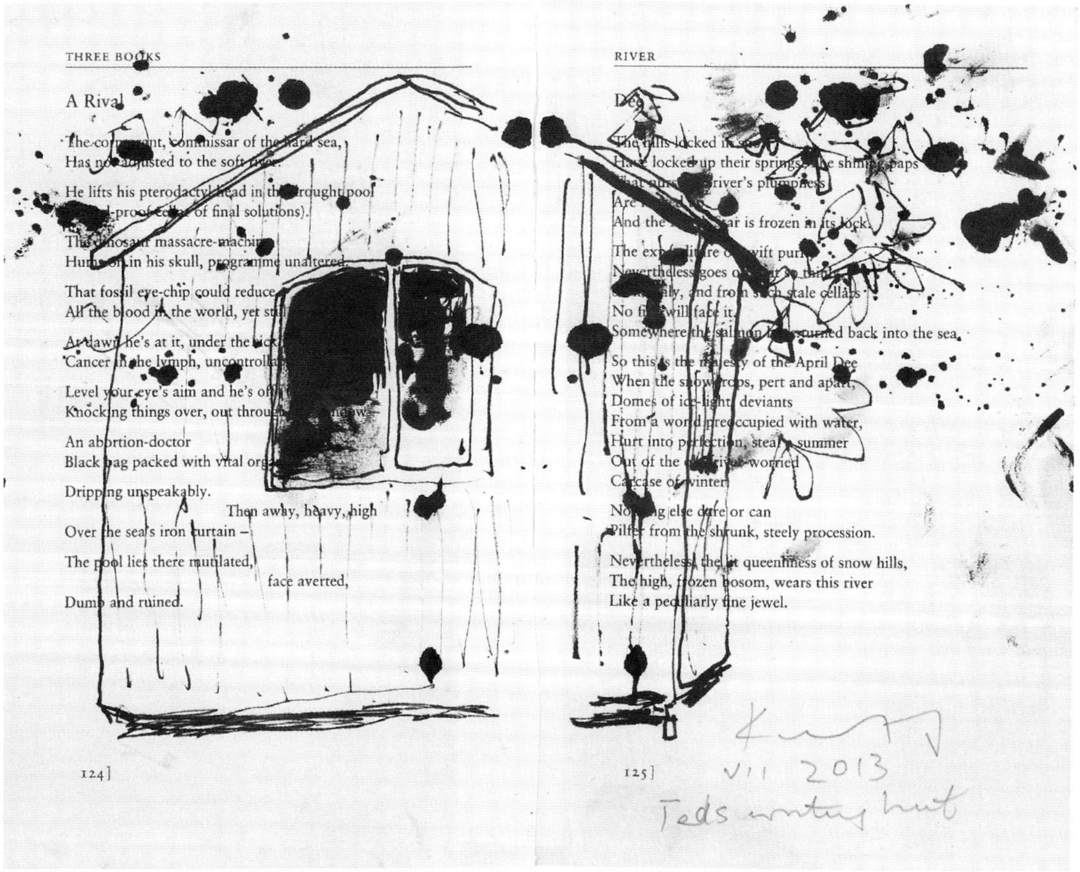

47. **Ted's writing hut**
July 2013
ink on Ted Hughes' book
19.5 x 25 cm (x4)

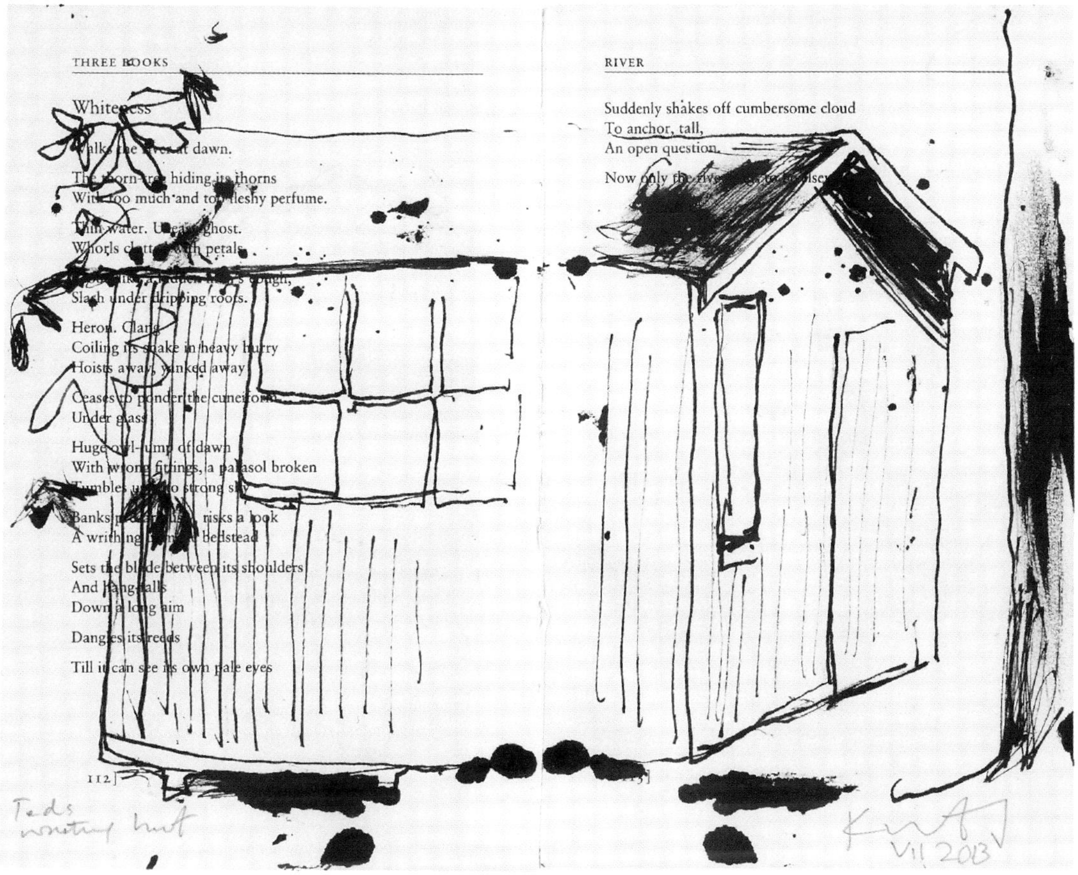
THREE BOOKS
RIVER
Suddenly shakes off cumbersome cloud
To anchor, tall,
An open question.
112]
Teds writing hut
VII 2013

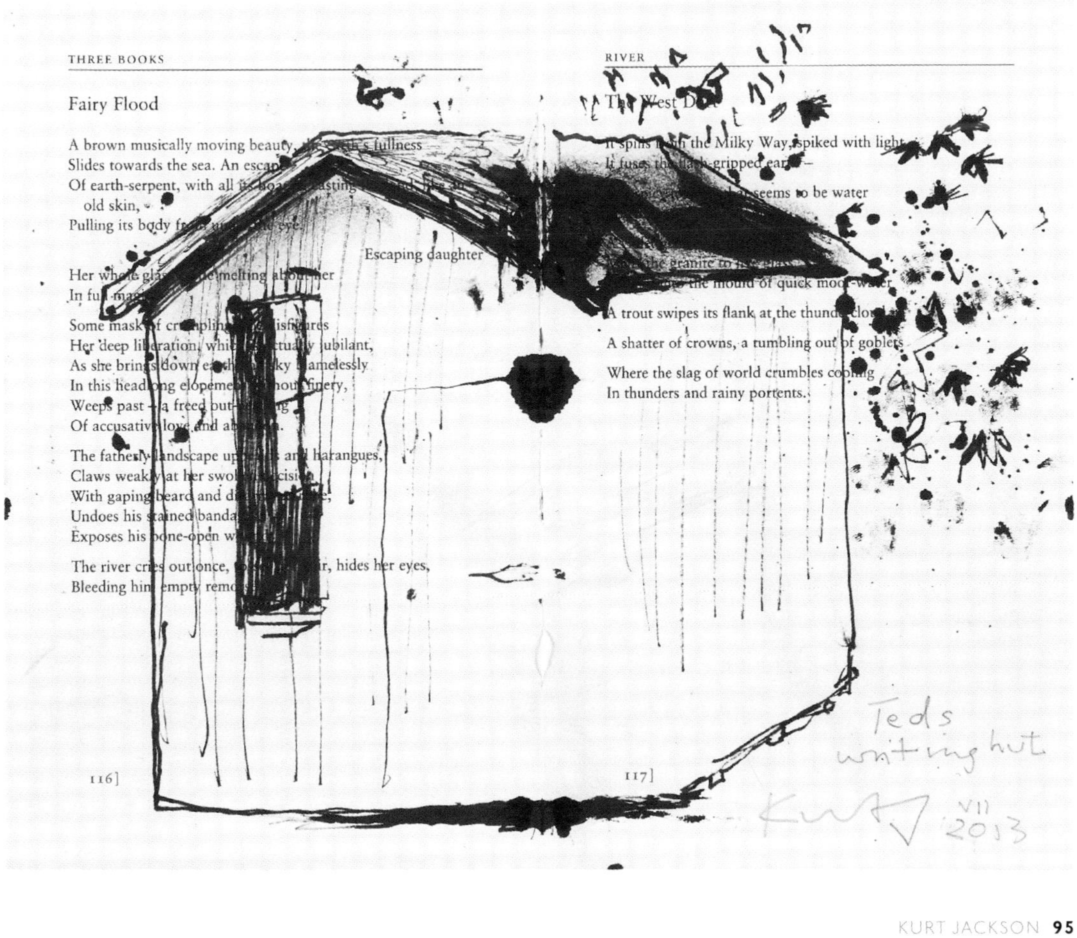
THREE BOOKS
RIVER
Fairy Flood
Escaping daughter
A shatter of crowns, a tumbling out of goblets
In thunders and rainy portents.
116]
117]
Teds writing hut
VII 2013

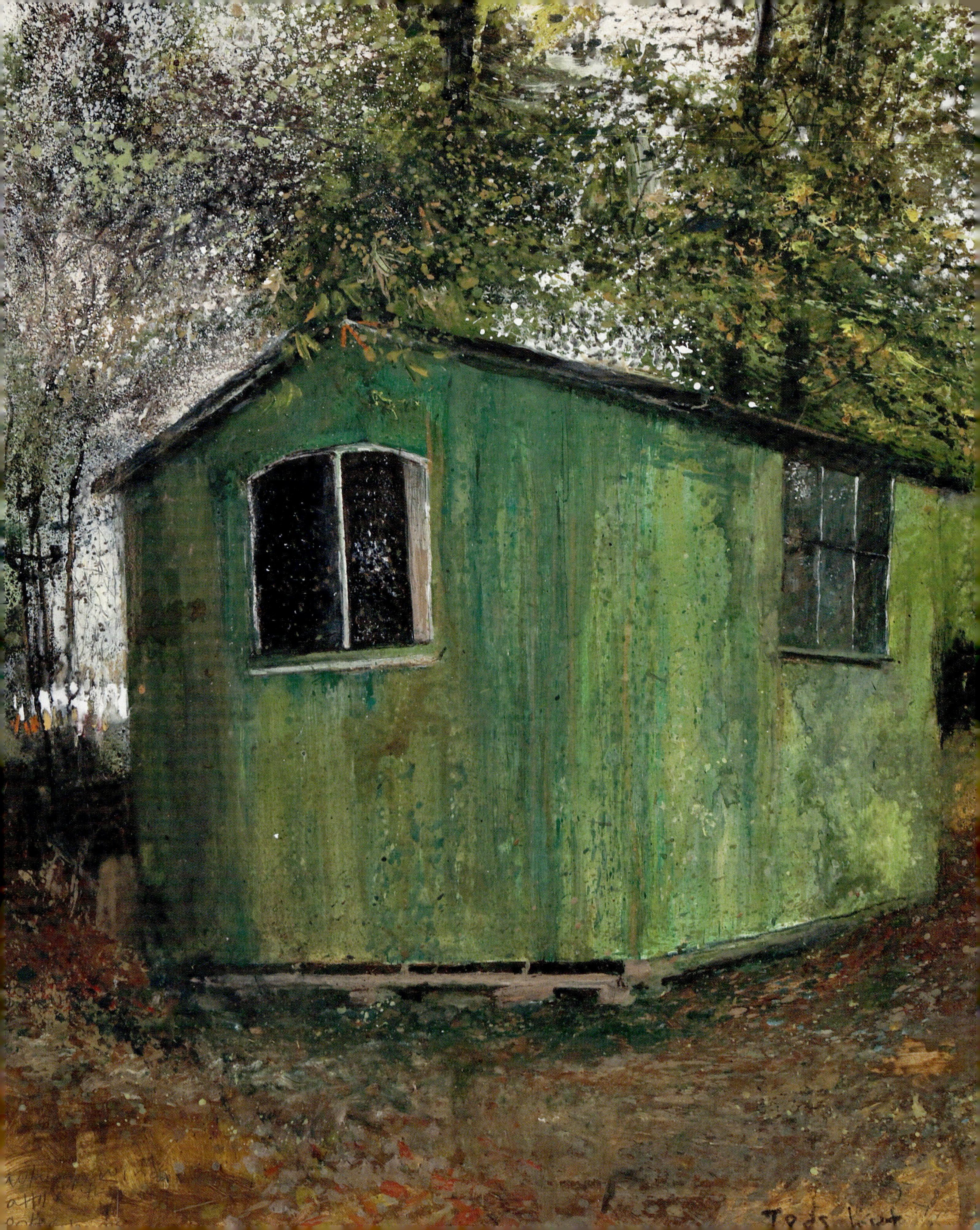
Tods hut

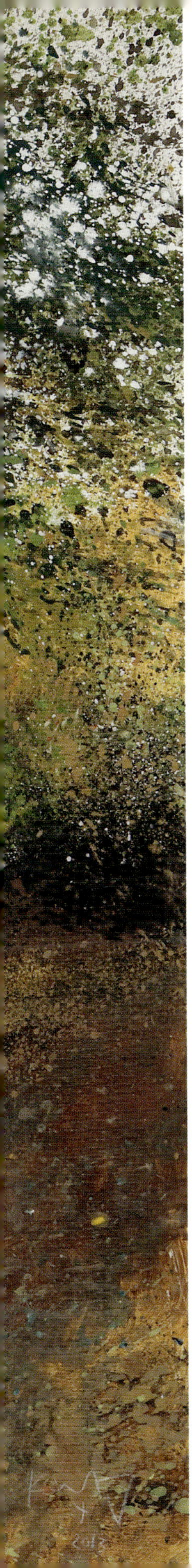

48. **Ted's hut. Autumn winds rattling the conker leaves**
October 2013 • mixed media on board • 65 x 65 cm

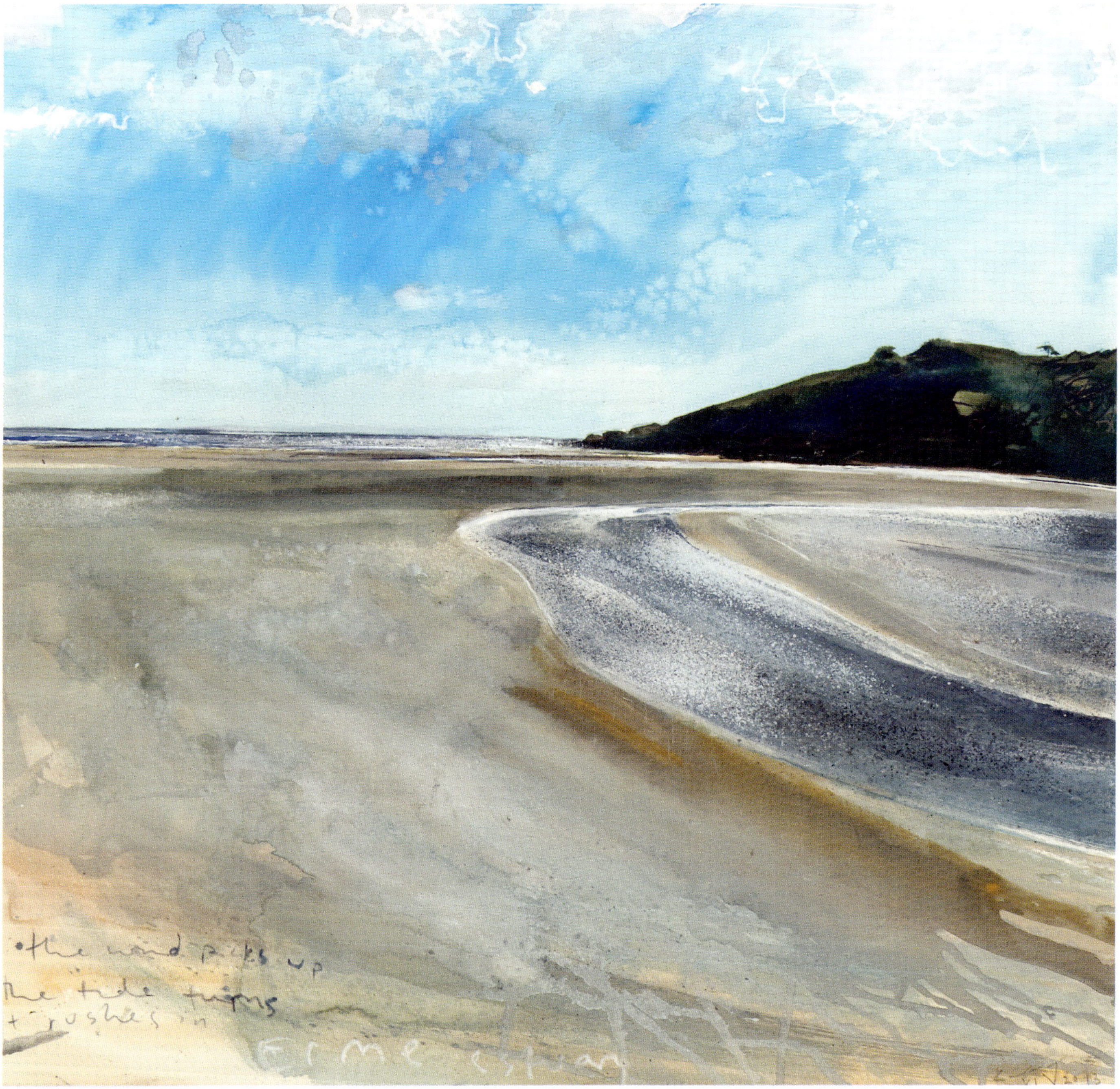

49. **The wind picks up, the tide turns and rushes in. Erme estuary**
June 2013 • mixed media on paper • 56 x 61 cm

17. An estuary, Devon

Robert Hurrell

The peaceful tranquillity of a wild estuary where the long passage of time is etched into the many trees growing along its steep wooded shores. The tide daily ebbing and flowing with the scent of the sea, as it meanders through creeks, mudflats, sand and saltmarsh. The calls of Curlew, Kingfisher, Wigeon, Grey Heron, Buzzard and now Little Egrets. The memories of people, some passed away, so many memories of such enjoyment, exploration, adventure and fun in this wild place. The massive splash in the darkness of Salar the Salmon heard leaping away upstream is now rare.

Paul and I pitting our instincts against the grey ghosts on the flooding tide; the mermaid found swimming in the salmon pool; wriggling elvers hiding by the old salmon trap; fish poachers; an encounter long ago in a small Avon dingy with a very real circling shark (but was it a Basking, Blue, Thresher or even a Porbeagle?); cold short swims (not all planned ones either). The unexpected Rainbow trout caught on bread whilst mulletting that was full of small Shore crabs and winged Red ants. Digging for slippery silver sand eels in the shifting sands or searching bladderwrack for peelers. The elusive, mythical Bass talked about so often but so rarely caught. Paul's one big bass. Shoals of trout smolts rippling the waters, awaiting the tide at sunset. Mullet becoming active many minutes before the flood tide had even reached their pools – they must have their own internal tide clock.

The beautiful arched estuary boat-house. Tiny Firecrests vanishing inside hanging curled-up dead oak leaves, searching for food in the winter.

Bathing house and beach log fires; bats flittering in low arcs over the water; making small boats with Mary and Andrew; flying my birthday kite on the beach in a February snowstorm; my brother's handcrafted wooden boat drifting away midstream on the fast incoming tide then remarkably finding it again many days later; hearing unknown footsteps in the darkness whilst fishing; several tall tales of lost fish; many young herons fishing the mudflats; the now long-gone mussel bed at the estuary mouth; making lime and mortar to repair the vertically slated external walls of the bathing house – challenging gravity.

An otter seal print left in the sand on the ebbing tide, shadowy ripples, holts, hovers, spraints and bird-like whistles – otters chasing their tails and chasing fish. Knowing you are in their place too. Sleeping on the water and learning to row. The streaking shooting star perfectly reflected in quiet, still waters.

Robert Hurrell *has been an Environment Agency fisheries officer since 1989. He is a rower of traditional Cornish wooden pilot gigs, skiffs and flashboats, a swimmer, fisher and photographer. A very keen observer and recorder of wildlife (especially birds, otters and bats) and of finding lovely natural forms, shapes and patterns in nature. He first met Kurt many years ago when he was seeking out Salar, the leaping Atlantic salmon.*

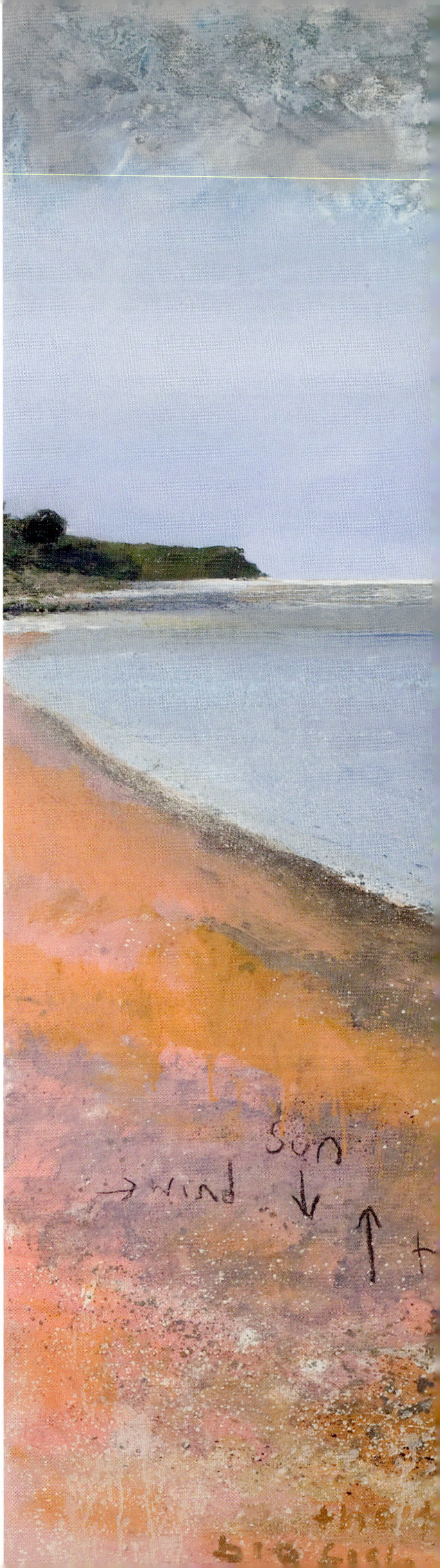

50. **The tide drops, big fish leap**
2013 • mixed media and sand on linen • 170 x 195 cm

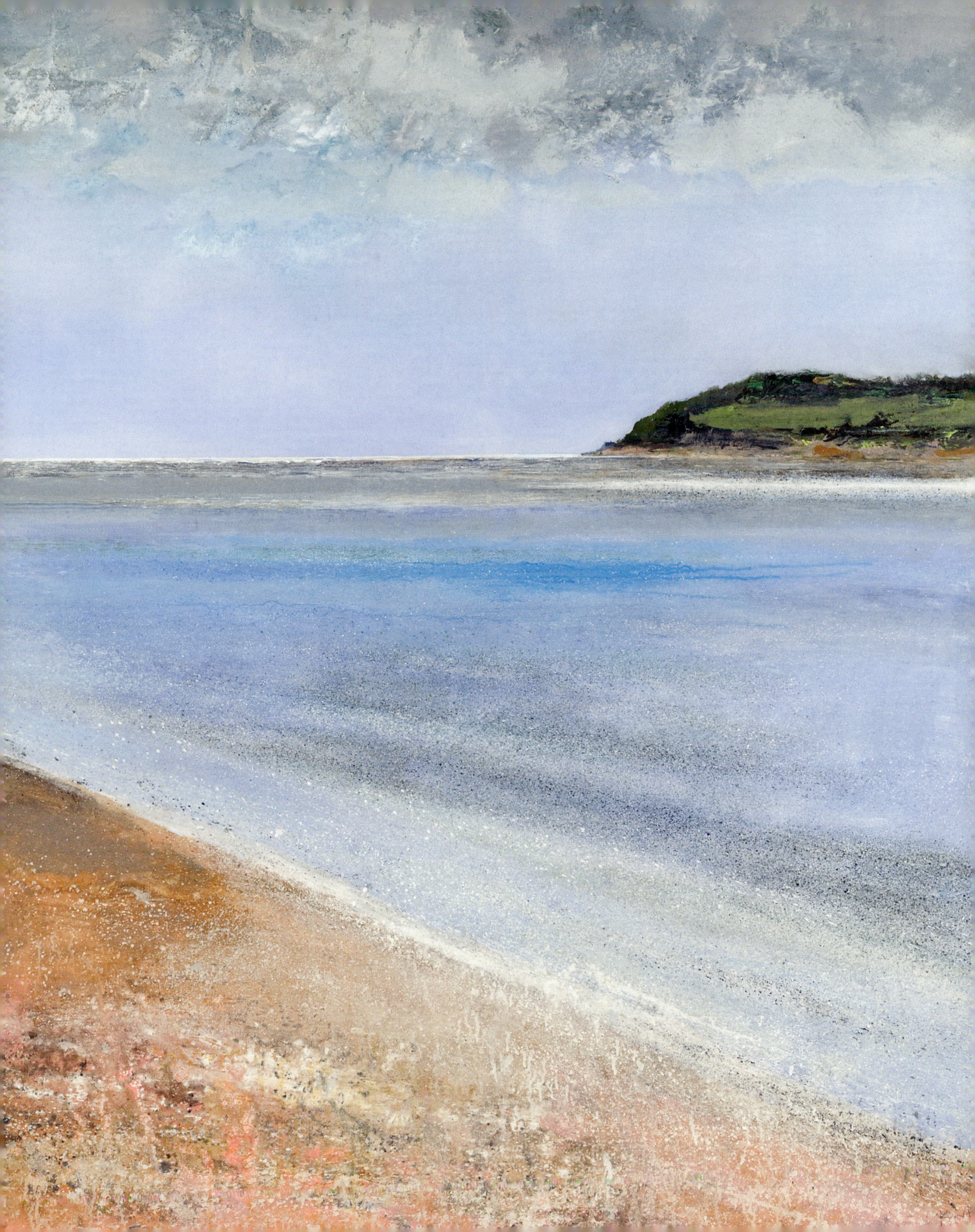

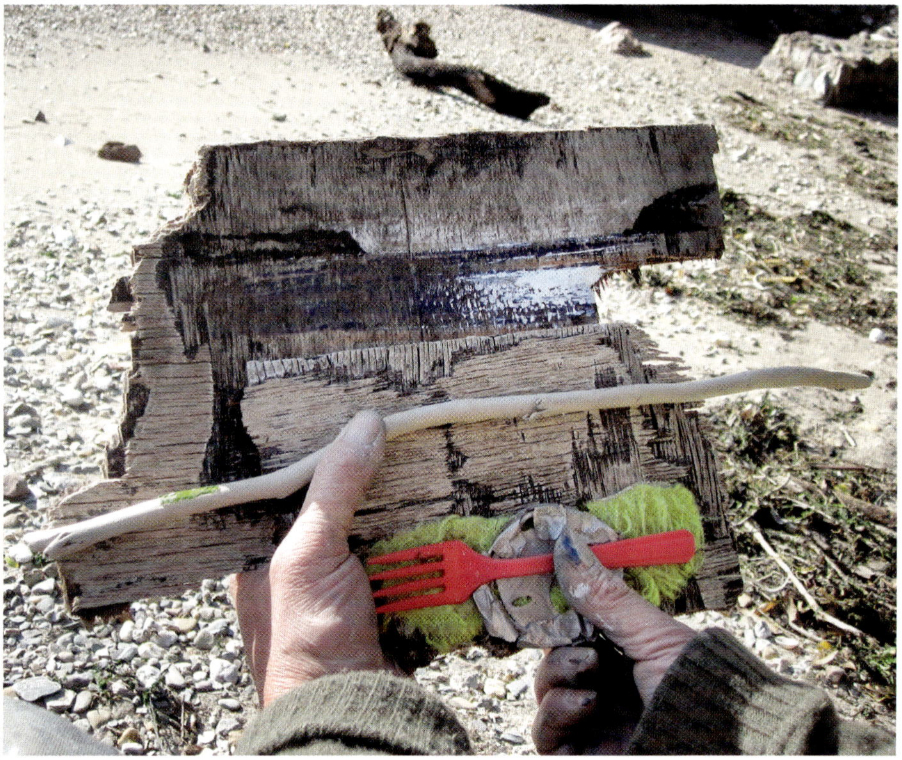

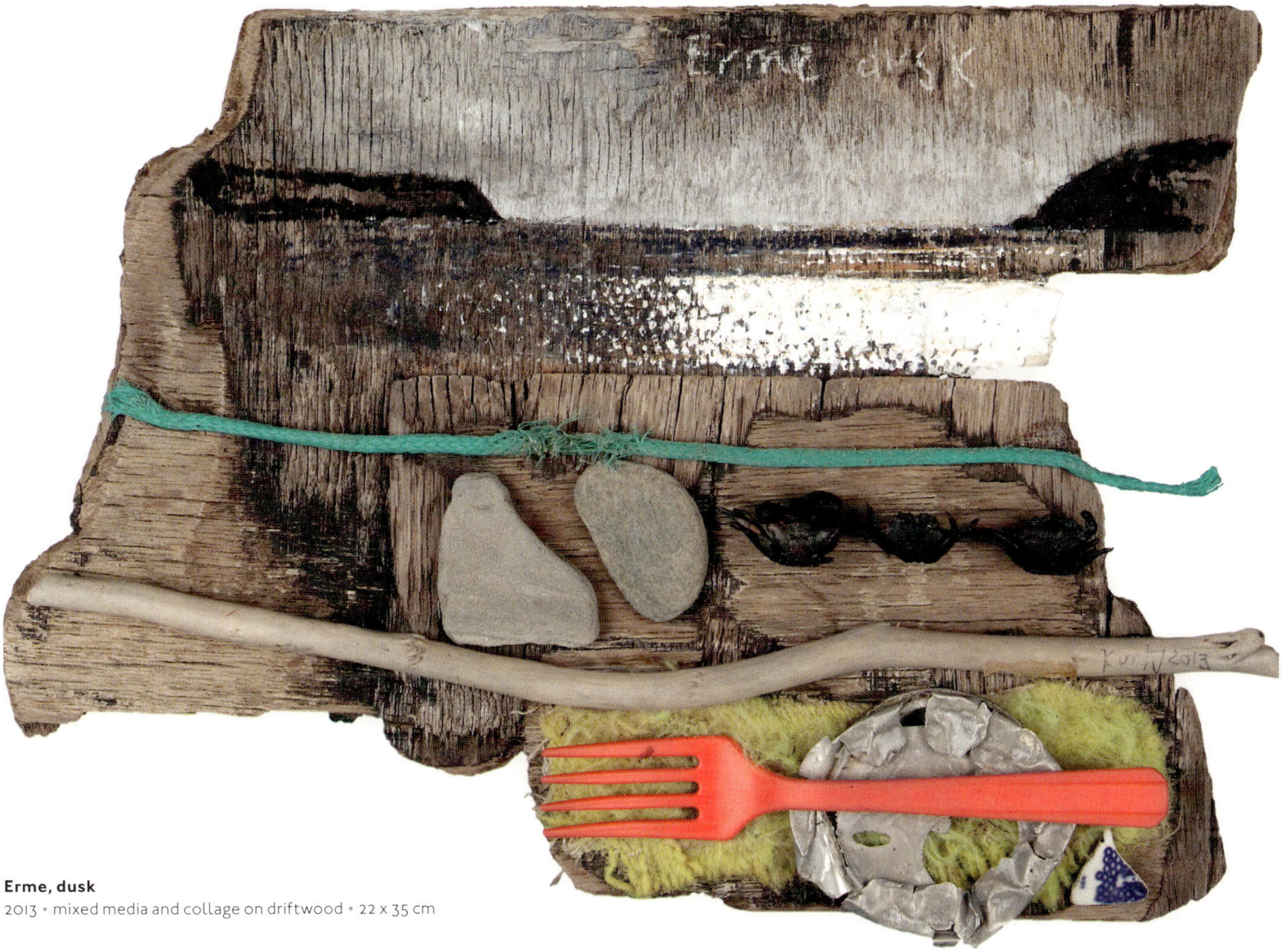

51. **Erme, dusk**
2013 • mixed media and collage on driftwood • 22 x 35 cm

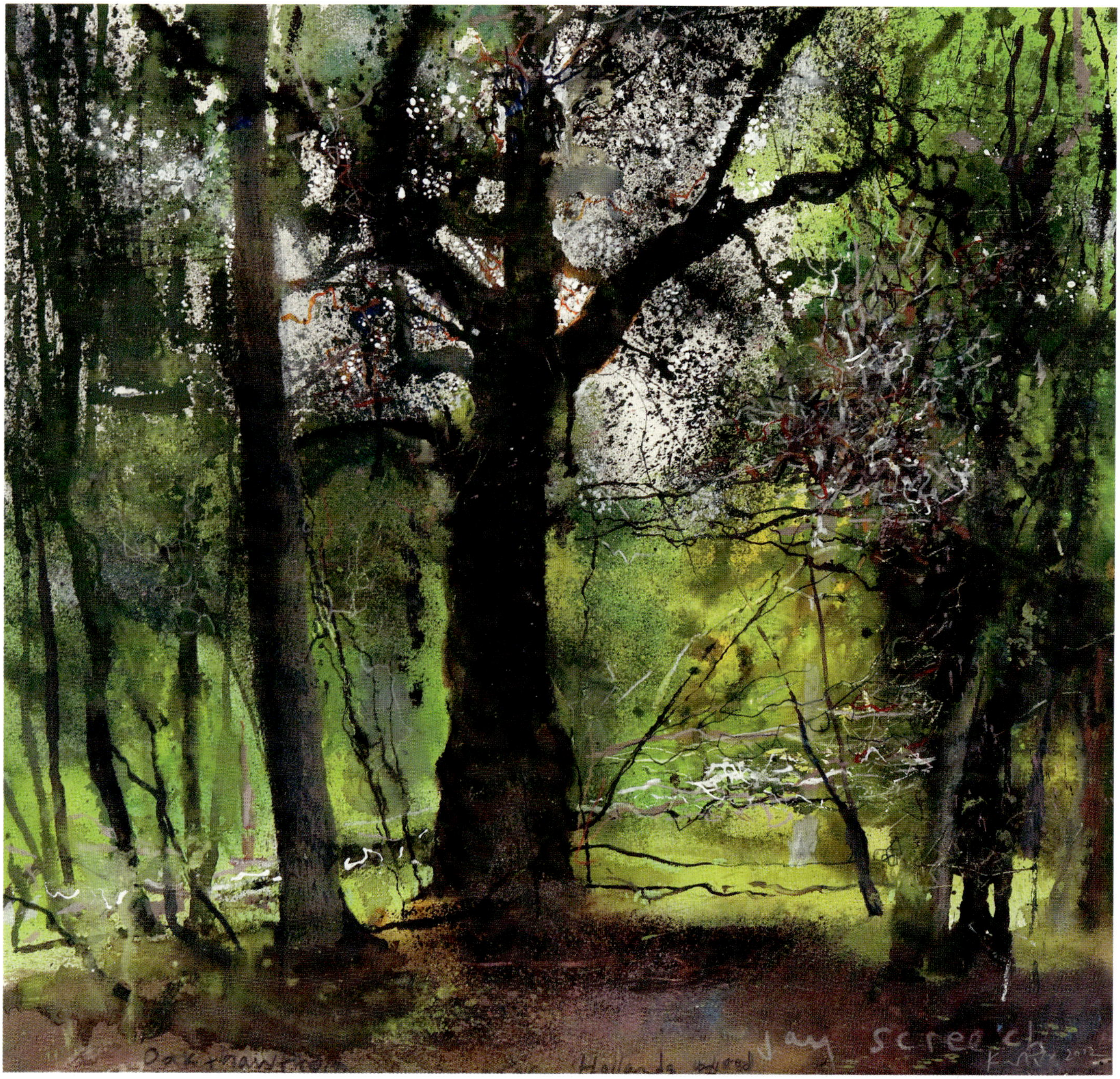

52. **Jay screech, oak and hawthorn, near Hollands Wood**
October 2012 • mixed media on paper • 57 x 61 cm

18. The New Forest – all of it

Caroline Jackson

My first strong memories ever are of the forest – camping at Backley Plain and then Pigbush: both in the depths of the Forest with ancient woods, heaths, bogs and rivers. I am from a large family and as such it defined me as a child: I was one of the Bradburys. When we camped we camped wild, as you did and as you could in the 1960s – seven of us children, the nine of us altogether, in a green Girl Guide-type ridge tent. The Bedford van driving out across the heath making its own road (the archaeological ruts still remain from those less populated times), then camping all alone in the wilderness, with just a few gypsies out there in the distance with their tell-tale fires.

The family campsite: the tent, a pit loo, cooking over the wood fire, full-English breakfasts – all smoky flavours. Dad would wake us early to walk quietly (all nine of us!) to catch sight of deer down a ride or ponies in the camp nibbling the cropped grass. Our days were spent jumping streams, playing follow the leader across fallen trees over rivers, dares … Then one year we arrived and all had changed: ditches had been dug, campsites had been created, and fires were banned. We had cold meals that year.

We continued with daytrips at weekends. My maths teacher father would set us orienteering courses that took us out across the heaths, through the ancient woods, the inclosures … following pony paths through that playground of kings. Then in the early 1980s I return with Kurt, and he starts to paint my place.

Fast forward ten years and we are back camping – but this time with my own family on a site near Brokenhurst a mile or two west of Pigbush, then at Stoney Cross. Seth, Zinzi and Chloë love it too; love the camping, the ponies, the forest rides, the expanse of it all.

Kurt paints the Forest throughout; a self-portrait in front of a majestic oak – stretched canvas and large mirror are all part of a family trip away; Lymington River, strong light, brown water (and our three off to play follow the leader across fallen trees …).

We return, but just the two of us, Kurt and I. This time to Bell's Hat, then Shave Green, for the 'Three Woods' project shown at the St Barbe Museum and Art Gallery, Lymington. Then, again-and-again we cross the New Forest on the A31 to visit our youngest, Chloë, at Southampton University.

Summer 2013 and I sit writing this under the oaks near Balmer Lawn next to Kurt as he paints the smooth beeches and gnarly oaks. We've got a robin for company, ponies munching nearby, leaves in the breeze, the earthy mossy scent of the woods around us, and the sun highlighting the bracken in the depths of the Forest. It is, to me, Paradise.

__Caroline Jackson__ met her husband Kurt at Oxford University whilst both were reading zoology and is mother to their three grown children. As the director of their company she has managed Kurt and his work for the last 30 years and is currently working on a project to build The Jackson Foundation near where they live in St Just. A committed feminist and environmentalist, she has planted her own wood and shares a passion with Kurt for growing their own veg.

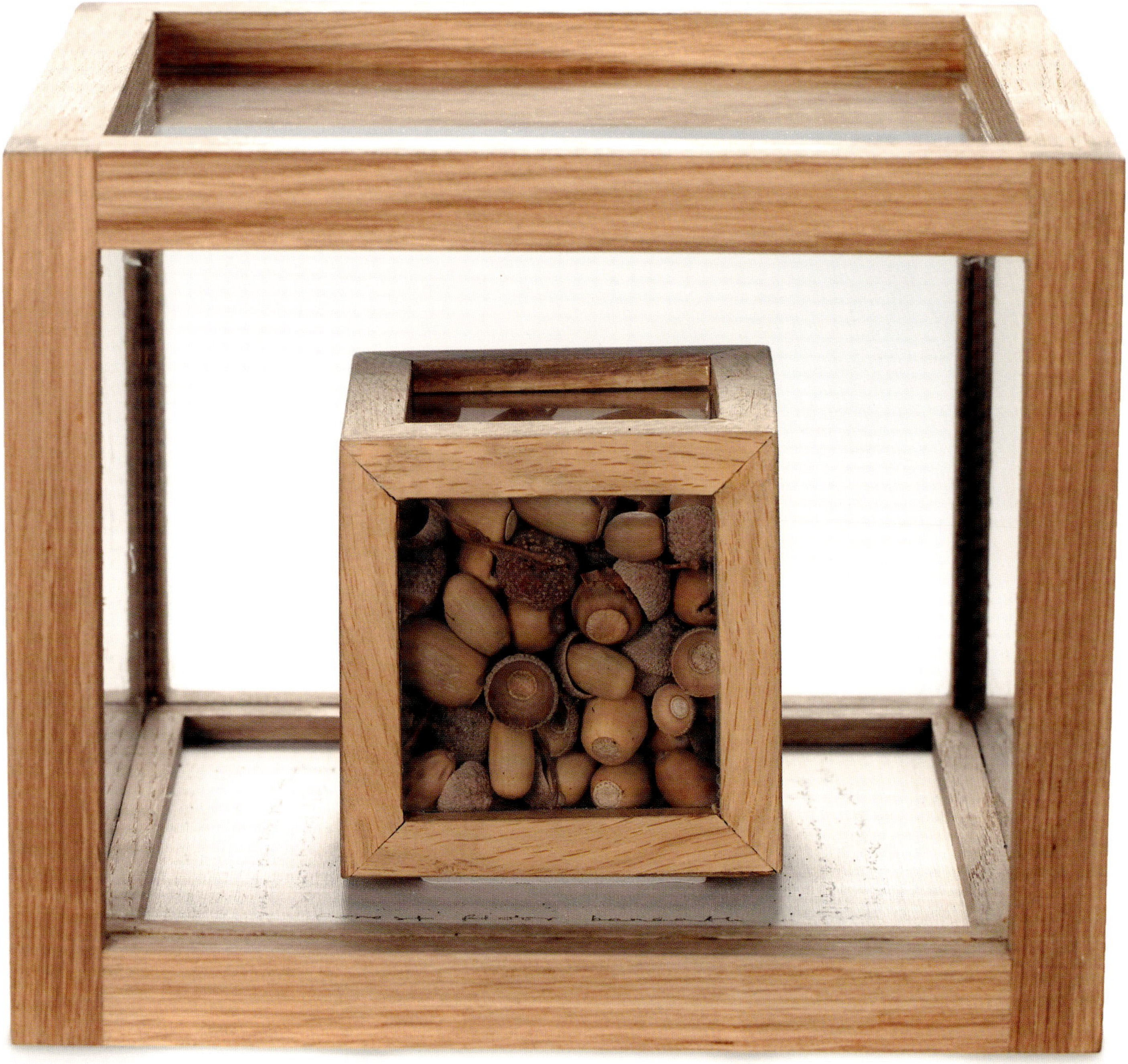

53. **New Forest box of oak**
autumn 2012 • acorns, oak and pencil • 19 x 24 x 24 cm

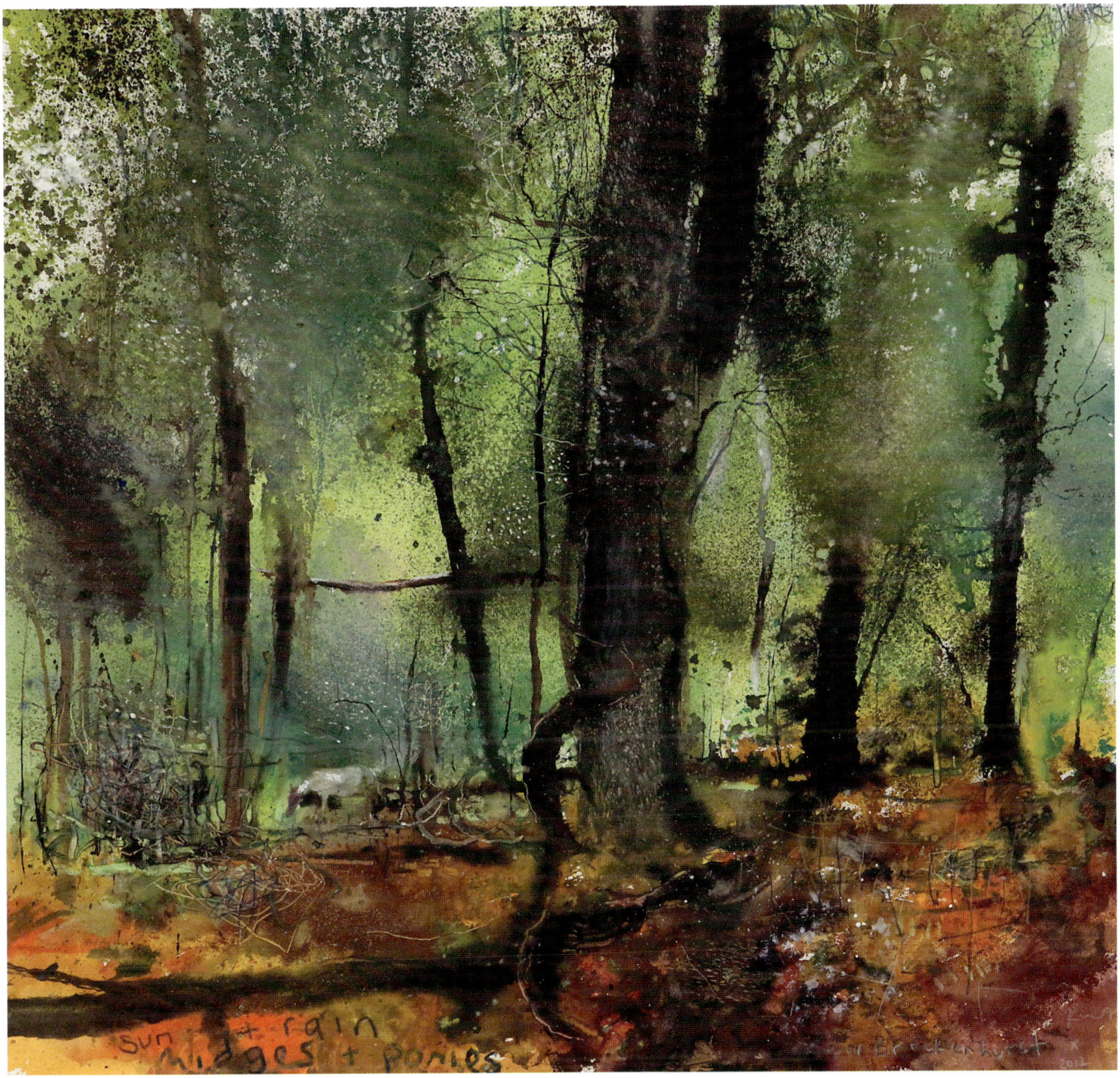

54. **Sun and rain, midges and ponies**
October 2012 • mixed media on paper • 56.5 x 61 cm

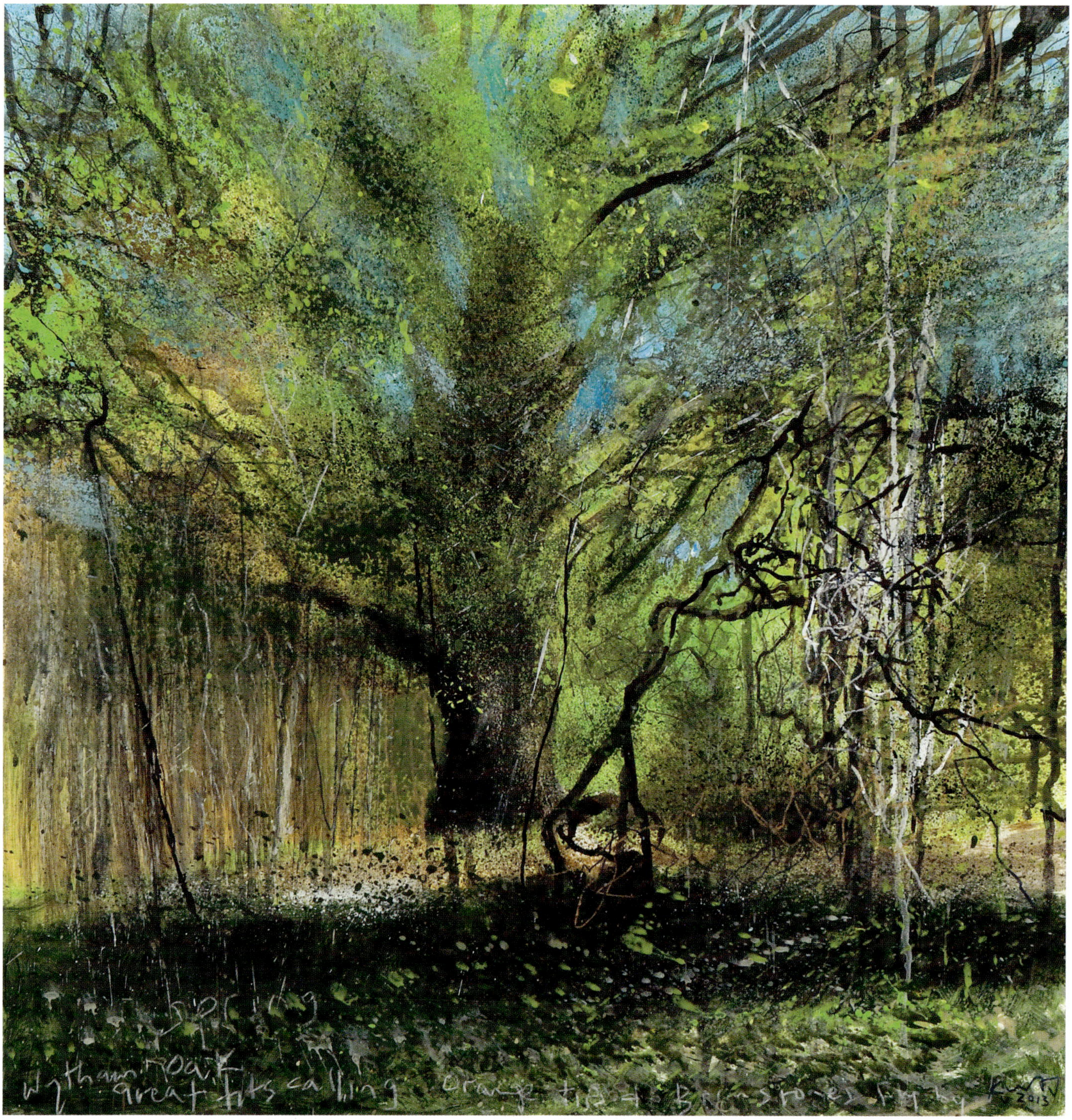

55. **Spring, Wytham Oak. Great tits calling, orange tips and brimstones fly by**
May 2013 • mixed media on board • 52 x 51 cm

19. Wytham Woods, Oxfordshire

John Krebs

If there were a Nobel Prize for Ecology, and if you could award it to a place rather than a person, Wytham Woods, near Oxford, would surely be a prime candidate. It is almost certainly unmatched anywhere in the world as a place of sustained, intensive, ecological research extending over nearly three quarters of a century. The ecological concepts and discoveries based on work carried out at Wytham read like a text book of ecology.

The Wytham Estate, encompassing 1250 hectares of which 400 are woodland, was donated to Oxford University in 1942 by Raymond ffennell, an Englishman who had made a fortune in the South African mining boom in the early twentieth century. The bequest asked the University to maintain the natural beauty of the woodlands and use them for instruction of students and for research. ffennell also requested that the woods be named the Woods of Hazel, after his daughter Hazel, who died in 1939.

The woods are ancient. The documented record goes back to 1100, when Henry I granted Abingdon Abbey the right to hunt deer from what was then called Cumnor Woods. But pollen records suggest that by 6000 BC oak, elm and hazel woodland was dominant at Wytham. In medieval times the woodland was harvested fuel, by coppice-cutting trees such as ash and field maple. Some of the coppice stools (the circle of young shoots surrounding the long-since decayed original trunk) are 4–6 metres across and may be 1000 years old. Today, the canopy is dominated by oak, ash and sycamore, with species such as hazel and field maple prominent in the under story. In the past seven decades, more than 150 scientists have carried out ecological research at Wytham, and I was lucky enough to be one of them. When I began my research career, in 1966, as a student working on populations of great tits, I felt as though I was following a long line of dauntingly important and clever predecessors stretching back to 1947. Now I realise that I was, if not in the pioneer group, at least one of the early settlers.

We now appreciate more than ever before that long-term ecological records have an intrinsic value that grows over time, yielding unique and crucial insights into the response of the natural world to climate change. As new techniques have developed – DNA fingerprinting, radio-tracking, satellite imagery – new questions have been asked and answered. When I built my first population model of the Great Tits, it was run on an electro-mechanical calculator, the computing equivalent of travelling by horse-drawn carriage. But for when I think back to the many hours, days and weeks spent working in Wytham Woods, often starting at dawn on cold wet winter mornings, I think of the beauty. For me, it is hard to match the sensation of inhaling the scent of a carpet of damp moss on a February morning and chewing 'bread and cheese' – the first, pale green, buds of hawthorn that foretell the arrival of spring, and another bird breeding season, in Wytham.

Lord John Krebs *studied zoology at Oxford University. He carried out his doctoral research in Wytham Woods on the ecology of great tits. He subsequently held academic posts at the Universities of British Columbia, Wales and Oxford. He has been chief executive of the Natural Environment Research Council, chairman of the Food Standards Agency, chairman of the Adaptation sub-committee of the Climate Change Committee and chairman of the House of Lords Science and Technology Select Committee. He is principal of Jesus College Oxford and is married to Sarah Phibbs.*

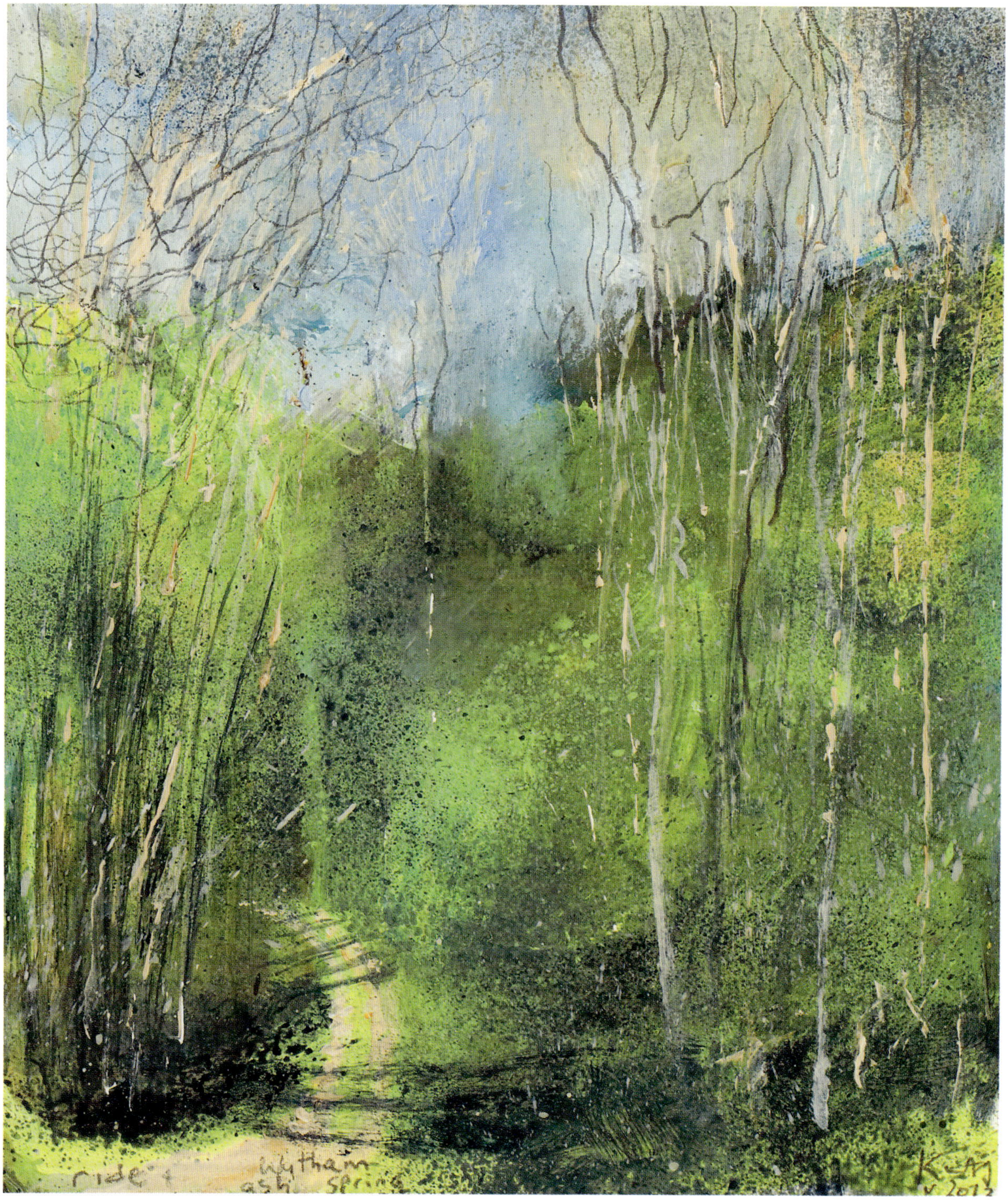

56. **Wytham ride, spring ash**
May 2013 • mixed media on board • 22 x 19 cm

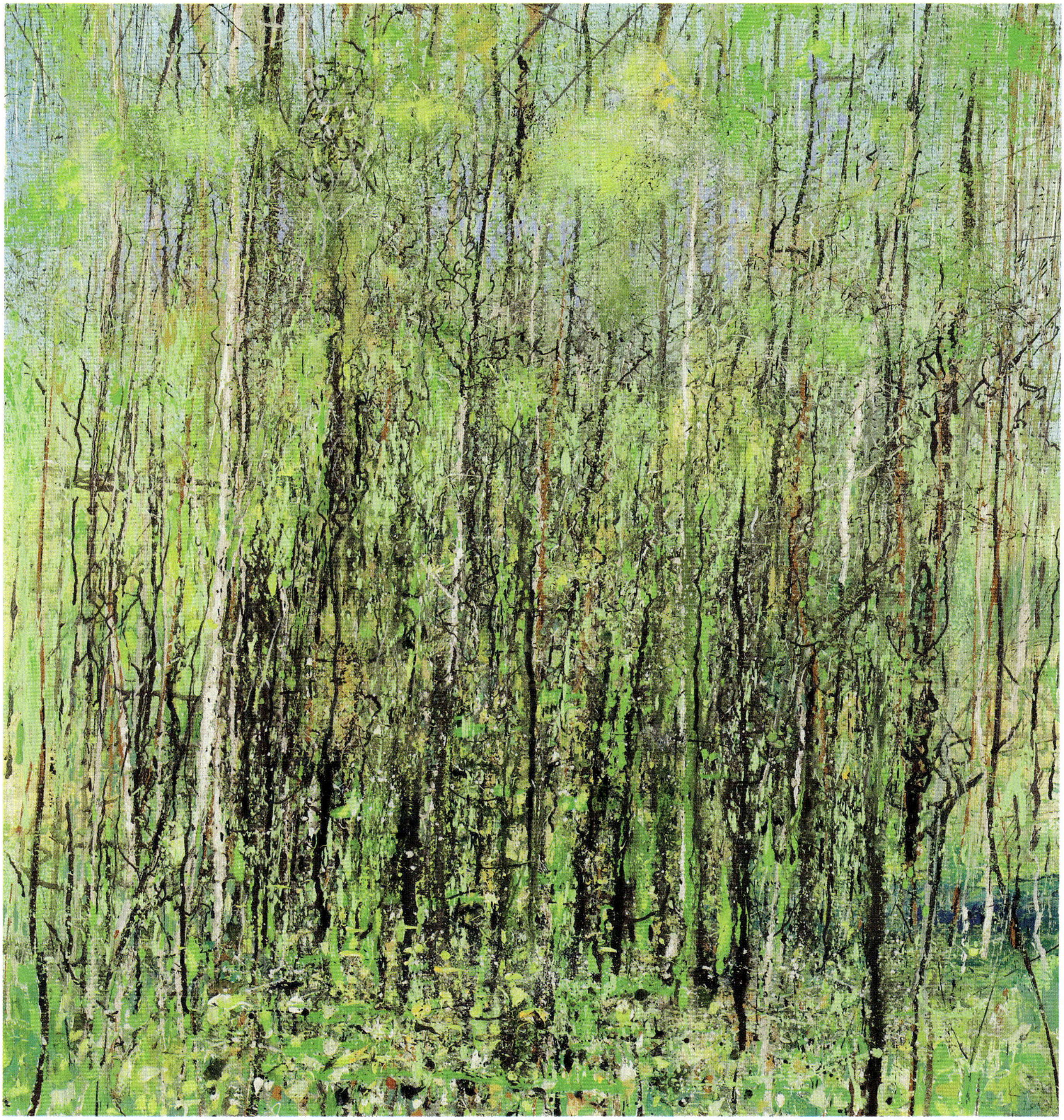

57. **Wytham bird song and spring greens**
2013 • oil on canvas • 92 x 92 cm

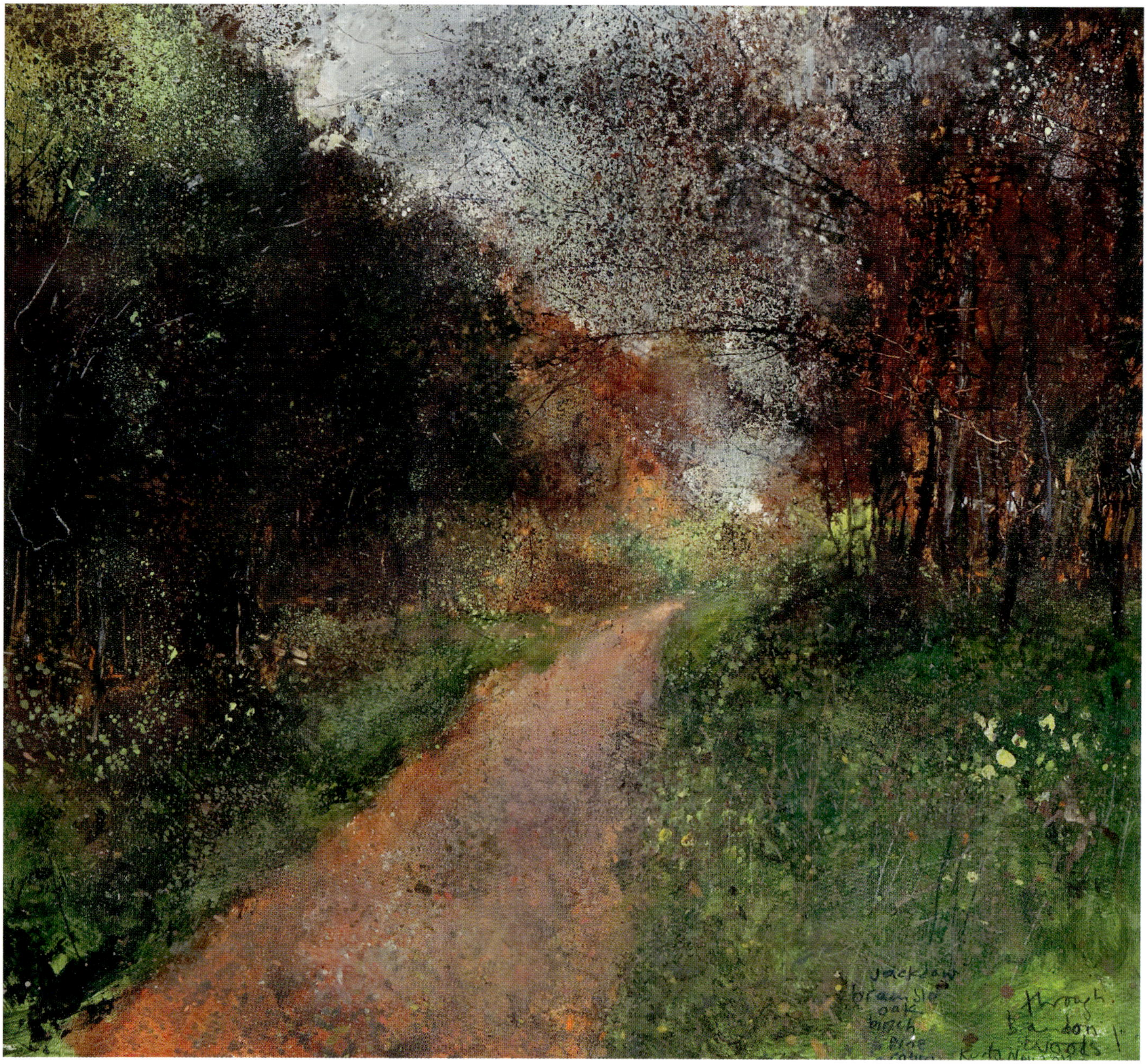

58. **Through Brandon Woods. Jackdaw, bramble, oak, birch, pine, robin**
November 2013 • mixed media on board • 54 x 60 cm

20. Brandon Woods, Warwickshire

Catherine Leyshon

It is late summer. Dad is lifting me up to reach the blackberries that are highest on the bush, its new canes bursting out from the old growth like an exploding firework stilled in mid-air. Hoisted between the exuberant brambles, I reach out for the berries, teasing away sheltering leaves and bravely ignoring spider webs and stink bugs. I am eight and my little purple-stained hands cannot hold many blackberries so I gather them against my rust-coloured jumper, knitted by Mum. Dad swings me down effortlessly and I tumble my bounty into the old ice-cream box that has stashed many seasons of fruit in the freezer. Mum would make apple and blackberry pie later, but most of these berries were destined for a higher purpose: homemade wine. My brother is further down the stand of blackberries, picking determinedly, his thick blond hair shining in the sun. We had walked into Brandon Woods early on a bright, cool Sunday morning, working through the lightless reach of evergreens to where the path opens out to admit sun and air beyond the daunting pines and conifers. The blackberry bushes are on the edge of the old growth from a time when the woods were part of the Forest of Arden, a sprawling medieval wood-land, itself a relic of a largely forested isle.

That Sunday morning, I was unwittingly connected to the trajectories that met there fleetingly in time and space and the many people who had walked along that track across the centuries. Working together to gather the berries, my dad created a place where we became part of his trajectory, his story. Dad was a person whose self-sufficiency and self-improvement were the cornerstones of a resourcefulness that brought us to the blackberry stands every year. He picked blackberries along the hedgerows of his Cambridgeshire boyhood, and along the edge of the U.S. airforce base where he worked as an apprentice electrician during the war, watching bombers land as he mended the runway lights. Now he's here with his children, lofting his little girl into the blue to reach the choicest fruit. By midday we are too hot and we're all thinking about going home for Sunday lunch, back through the trees to the forest gate. When we walk in to the house, Mum will be amongst the steam and heat of preparations, and the smell of the roast will lure us further in. Dad will pour a can of bitter into a pint glass with a sturdy handle, and have a handful of roasted peanuts before lunch. Later, the wine-making equipment will appear for the peculiar alchemy of blackberries, water, sugar and yeast. At some point in the winter, Dad will enter the cupboard under the stairs – a complex laboratory of demi-johns, hygrometers, tubes, and buckets – lit with a single bare bulb. Our distant late-summer fruit forage will be recalled as he emerges with a bottle of red wine. Time will pass and we will all fly apart in different directions, along different trajectories.

I haven't been back to Brandon Woods for 25 years, perhaps more. But from a single blackberry bush on a single late-summer day grows this tangle of memories, anchoring a set of stories about childhood, place, identity, family and – as the years pass – loss and longing. It is not necessary to return to be able to hold the place in my imagination, to recall my Dad's sturdy grip, his work-hewn hands, his quiet satisfaction at the harvest. It is enough that the imbrications of place and memory are irresistible and sustaining.

Catherine Leyshon *was born and grew up in Warwickshire. She is a geographer interested in place, landscape and identity in the mediums of art, writing and film. Catherine's piece of writing is dedicated to John Brace, 1934–2012.*

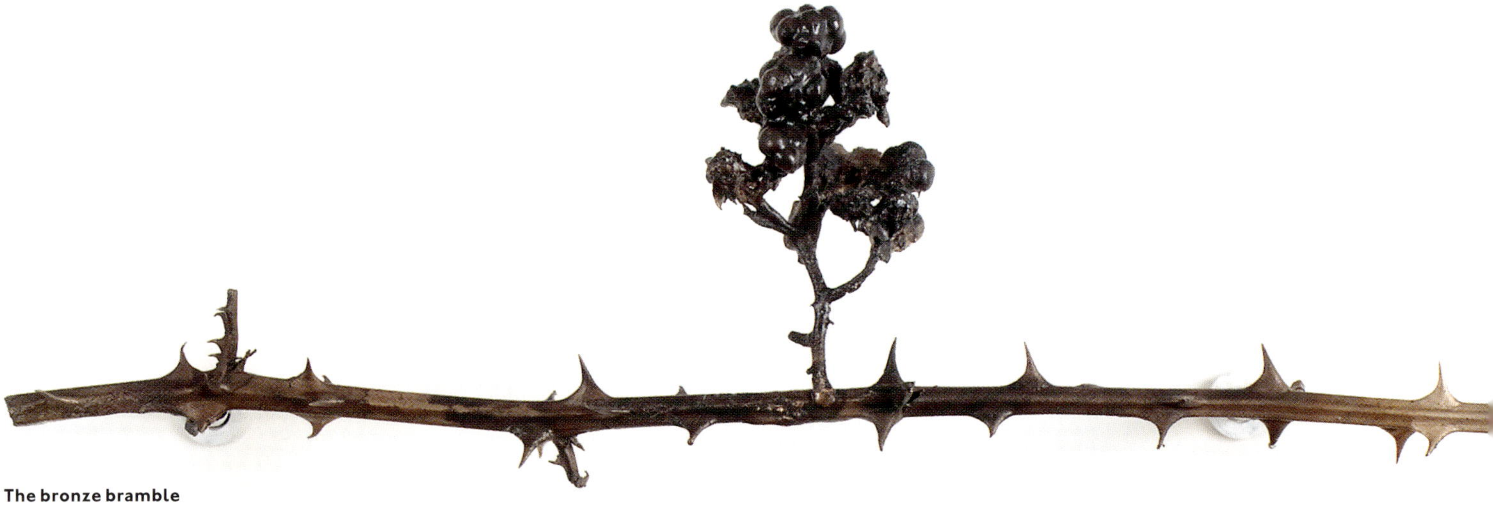

59. **The bronze bramble**
2012 • bronze • 23 x 46 cm

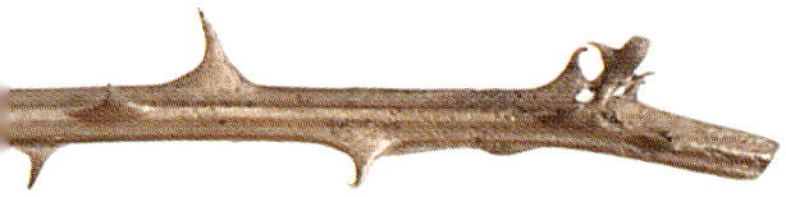

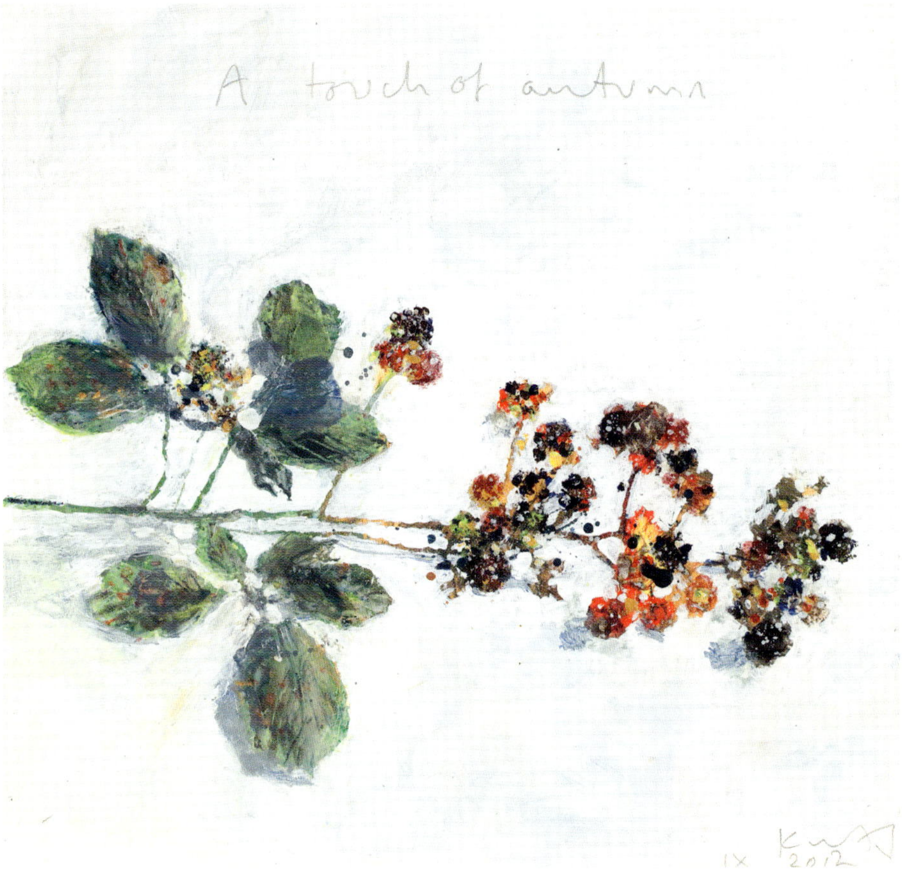

60. **A touch of autumn**
September 2012 • acrylic on board • 21 x 22 cm

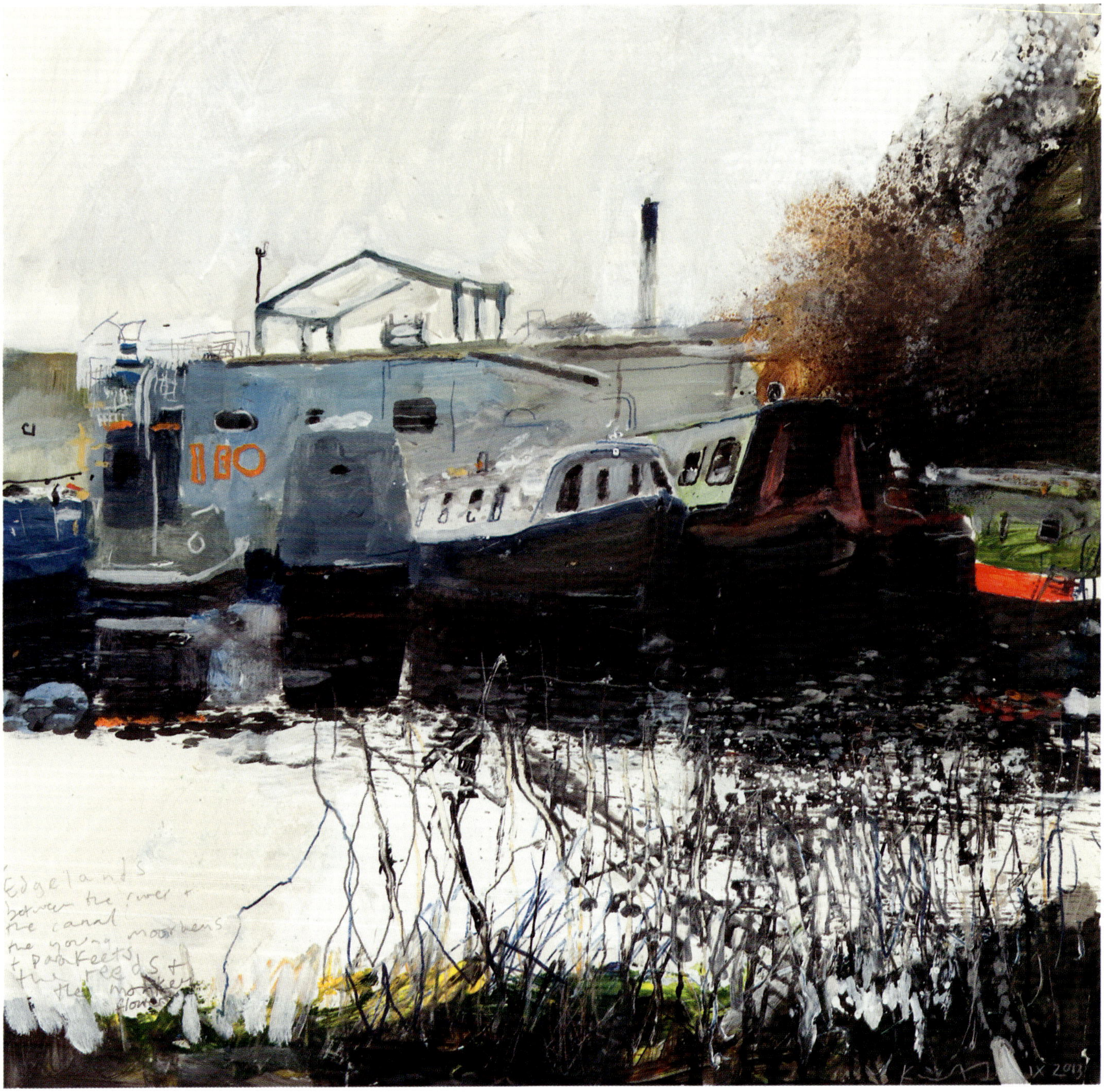

61. **Edgelands, between the river and the canal. Young moorhens and parakeets, reeds and monkey flowers**
September 2013 • mixed media on board • 50 x 54 cm

21. Grand Union Canal/River Colne

Richard Mabey

I discovered this Dadaist patch of urban wild in the late summer of 1972, when I was struggling to find a shape for the introductory chapter to *The Unofficial Countryside*. Raddled from a day cooped up in an office, I'd left a traffic jam on the Uxbridge–Rickmansworth road on impulse, dropped down to a valley where the River Colne and the Grand Union Canal run in tandem, and had found myself in this unclassifiable breathing space, with a sprawling sewage works to the west and sheep-grazed chalk hills rising up towards Moor Park Golf Course to the east. The omens were encouragingly incongruous: bad puns on pub signs ('The Coy Carp'), a white-water canoe slalom improvised by the edge of an industrial weir. There were swallows looping under the giant pipes that carried the sewage across the canal and spikes of purple loosestrife (*Lysimachia* – the deliverer from strife!) along the water's edge.

I've come back again, 40 years later, and I'm astonished by how little the place has changed. 'Yellow water lilies drooped like balls of molten wax', I'd written in 1973, and so they still are, in crystal-clear water. Naturalized buddleia, from China, is growing next to impeccably native yellow iris. A grey wagtail loops across the cut towards the weir in the exact same place it had four decades ago. What is different is the influx of people, especially boat people. The gentrification of Chorleywood has seeped south, picking up bohemian and dissident shades on the way. An old bargeman's cottage with a glass-walled Bauhaus-style extension sits not 100 yards from the narrowboat *Pisces*, emblazoned with the slogan 'Affordable boating for the community'. A pair of cormorants perform synchronized underwater dives in front of a lawn decked out with a geodesic climbing frame. There are fisherman's day-boats, floating weekend hideaways, houseboats done up in hippy baroque. Iain Sinclair, tramping the canal a mile or so further north in his circumnavigation of the M25, *London Orbital*, spotted a boat with the strapline 'Viscount Sasha, International Physiotherapist to the President of the USA'. I spotted a launch with a map of the entire solar system tricked out in transfers on the windscreen.

I can see the attractions of this aquatic commune. But why do I find this compromised edgeland so invigorating, when I could be sauntering in 'real' countryside' a mile away? Is it a touch of inverted snobbery, the ecological equivalent of the fashionable taste for 'shabby chic'? Maybe, but I think there's also a glimpse of redemption in these unkempt borderlands.

Nearly a century ago, the Metropolitan Railways publicity brochures on this patch boasted of 'the song of the nightingale for which the neighbourhood is renowned ... the network of translucent rivers traversing the valley, render Rickmansworth a Mecca to the city man pining for country and pure air.' The nightingales are long gone, and the air rather less than pure, but the riot of wild life pushing against the urban edges seems to me rather hopeful. It's neither pugnacious nor pet-like, just possessed of a sublimely indifferent neighbourliness. 'Do your best, do your worst, we'll muck along.'

***Richard Mabey**'s books include* The Unofficial Countryside *and* Nature Cure.
He is a fellow of the Royal Society for Literature and lives in Norfolk.

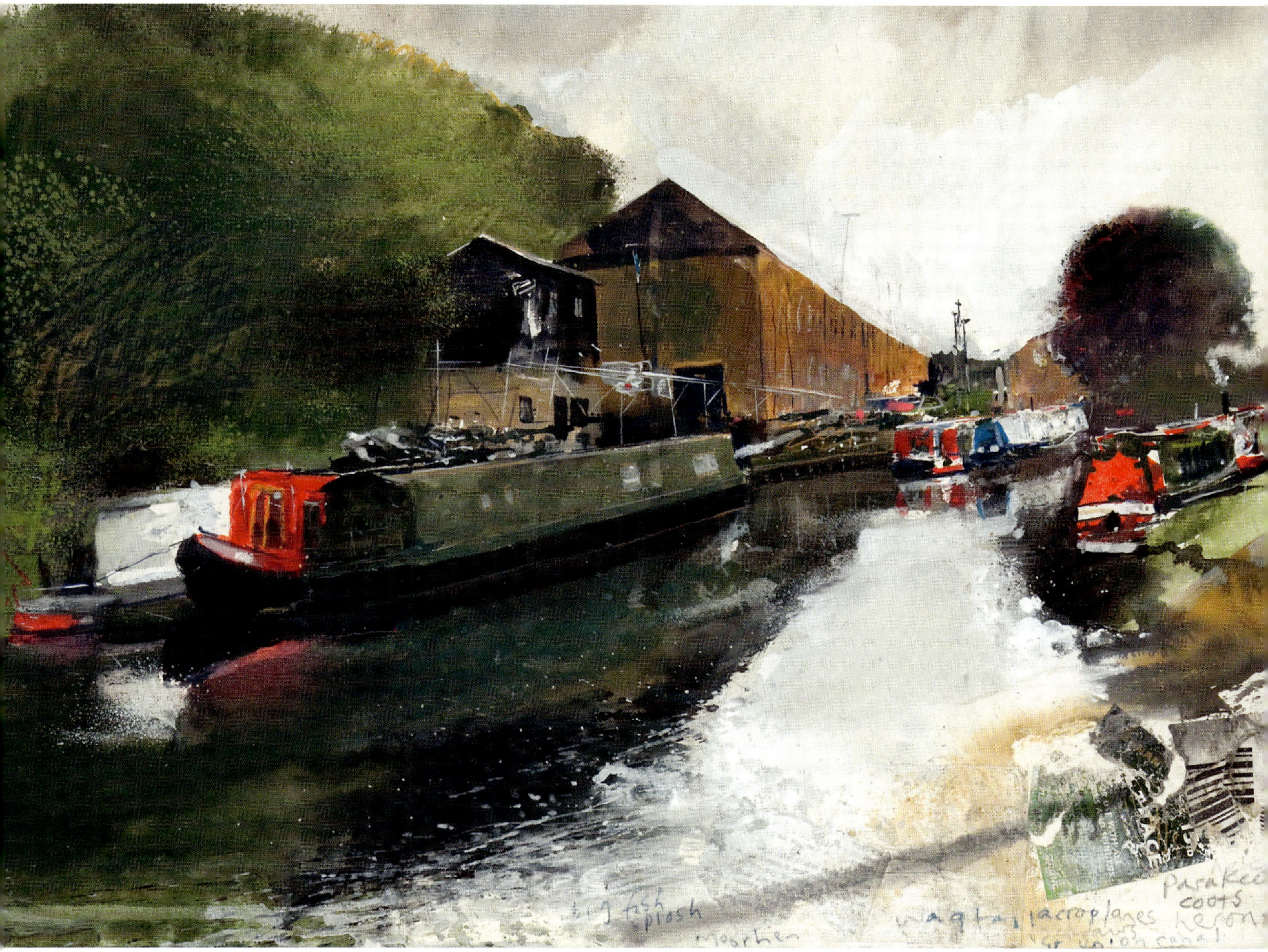

62. **Grand Union canal. Big fish splosh, moorhen, wagtails, aeroplanes, jackdaws, helicopters, parakeets, coots, heron**
September 2013 • mixed media and collage on paper • 42 x 62 cm

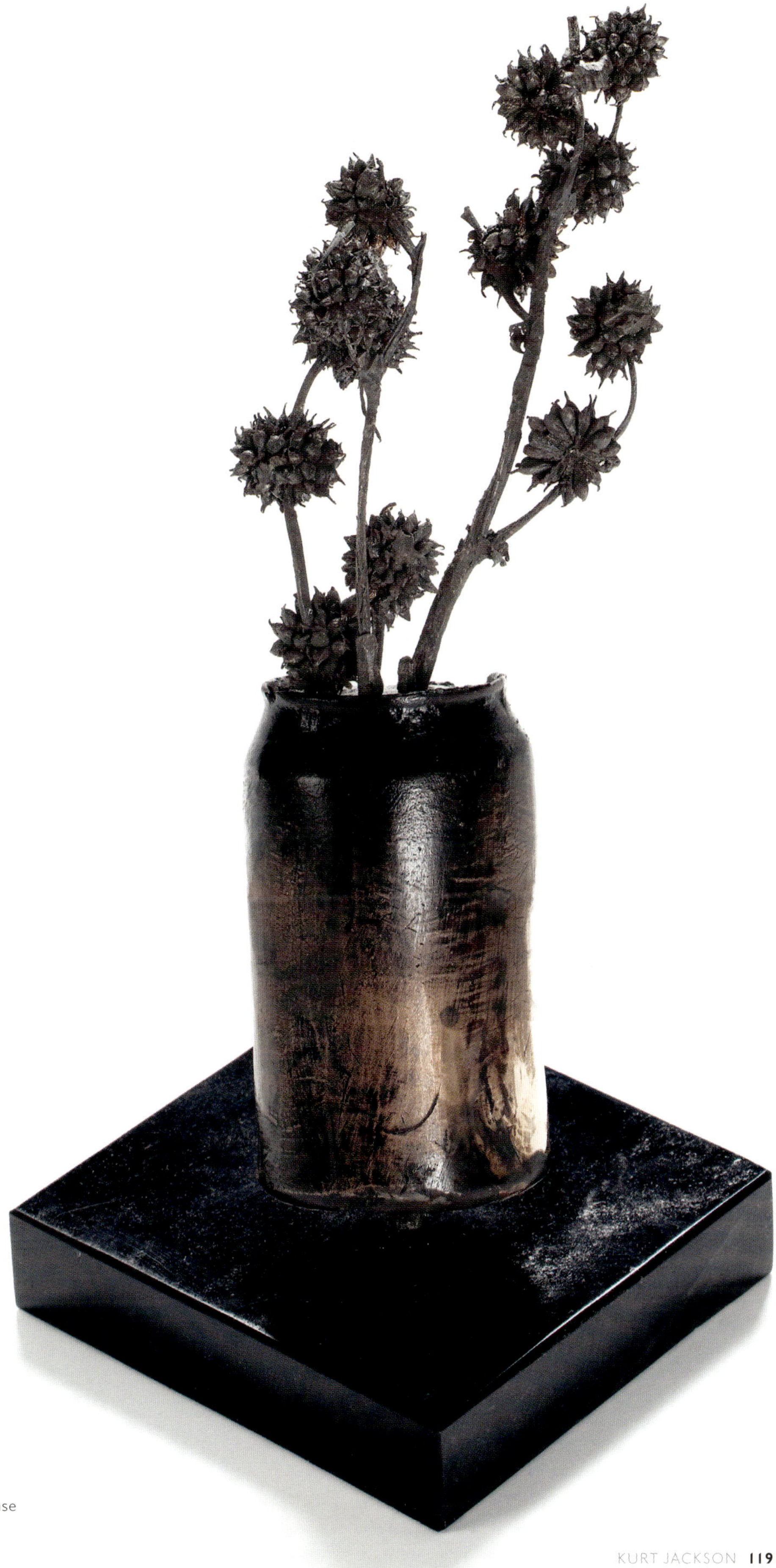

63. **Coke can and bur-reed**
2014 • bronze on stone base • 13 x 16 x 29 cm including base

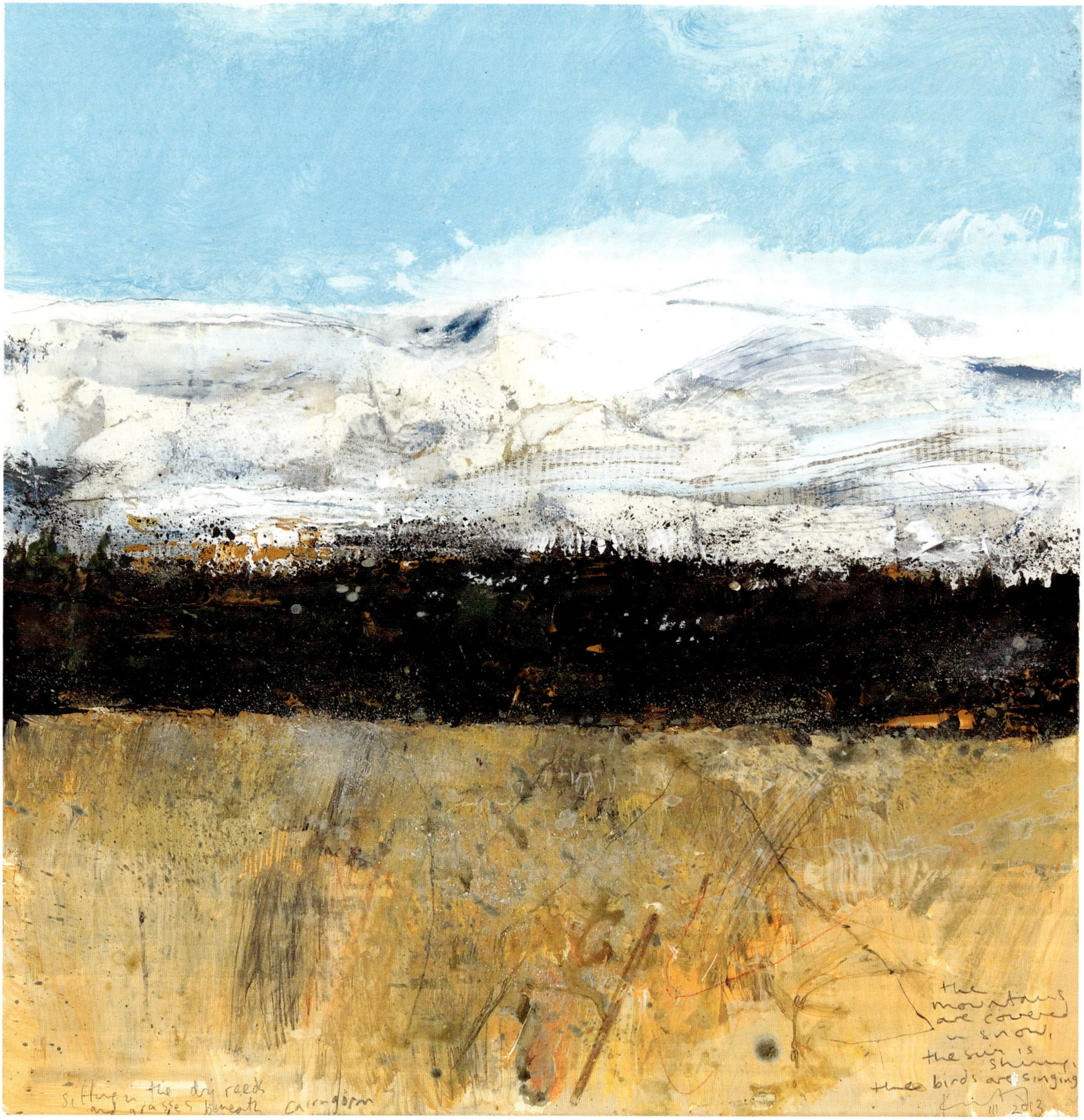

65. **The mountains are covered in snow, the sun is shining, the birds are singing. Sitting in the dry reeds and grass beneath Cairngorm**
March 2013 • mixed media and collage on board • 51 x 51 cm

22. The Cairngorms

Robert Macfarlane

The Cairngorms are Britain's Arctic. In winter, storms rasp the upper shires of the range and avalanches scour its slopes. Even in high summer, snow often lies in the coldest corries, sintering slowly into ice. The wind is such a shaping power there that up on the plateaux are bonsai pines, fully grown at six inches, and juniper bushes which flatten themselves across the rocks to form densely woven dwarf forests. The range itself is the eroded stump of a mass of magma that rose up through the earth's crust in the Devonian period, cooled into granite, then emerged out of the surrounding schists and gneiss. The Cairngorms were once higher than today's Alps, but over aeons they have been eroded into a low-slung wilderness of whale-backed hills and shattered cliffs. Born of fire, carved by ice, finessed with wind, water and snow, the massif is a terrain shaped by what the Aberdonian writer Nan Shepherd called 'the elementals'.

The Cairngorms were my first mountain range, and they are still the hills I know best. My grandparents lived in a converted forestry cottage on a rare limestone upsurge on the north-eastern slopes of the massif, and the field of rough pasture which they owned ran down to the banks of the River Avon. From a young age, I visited them with my family, usually in the summers. On a wall of the house hung a vast laminated Ordnance Survey map of the whole massif, on which we would finger-trace walks done and walks planned. My grandfather was a diplomat and mountaineer who had spent his life climbing around the world, and it was he and his Cairngorm world which cast the spell of height upon me as a child.

His yard-long wooden-hafted ice-axe and his old iron crampons seemed to my young imagination like the props of wizardry. I was shown black-and-white photographs of the peaks he had climbed in the Alps and the Himalayas, and it was miraculous to me that such structures could be ascended by humans. I have since crossed the massif on foot and ski many times, and my maps of the region are spidery with the marks of tracks followed and routes attempted.

I have seen dozens of blue-white snow hares, big as dogs, popping up from behind peat hags over the back of Glas Maol, I have followed flocks of snow buntings as they gust over the Braeriarch plateau, and I once spent hours sheltering in a snow-hole above the Northern Corries while a blizzard blew itself furiously out. Up on the wide summit plateau of Ben a' Bhuird, I found myself in the purest white-out conditions I have ever experienced. Snow, cloud and blizzard combined such that the visible world dissolved into a single pallor. Scale and distance were impossible to discern. There were no shadows or waymarks. Space was depthless. Even gravity's hold felt loosened: slope and fall-lines could be inferred only by the tilt of blood in the skull.

The Cairngorms are my heartland, and if they themselves have a heart then it is the Pools of Dee, which lie just to the south of the high point of the Lairig Ghru, the great pass that cleaves the massif into its western and eastern halves. The Pools are the headwaters of the Dee, which river eventually finds the sea at Aberdeen 50 miles to the east, and they contain the clearest water into which I have ever looked.

***Robert Macfarlane** is the author of* Mountains of the Mind, The Wild Places *and* The Old Ways.

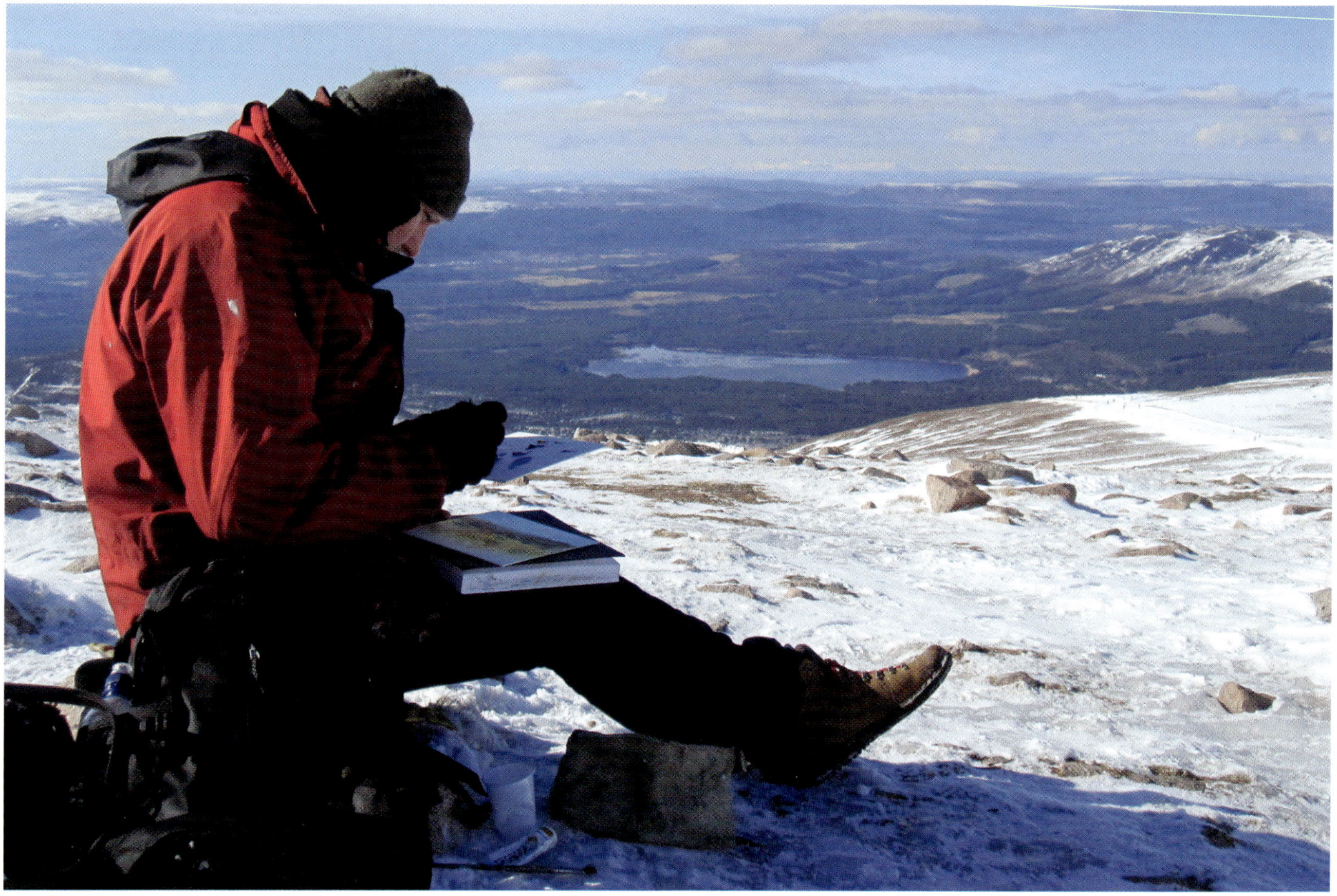

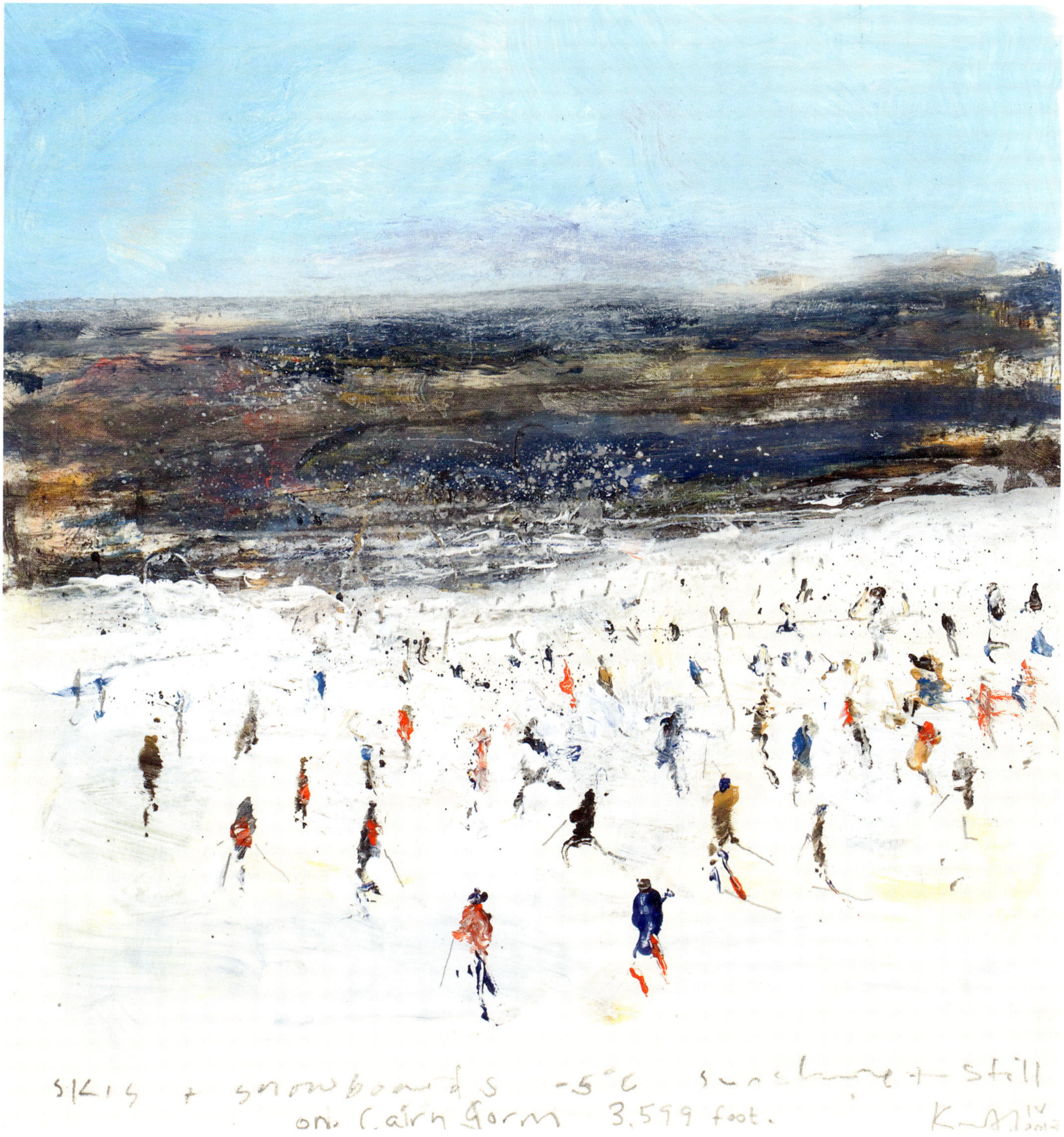

64. **Skis and snowboards, -5°c, sunshine and still. On Cairngorm, 3599 feet**
April 2013 • mixed media on board • 21 x 20 cm

66. **Frozen Loch Morlich, ice crack, chaffinch song, geese honk**
2013 • mixed media on linen • 173 x 193 cm

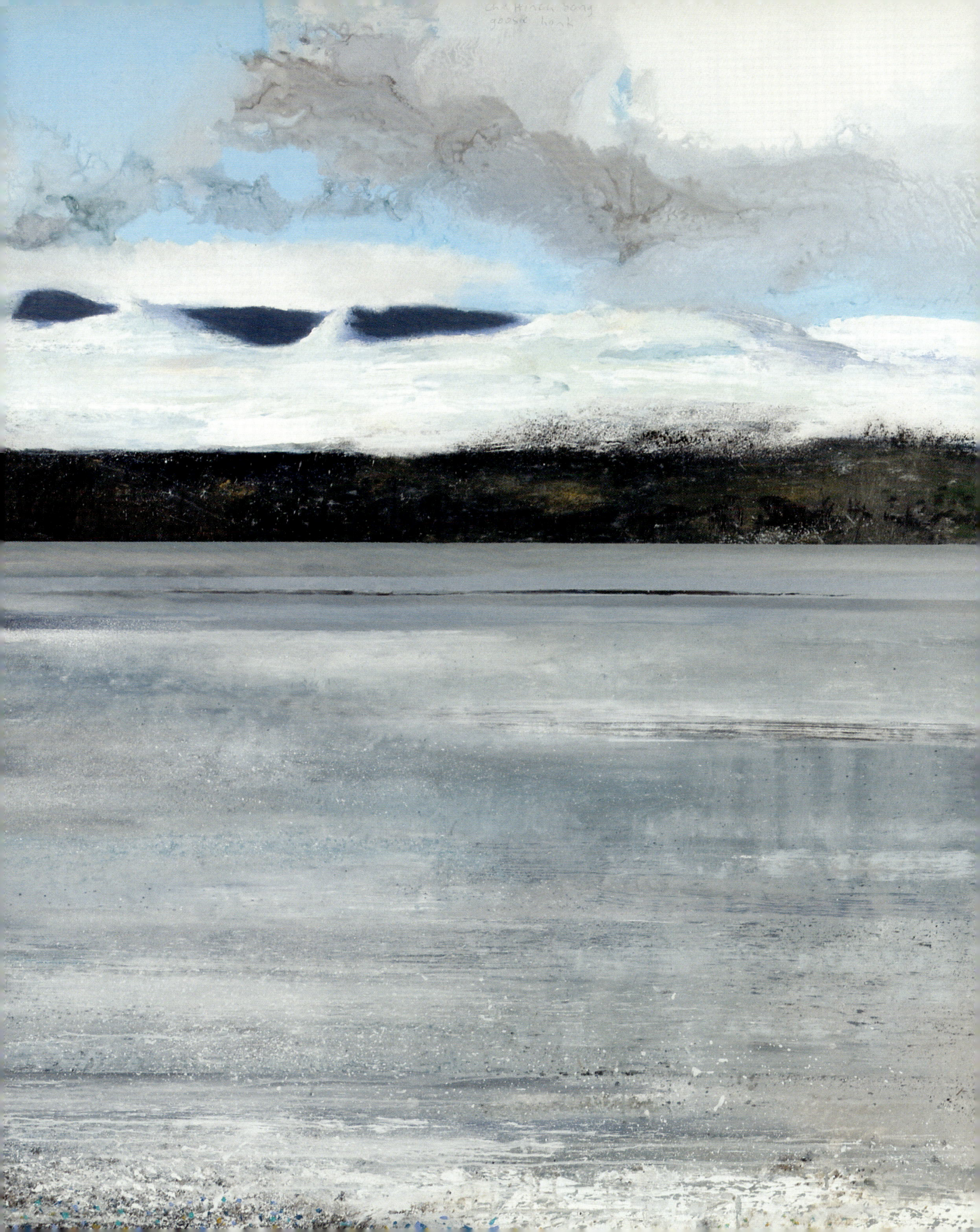

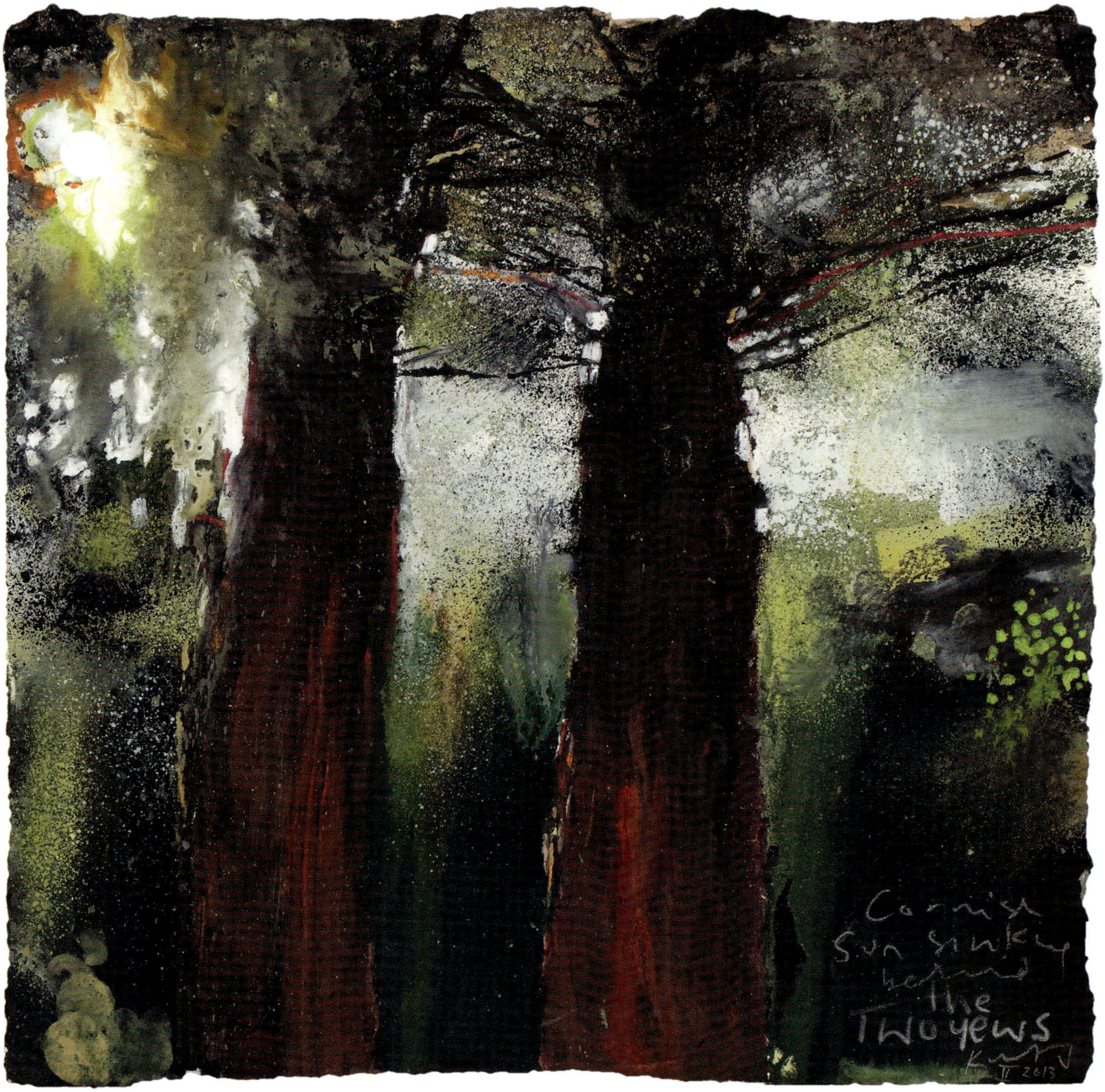

67. **Cornish sun sinking behind the two yews**
2013 • mixed media and collage on paper • 28 x 30 cm

23. **Yew trees, Lambessow**

Jessica Mann

Two yew trees flank the footpath that leads from the far end of our long front garden, through a shrubbery and across a lawn to the bright blue door. Nowadays one drives to a different entrance, but in the past, visitors approaching Lambessow would see it framed between the huge trees. It is a rambling house, much altered over the centuries. A traditional Cornish farmhouse, probably mediaeval, was incorporated into a larger building when an H-shaped house was built on in the seventeenth century. Over the years Lambessow has been alternately a working farmhouse and a 'gentleman's residence.' The place was a tenanted farm in the 1960s when its landlord, the Duchy of Cornwall, amalgamated the fields with the neighbouring farm and sold the house to the playwright Ken Taylor and his wife Jill.

We bought Lambessow from them in the early 1970s. My husband, the archaeologist Charles Thomas is the author of countless books and articles, and I am a novelist and journalist. So in the last half century millions of words have been written under this roof. But Lambessow has an earlier association with literature. In the eighteenth century it was the country house of the Foote family, their elegant Truro town house (which later became the Red Lion Inn) being every bit of a mile and a half away. Samuel Foote, born at Lambessow in 1720, became a successful playwright and a flamboyant, notorious figure in fashionable London. In his play *The Maid of Bath* (1761) the hero describes his capacious country house. 'You may stretch your legs without crossing the threshold: why we go up and down stairs to every room of the house.' As for his 'good gardens': 'Why, before the great parlour window there grows a couple of yews, as tall as a mast and as thick as a steeple; and the boughs cast so delightful a shade, that you can't see your hand in any part of the room.'

It is notoriously difficult to assess a yew tree's age but evidently these two were already enormous in Sam Foote's day. Even then cutting them down must have seemed unthinkable. So the trees still cast a shade over the front rooms (and we still go up and down steps to nearly every room in the house).

Sometimes elderly visitors call in to look at the place where they had grown up long before; one lady remembered Lambessow being so isolated that news of the outbreak of the first world war only reached her parents a week later. Another told us that the yew trees were traditionally given the names of the daughters of the house – luckily we have two. How often the trees' names must have changed over the unmeasured centuries. They may be inconveniently placed and force us to keep the lights on by day, but the yew trees are untouchable. They seem to be the ancient guardians of the house where I have lived for more than half my life.

Jessica Mann *writes crime fiction, non-fiction and journalism; broadcasts on book, quiz and current affairs programmes; grew up in London and now lives in Cornwall with her husband, the archaeologist Professor Charles Thomas; they have two sons, two daughters and eleven grandchildren.*

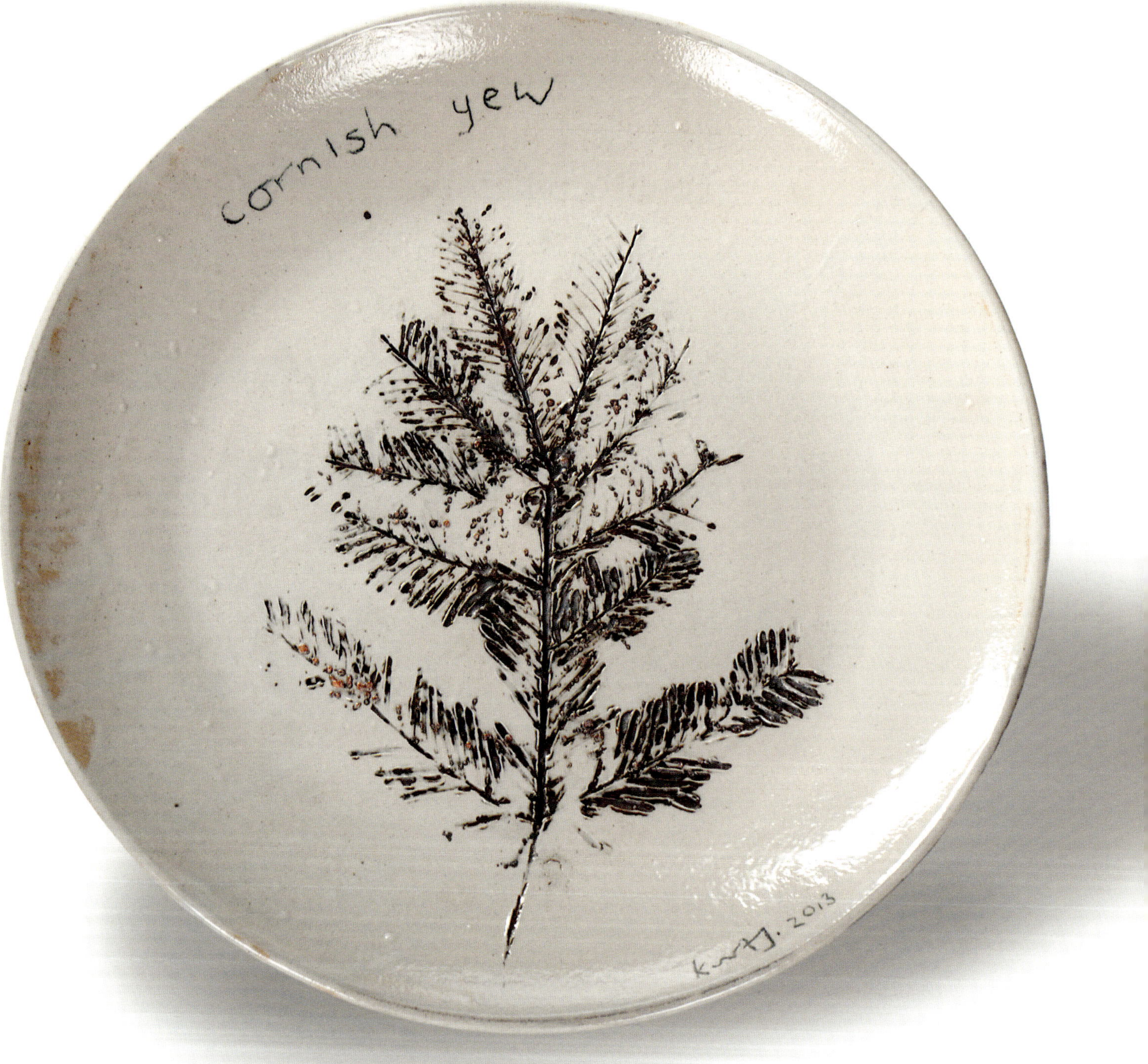

68. **Cornish Yew diptych**
2013 • stoneware • 34 cm diameter (x2)

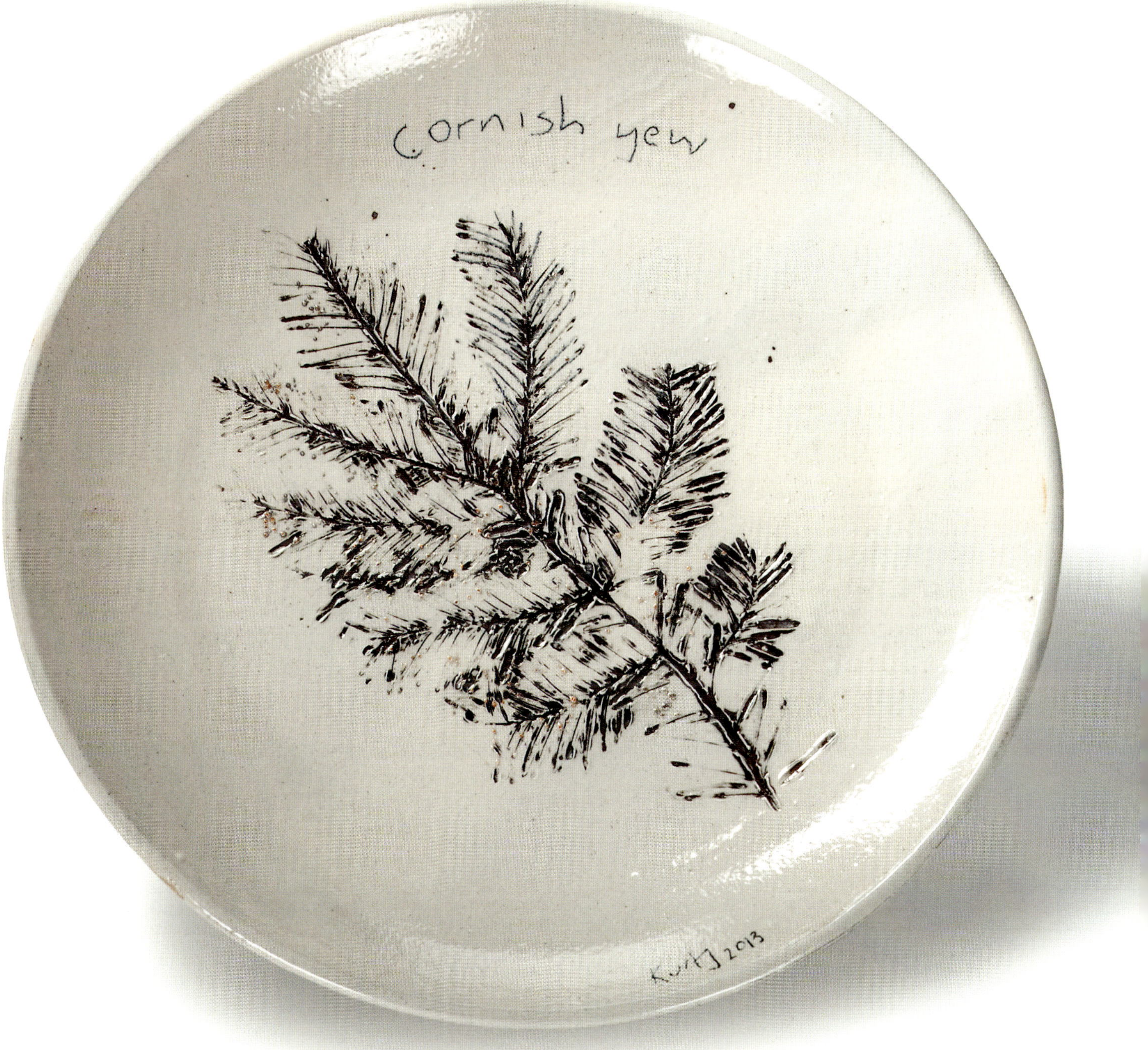
Cornish yew
Kurt J 2013

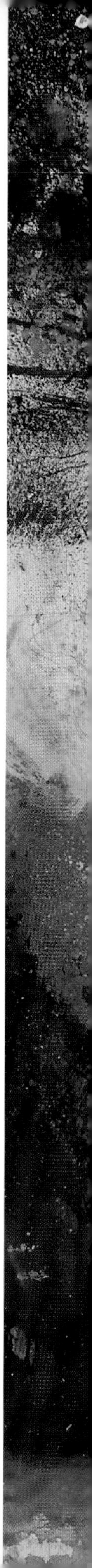

69. **The two yews of Lambessow**
February 2013 • mixed media on paper • 60 x 56 cm

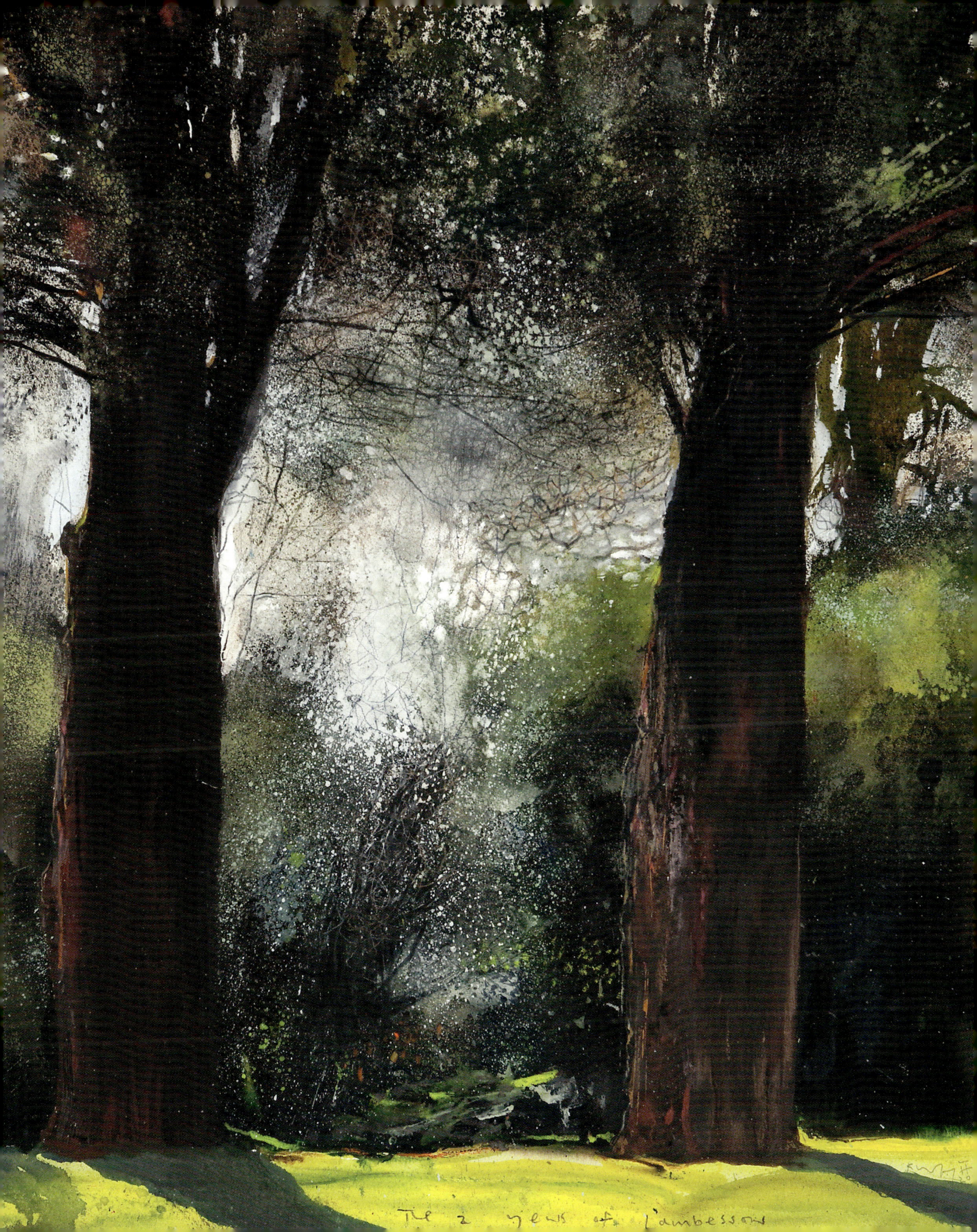
The 2 yews of Lambessow

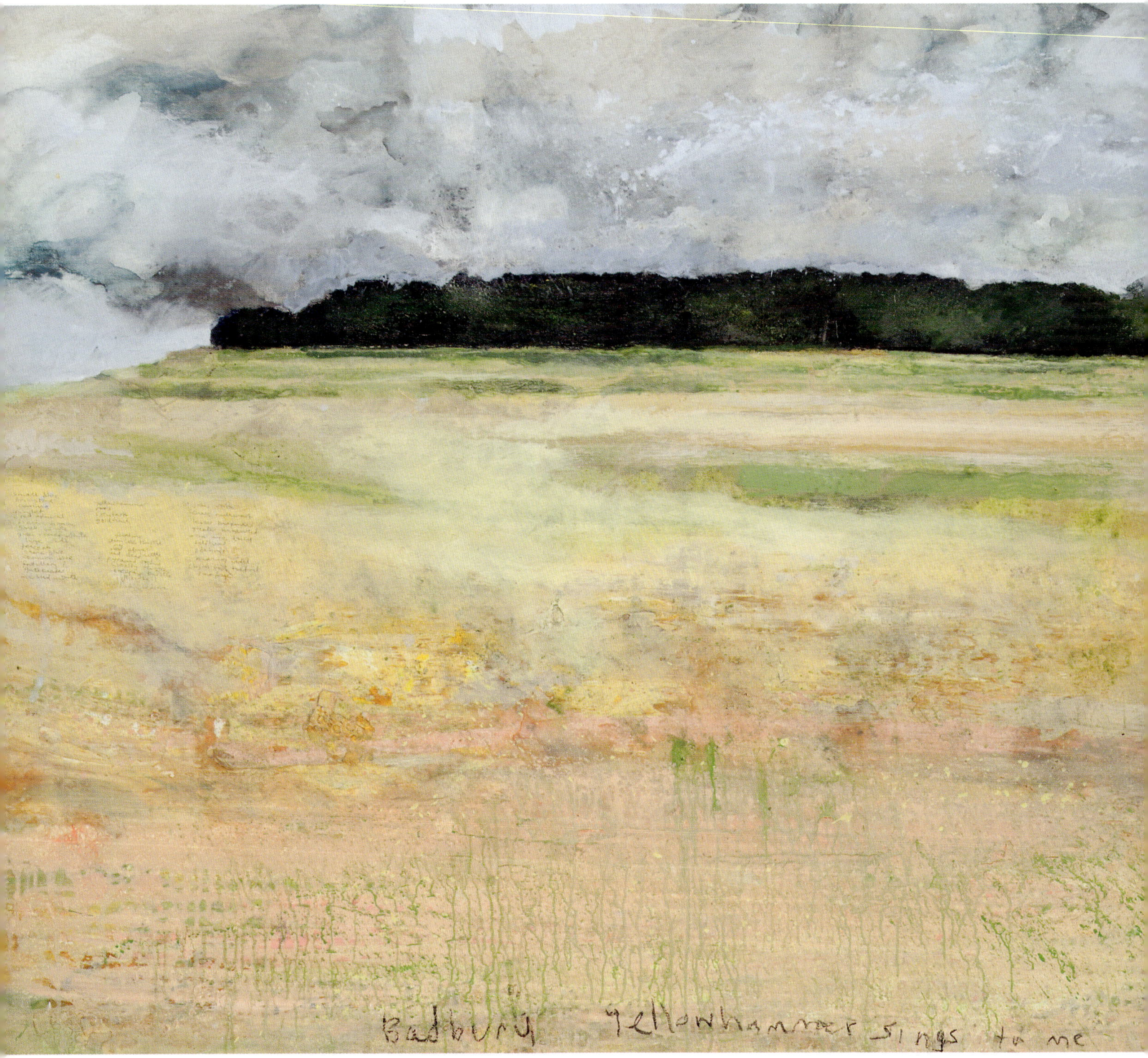

70. **Badbury yellowhammer sings to me**
2013 • mixed media on linen • 127 x 201 cm

24. **Badbury Rings, Dorset**

Steve Marshall

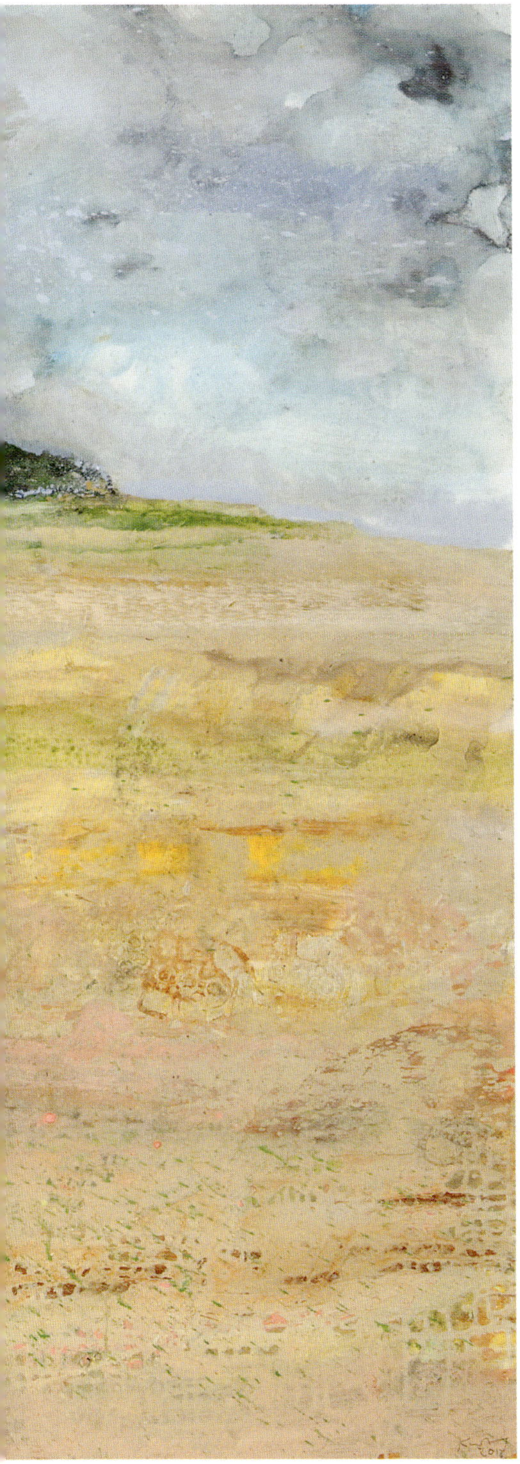

I first came to Badbury Rings on family expeditions as a child, with my brother, parents and grandparents. I remember flying kites, playing football and even cricket outside the rings, but the biggest excitement was the imposing ramparts which had to be scaled to reach the secret places within. Memory can be unreliable, but I look back on the interior of the rings as overgrown, dark, mysterious and enticing, wonderful for hide-and-seek but not without risk: one could venture in and not return, or emerge somehow changed by a brush with the ancient past.

My grandfather would recall his time with the RAF at nearby Tarrant Rushton airfield during the Second World War: cycling under the magnificent beech avenue that runs beside the rings, passing lines of vehicles hidden under the canopy before D-Day. But even beeches are ephemeral and when a new line of trees was planted to take their turn when the current guardians fail, my grandfather sponsored one as a marker for his own association with the place.

My own connection with Badbury Rings has helped me to appreciate the peculiarly British artistic obsession with the idea of *genius loci*, the spirit of place. Palmer had Shoreham, Paul Nash the Wittenham Clumps and others have relentlessly explored a cherished landscape.

Familiarity does not dilute mystery, but deepens it. For each of us there are layers of associations. There is the mystique created by romantic traditions: Badbury was Mount Badon the site of Arthur's great victory over the Saxons, and after his death his soul returned to the scene in the body of a raven. Then there are the subconscious connections we make with familiar landscapes, reinforced by the cherished memories of time spent in our special places.

Badbury Rings endures, impassive, while the generations slip by. I brought my children to charge gleefully around the earthworks, my parents became the grand-parents. Yet even the rings are not immune to change. The interior has been tidied, the undergrowth cleared, the trees thinned: a beautiful spot for a picnic, but the air of mystery is diminished and sun-dappled calm has replaced the wild unknown.

Paul Nash visited in 1935 while writing a *Dorset Shell Guide* and eloquently reassures me that there was indeed some truth in those early memories: 'I have read of enchanted places, and at rare times come upon them, but I remember nothing so beautifully haunted as the wood in Badbury Rings.'

__Steve Marshall__ is the former director of St Barbe Museum & Art Gallery, now a freelance arts and heritage consultant and exhibition curator. He was born and raised near Wimborne in Dorset and has a particular love of the British landscape and its representation in painting during the 20th and 21st centuries.

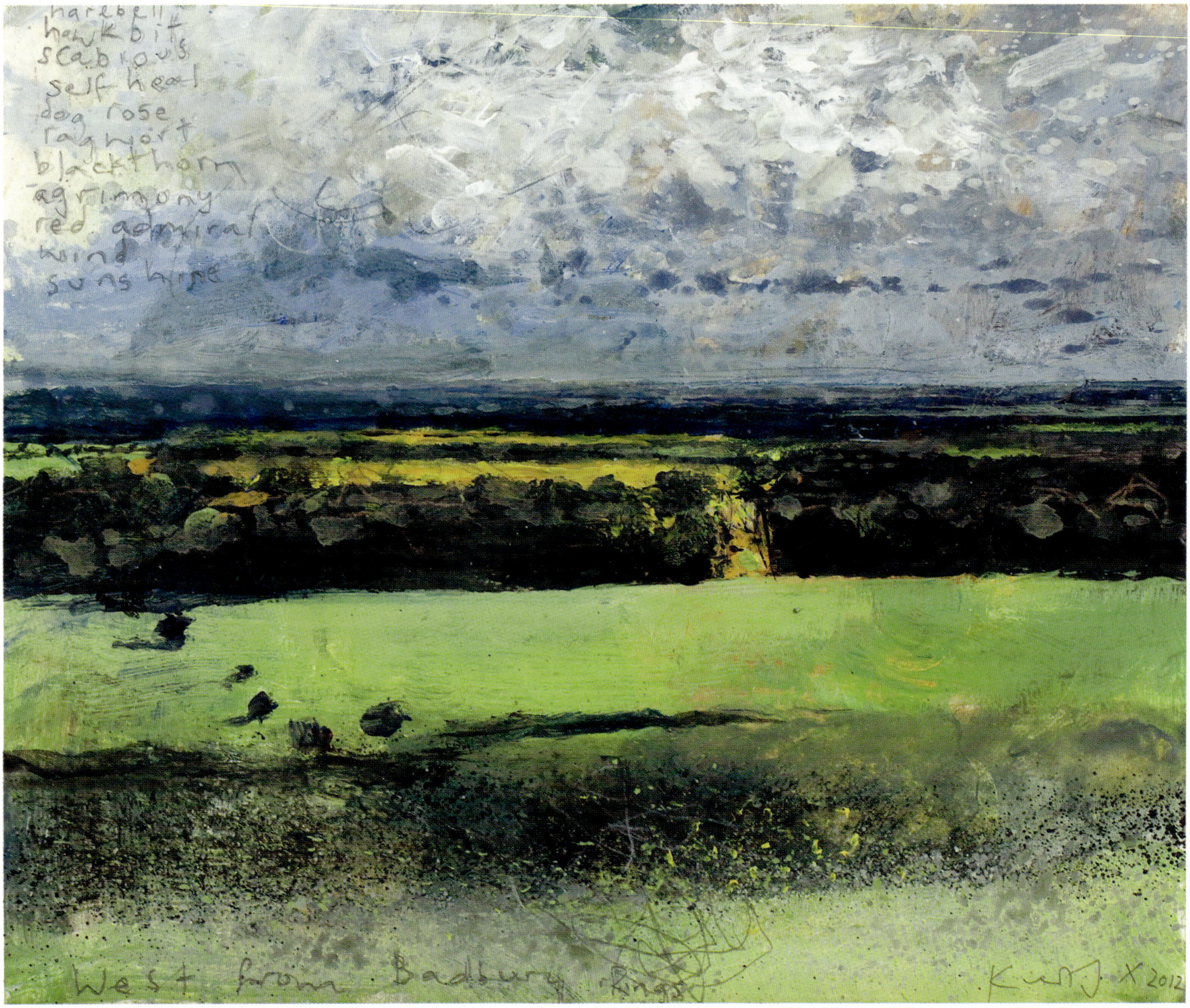

71. **West from Badbury rings**
October 2012 • mixed media on board • 19 x 23 cm

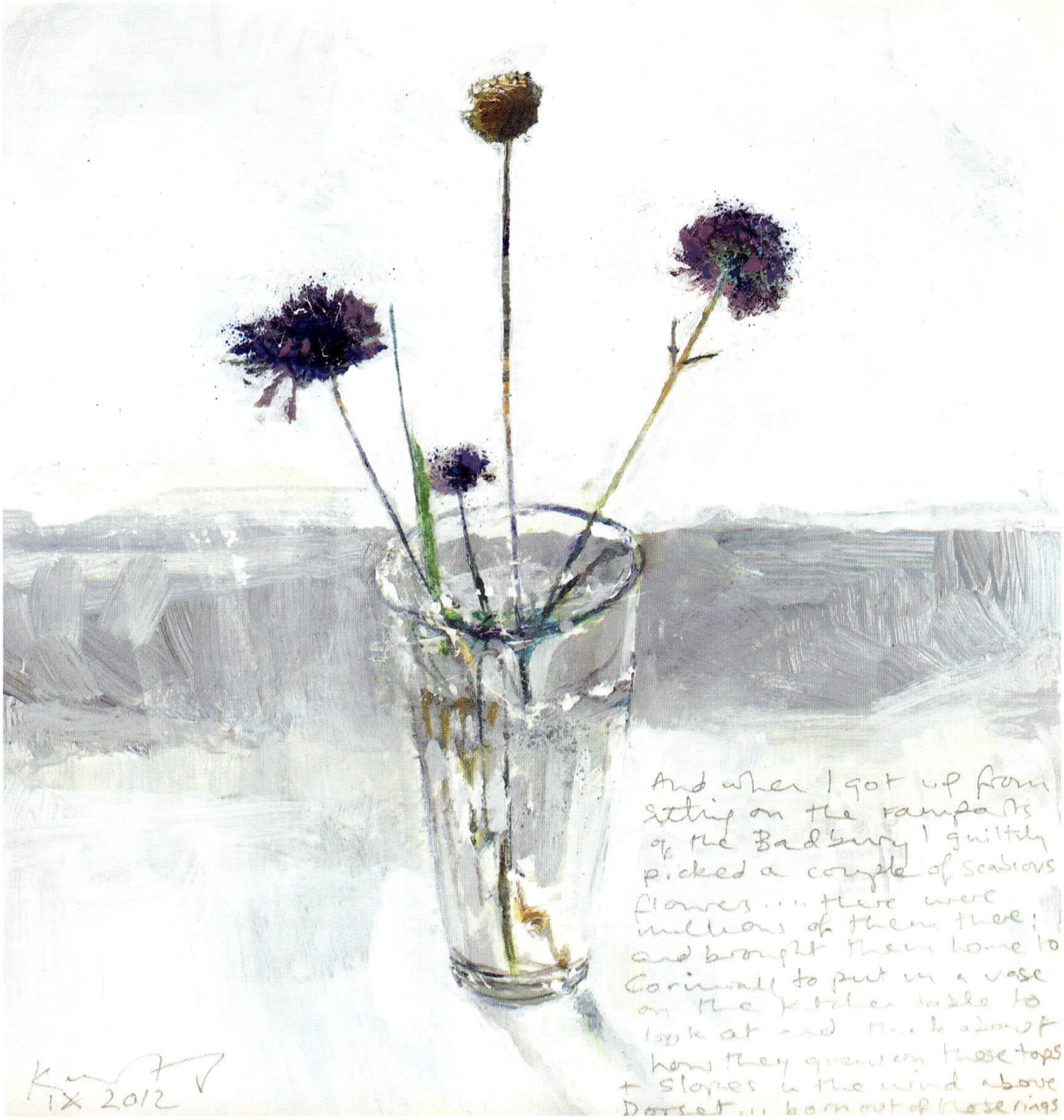

72. **Scabious from the ramparts of the Badbury Rings**
September 2012 • mixed media on board • 21 x 20 cm

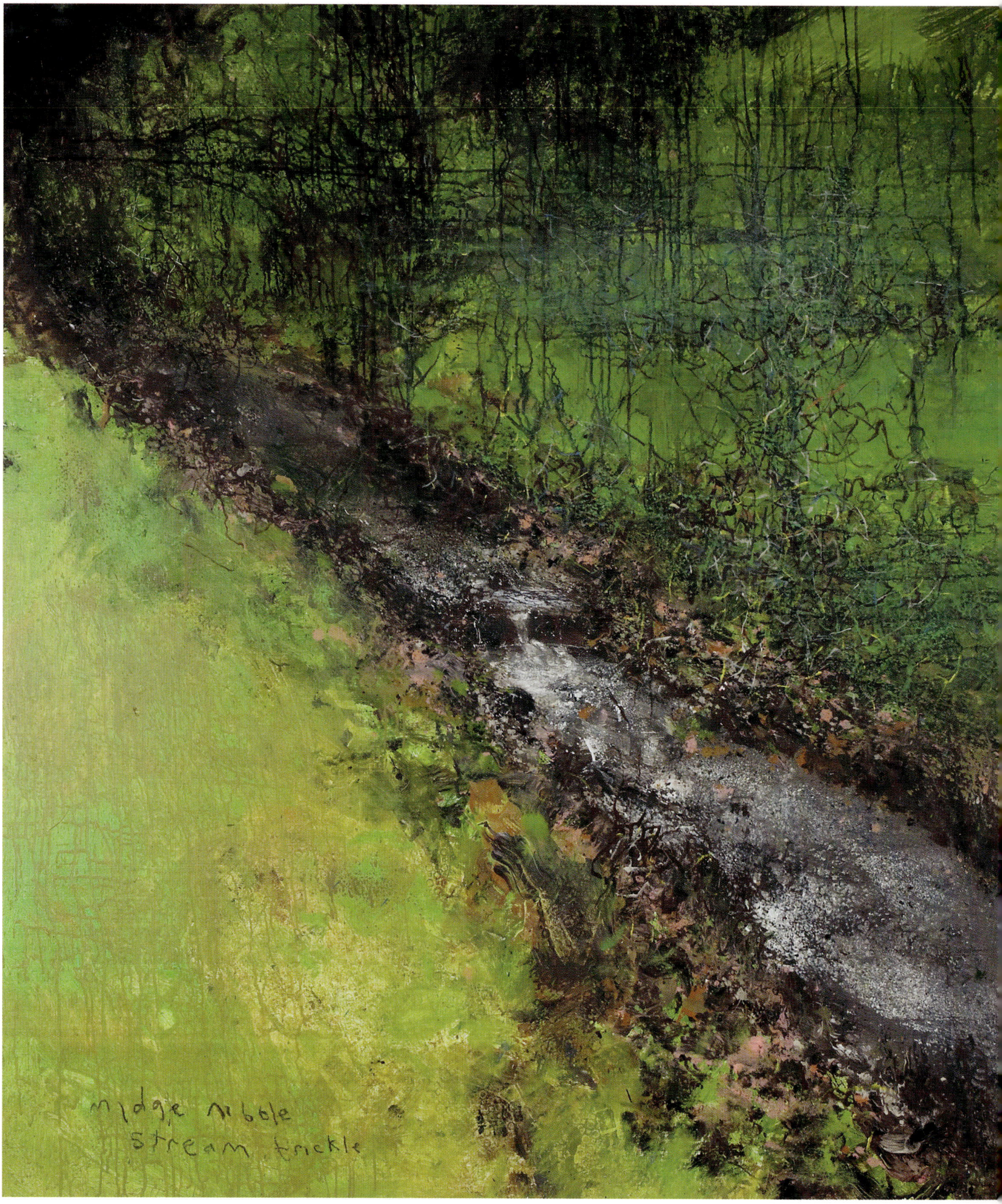
midge nibble
stream trickle

25. Chalk Ford, Scorriton, Dartmoor

Alice Oswald

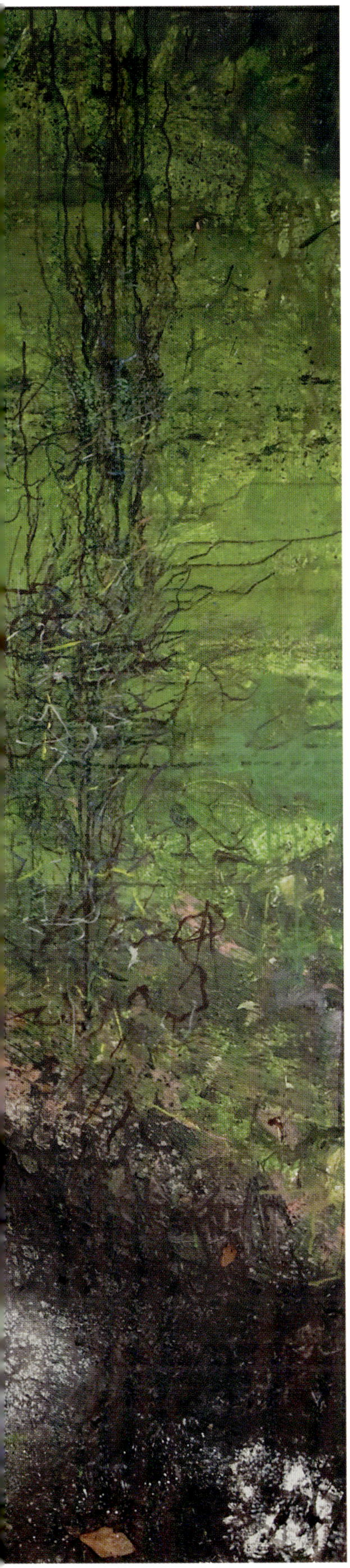

Cold Streak

I notice a cold streak
I notice it in the sun
All that dazzling stubbornness
Of keeping to its clock

I notice the fatigue of flowers
Weighed down by light
I notice the lark has a needle
Pulled through its throat

Why don't they put down their instruments?
I notice they never pause
I notice the dark sediment of their singing
Covers the moors like soot blown under a doorway

Almost everything here has cold hands
I notice the wind wears surgical gloves
I notice the keen pale colours of the rain
Like a surgeon's assistant

Why don't they lift their weight
And see what's flattened underneath it?
I notice the thin meticulous grass
Does well in this place

Alice Oswald has published six volumes of poetry and two anthologies. She lives in Devon.

73. **Midge nibble, stream trickle. Chalk Ford stream**
2013 • mixed media on linen • 170 x 195 cm

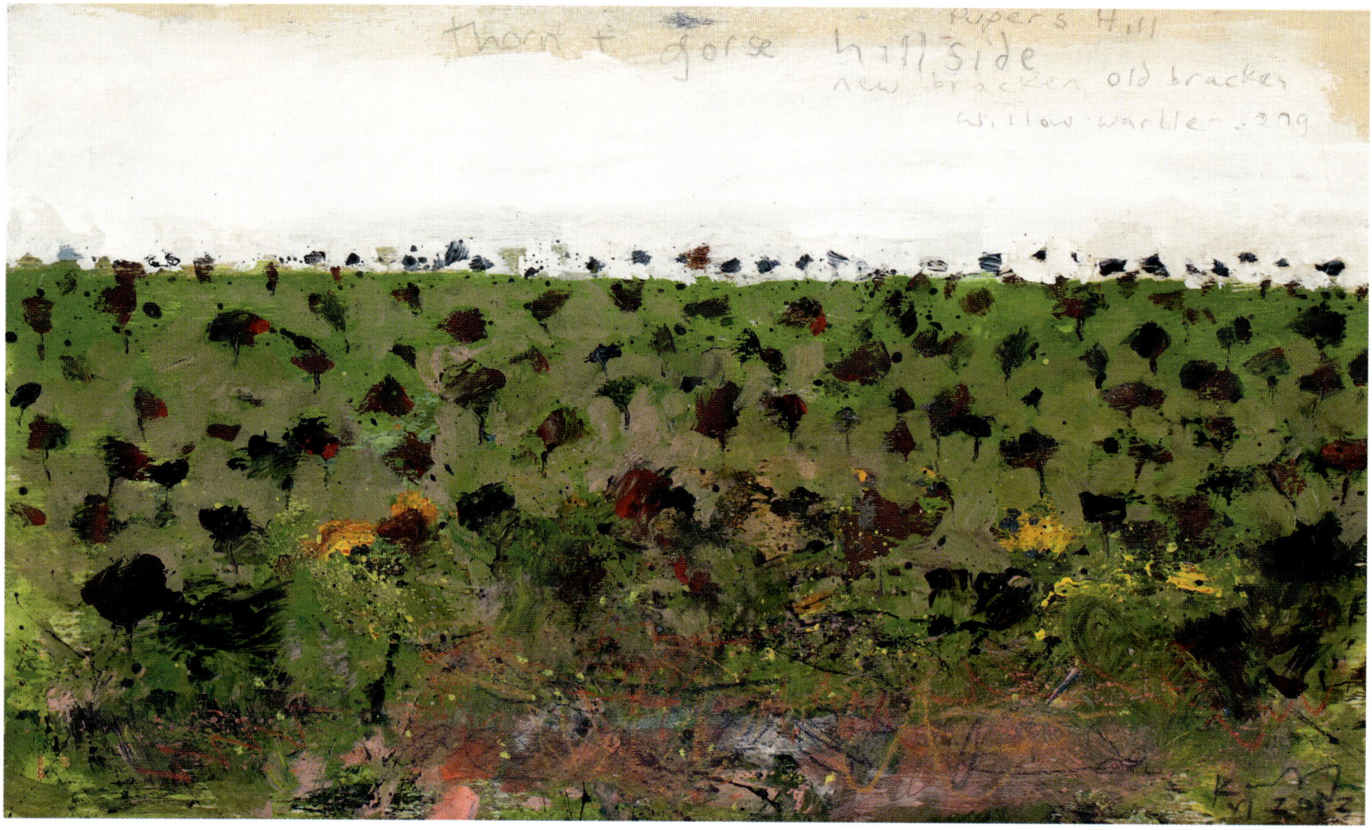

74. **Thorn and gorse hillside, new bracken, old bracken. Pupers Hill**
June 2013 • mixed media on wood panel • 20 x 35 cm

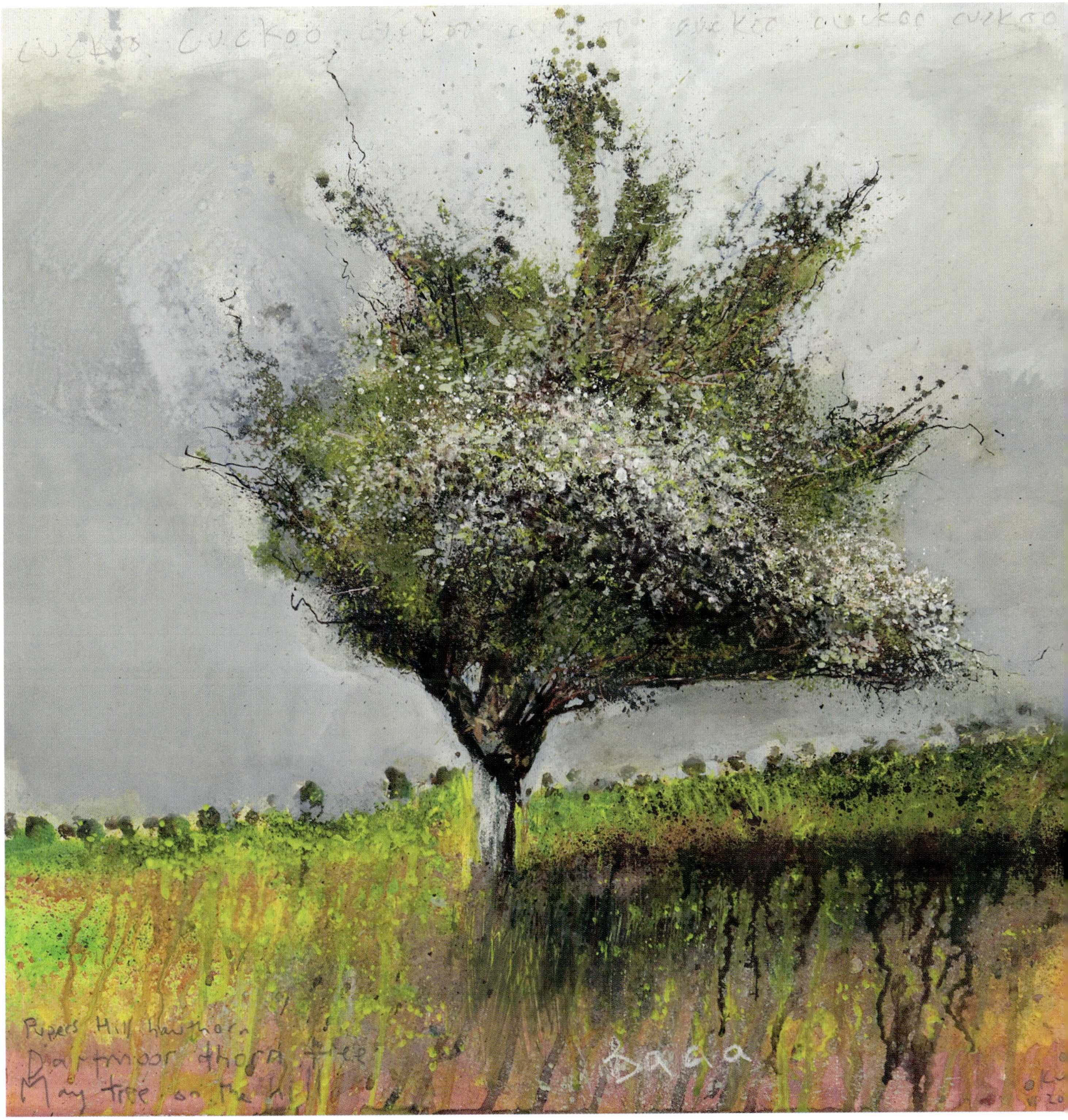

75. **Pupers Hill hawthorn, Dartmoor thorn tree, may tree on the hill**
June 2013 • mixed media on paper • 56 x 58 cm

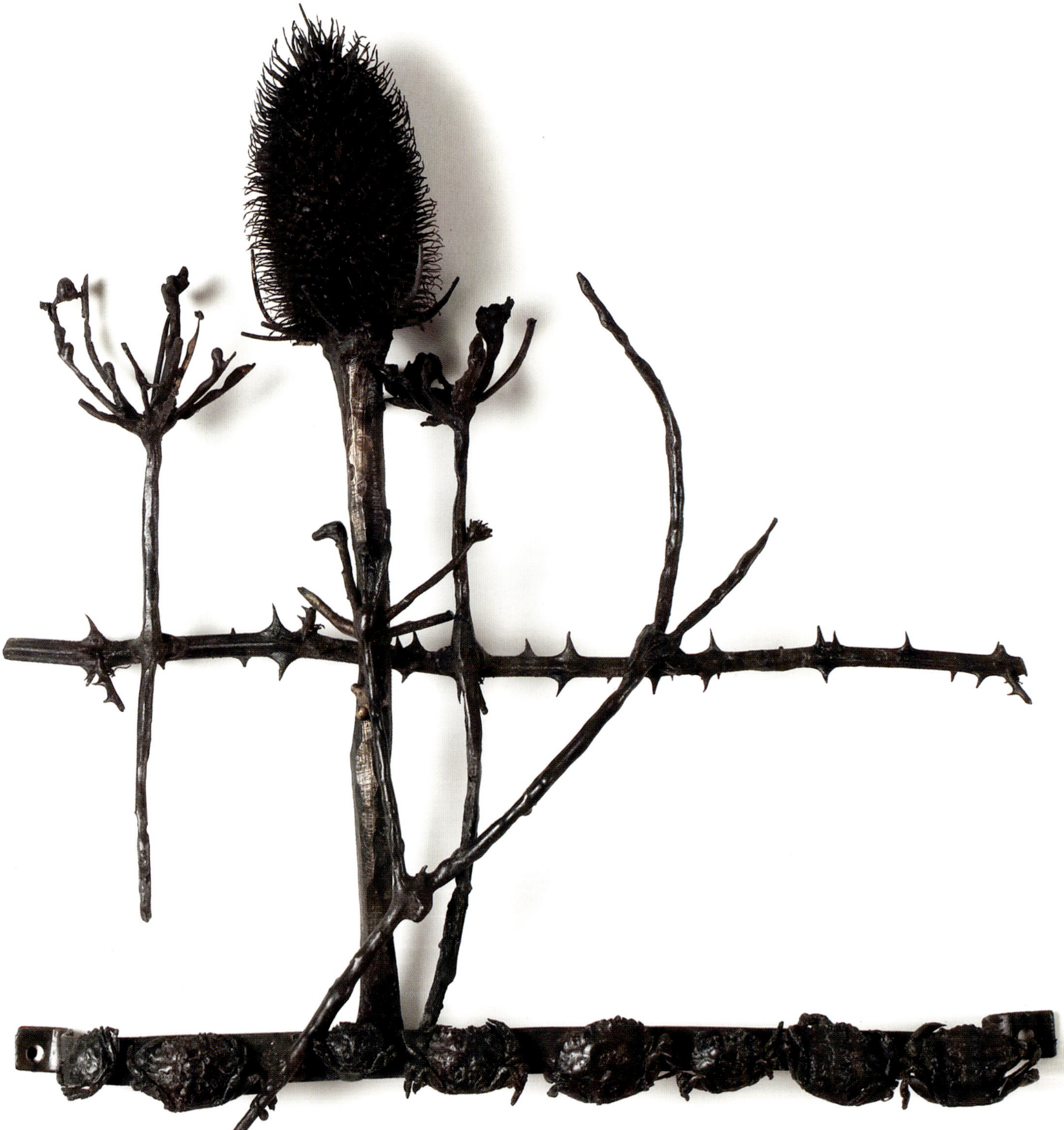

76. **Queen Anne's lace, teasel, bramble, shore crabs. Eel Pie Island**
2014 • bronze • 28 x 28 cm

26. Eel Pie Island, Twickenham

Annie Robinson

'So this is the famous Eel Pie Island?' she says, raising her sweet, rain dropped face.

'Dickens called it "a place of ill repute".'

As they cross the bridge; 15 paces from town to country, he points to a small beach on the bank. 'I learned to swim in the Thames, it's not sand at all but squelchy mud; you should have heard us squealing like the pigs in a shed as our toes, heels, ankles, knees and skinny white thighs dissolving in milky tea up to our chins, floating away, still holding hands as if we were asleep on the water. I went under but I kept my mouth shut and drifted along and later the kids said I was lucky to escape alive before the river carried me over the big weir down, down, down into a whirlpool to be sucked into a vortex where the skeletons of all the dead ducks, swans, herons and fish swirl round and round forever. But I grabbed a branch of willow along the bank and pulled myself in under its leaves startling a heron that turned into a grey dart and whistled past me along the river flapping slow wings against my cheek, legs hanging helpless as old woman's hands.'

Rose, in her little hut, stretches fierce grubby claws to grab the toll. 'Hello dear!' she croaks.

'Summer's coming, Rose, time to pack away your mittens,' he says.

'She's getting on a bit,' he whispers 'she was there in Dickens's time.' Sometimes he wonders if he misses the country: blossoms shake little fists along their path, a robin sings as they walk along a lane of soft black mud, trying to avoid the puddles on the path, winding past the boat yard that sprawls untidily down to a khaki river where smart moorhens bob black tie and tails among the reeds. The air buzzes with birds too busy for bed and bees too sozzled to sting.

It's light until late now and the sun – a red hot cannonball – lies in wait behind a hedge fizzy with elderflower and white blossoms, 'Break your Mother's Heart' he says.

'What do you mean?' A little frown. 'I hope it won't come to that!'

'Sorry,' he says 'that was Faye's name for cow parsley. When I was a kid two old women looked after me – I can see them now – after school they'd meet me by the gate: a tall one who'd say stuff like 'That's *Anthriscus sylvestris*, a member of the umbeliffer or carrot family; commonly known as Queen Anne Lace,' and a short one who got drunk on words. The way Faye talked made pictures in your mind; she said call them what you like but those flowers are the most flagrant flirts; barely out in polite society and popping their corks; will you look at their champagne bubbling all over those green green leaves!

She fetched me a big slice of cake and a glass of milk and set her easel near the vegetable garden to paint the flowers in the hedge saying she didn't know why she bothered for no paint on earth could match them and wasn't he the lucky, lucky boy to be leafing through the book of spring and still on the first pages while she was trying not to turn to the back to see how it all ended. At least she knew where it all began, she said. Look at this iris showing us its privates. It's all about sex you know. And Marjory set her grumpy hoe back among the real weeds, scritch scratch, scritch, scratch and I went red and changed the subject. I remember asking about the gold she painted on the shiny surface of a pattern of flowers, laid one upon the other.

'The glittering go-betweens,' she called them 'can't you hear the buzzing?'

Rounding the corner he catches his breath at the sight of the magnificent dowdy dilapidated hotel with its lawn sloping down to the Thames. Any moment now a steamer will paddle by and Tom Sawyer will wade through the mud looking for Jim; it's Mississippi without the segregation; all over the grass couples kiss and cuddle. What would Dickens think?

Annie Sagar Robinson is a mother, wife, writer, teacher, gardener, singer who lives beside the sea in Cornwall and writes books.

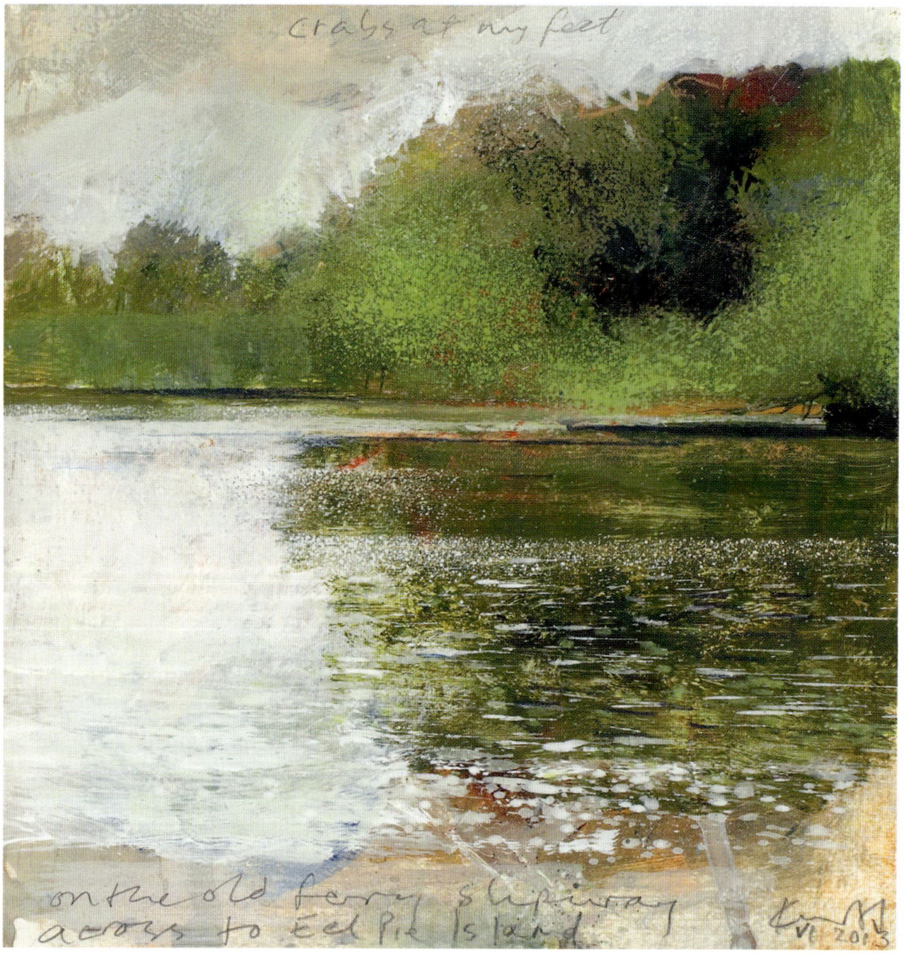

77. **Crabs at my feet, on the old ferry slipway across to Eel Pie Island**
June 2013 • mixed media on board • 22 x 22 cm

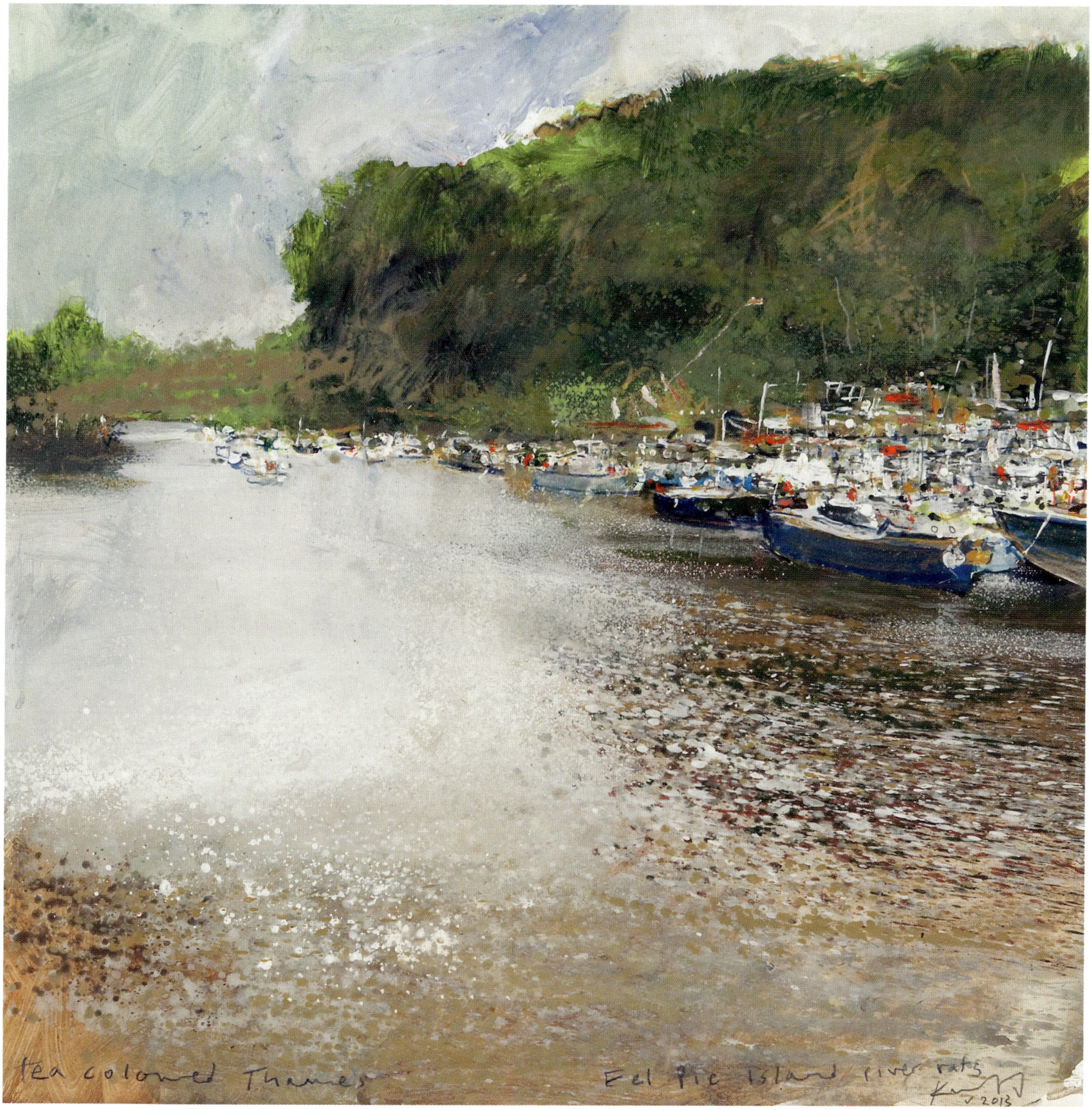

78. **Tea coloured Thames. Eel Pie Island river rats**
May 2013 • mixed media on board • 53 x 54 cm

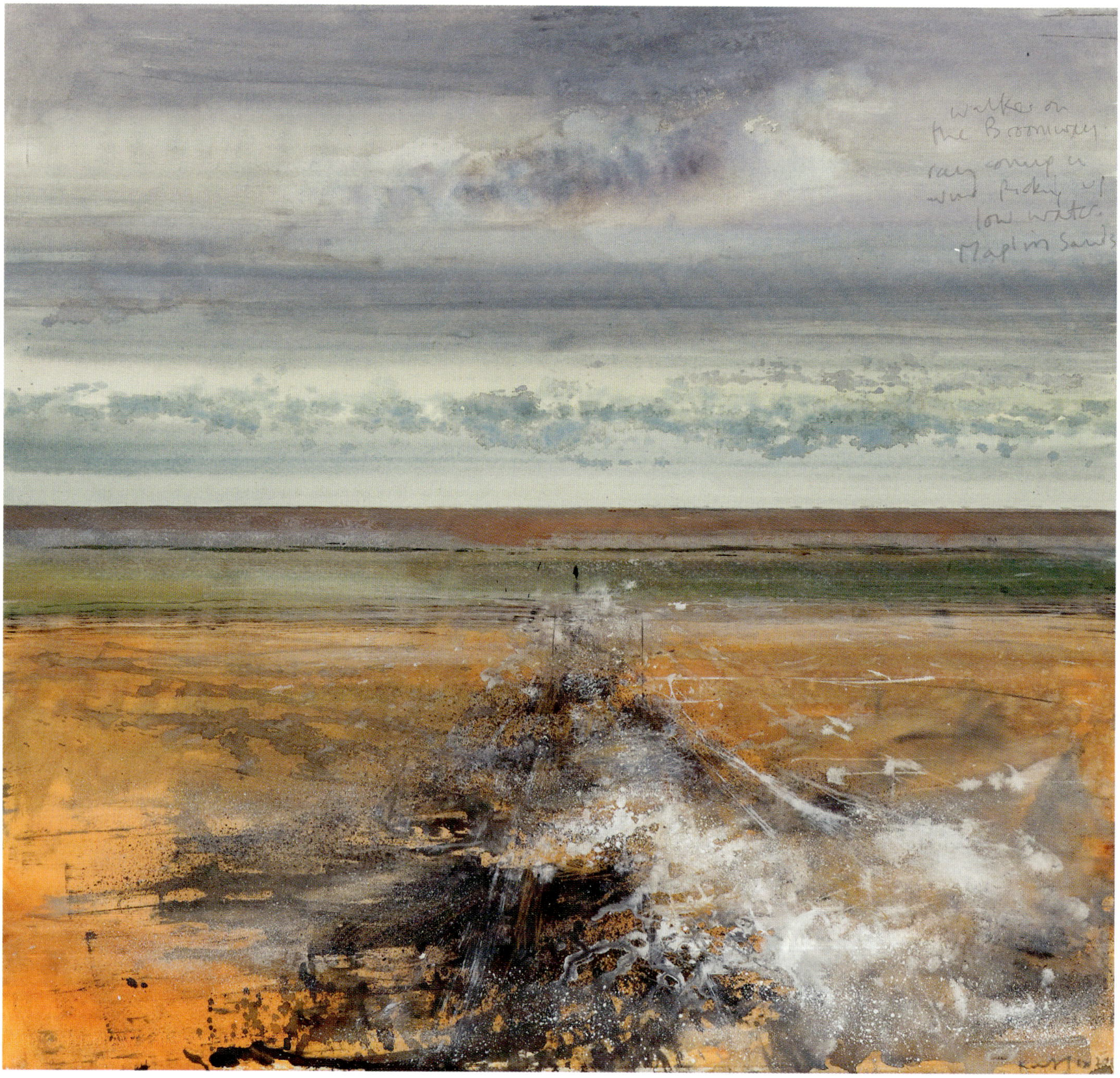

79. **Walker on the Broomway, rain coming in, wind picking up. Low water. Maplin Sands**
September 2013 • mixed media on paper • 57 x 61 cm

27. **Broomway, Essex**

John Sauven

But if you judge safety to be the paramount consideration in life you should never, under any circumstances, go on long hikes alone. Don't take short hikes alone, either – or, for that matter, go anywhere alone. And avoid at all costs such foolhardy activities as driving, falling in love, or inhaling air that is almost certainly riddled with deadly germs. Wear wool next to the skin. Insure every good and chattel you possess against every conceivable contingency the future might bring, even if the premiums half-cripple the present. Never cross an intersection against a red light, even when you can see all roads are clear for miles. And never, of course, explore the guts of an idea that seems as if it might threaten one of your more cherished beliefs. In your wisdom you will probably live to be a ripe old age. But you may discover, just before you die, that you have been dead for a long, long time.
from *The Complete Walker*, an in-depth guide to backpacking, by Colin Fletcher.

The location for this work of art is a short ramble along the east coast of England. The walk takes you along a route about as remote, empty and lonely as you will find in the UK, yet it is only 40 miles from London.

It's been described as one of the most treacherous coastal paths in the UK. The path is underwater for a couple of hours each side of high tide. And while the path used to have posts or stakes every ten metres or so, today they are all gone. In fact if you see posts don't follow them as they don't mark the route of the path.

The path got its name from the bundles of sticks that were tied to the top of the posts making them look like a witch's broom, hence the name 'Broomway'. But the path is more commonly referred to as the 'doomway' because of the hundreds of lives it's claimed.

The sands can sink under foot. The mist can roll in without warning, creating virtual whiteouts. Try to avoid misty days. The tide can appear suddenly and at speed. Timing is everything. And due to the MoD firing range in the area you run the risk of treading on 'unexploded objects'. To avoid live rounds you need to walk it on a Sunday when the MoD have a day off.

Ideally you should do it in bare feet, as feeling the texture of the path is important, and don't forget your compass.

No one knows for sure if the path was made by man or nature but it's quite rigid and fixed. In fact the path used to be used by postman with a horse cart to deliver the mail to the islanders.

And it is a legal, public right of way.

The area is an important site for migrating and breeding birds including the second largest colony of avocets. These black-and-white waders have a strange looking long, curved beak usually seen here in the summer. Brent geese from Russia spend the winter on the mud flats. But depending on the time of year you will come across a wide variety of birds.

Today it's mainly used by ramblers on foot, quaintly referred to on MoD hazardous warning signs at the start of the walk as 'pedestrians'.

British writer Robert Macfarlane described the 'Broomway' as 'the eeriest, the unearthliest and the most memorable walk' he's ever undertaken.

I have always been drawn to wilderness. Forty miles from London this place is hard to beat. And best to do it before someone comes up with the idea of building a new airport in the area. Wilderness usually means wasteland to developers. Ah, I forgot. Boris Johnson, the Mayor of London, has already come up with the idea.

And as for Colin Fletcher, the founder of the modern back-packing movement, he was knocked down and nearly killed by an SUV in 2001. He eventually died as a result of the head injuries he sustained from being hit by the 4x4 gas guzzler. But his legacy lives on every time someone picks up their backpack and their walking stick.

John Sauven *has been executive director of Greenpeace UK since September 2007. Before that he was the director responsible for Greenpeace communications and working on solutions with businesses. With a background in forests he was instrumental in getting protection for the Great Bear temperate rainforest on the west coast of Canada and achieving a moratorium on deforestation from soya production in the Amazon. More recently he has been working to protect the rainforests in Indonesia.*

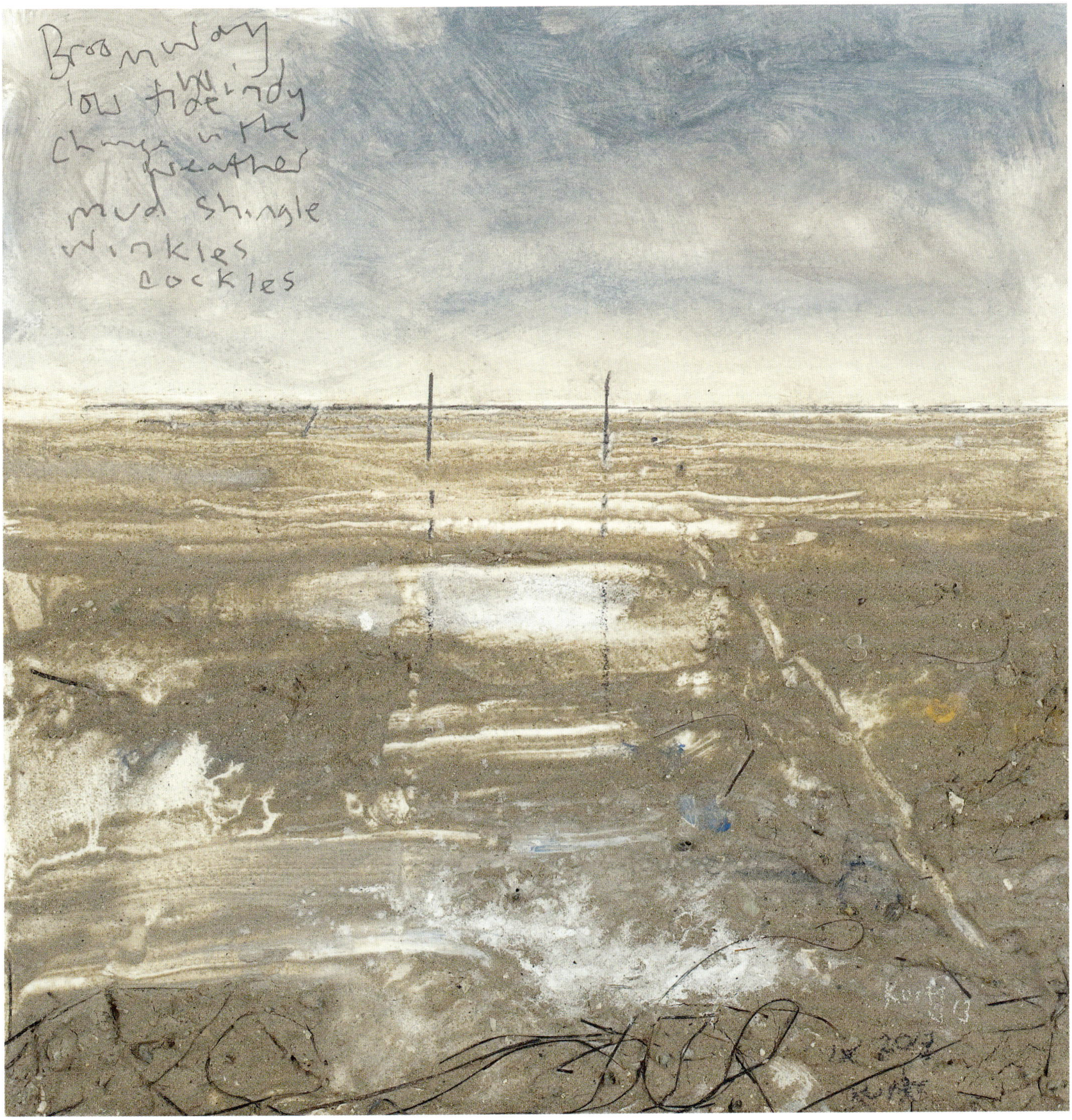

80. **Broomway, windy, low tide. Change in the weather**
September 2013 • mixed media and mud on board • 23.5 x 23 cm

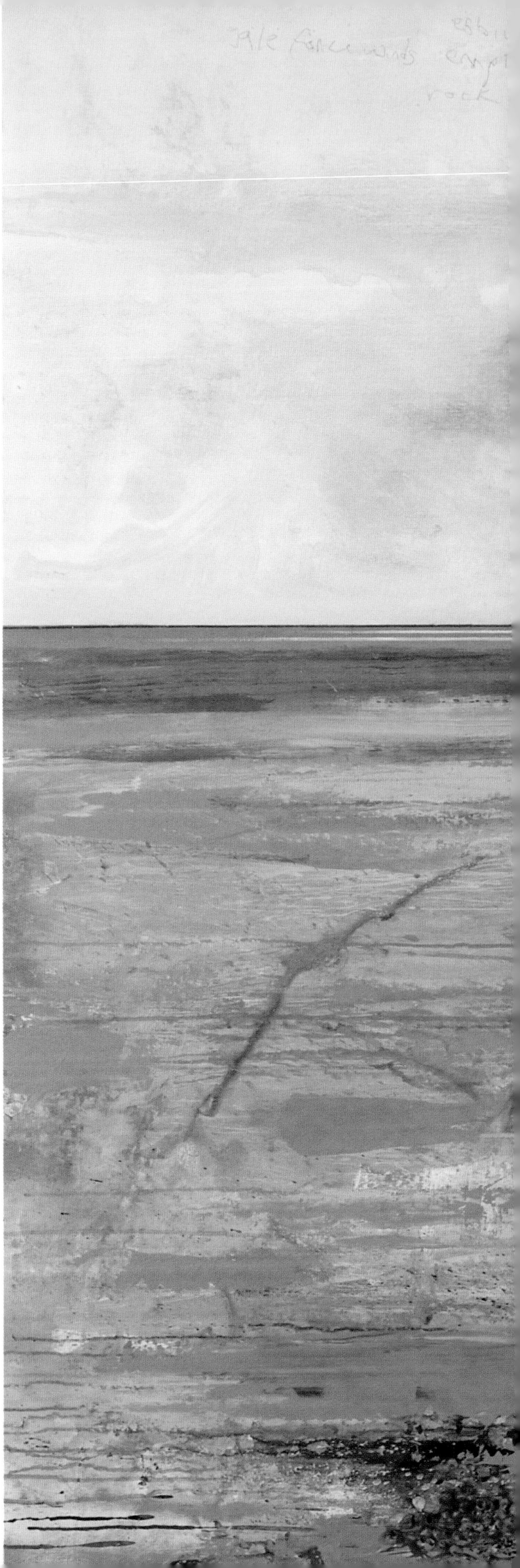

81. **Broomway – the most dangerous footpath in Britain**
2013 • acrylic, oil and collage on linen • 170 x 203 cm

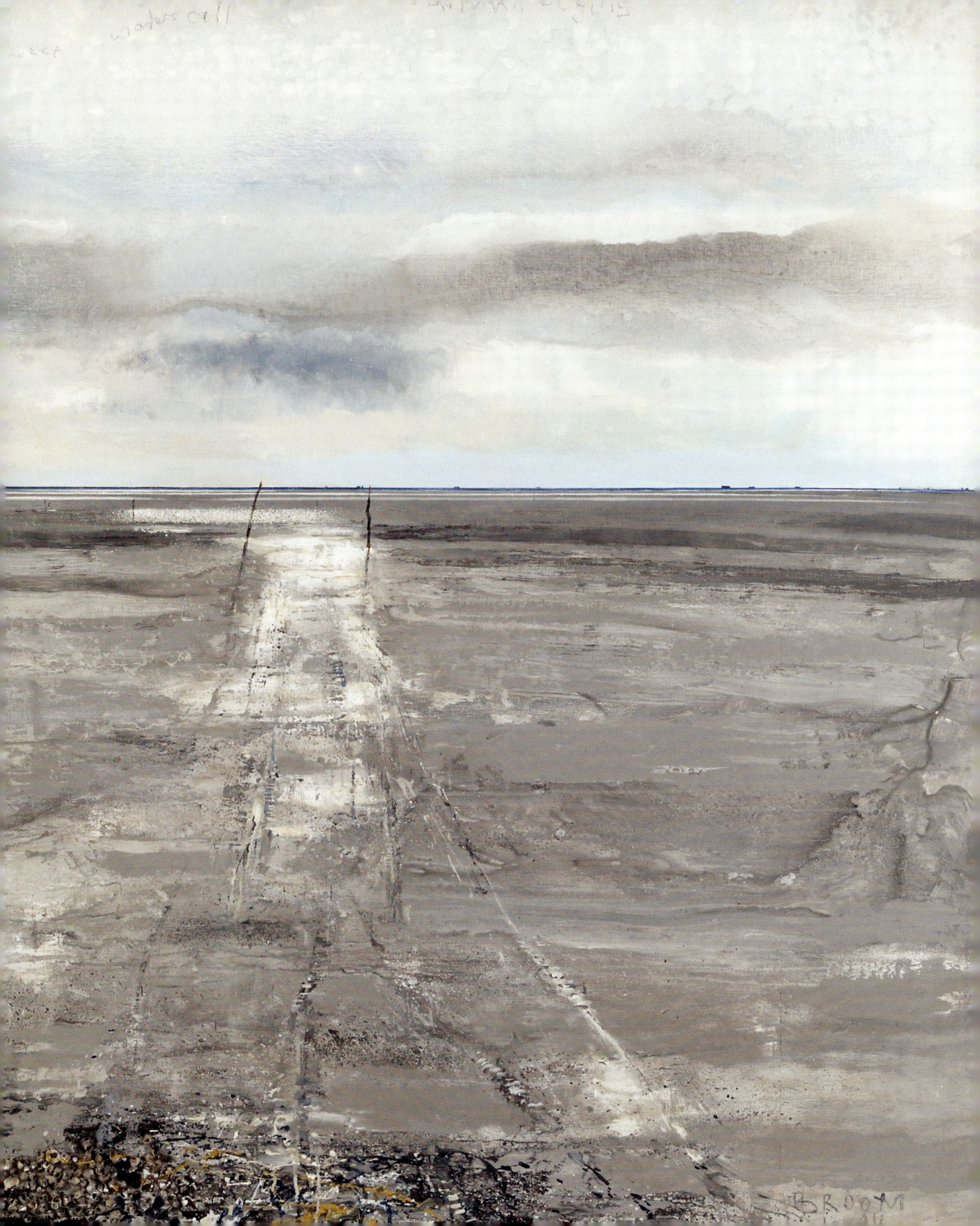

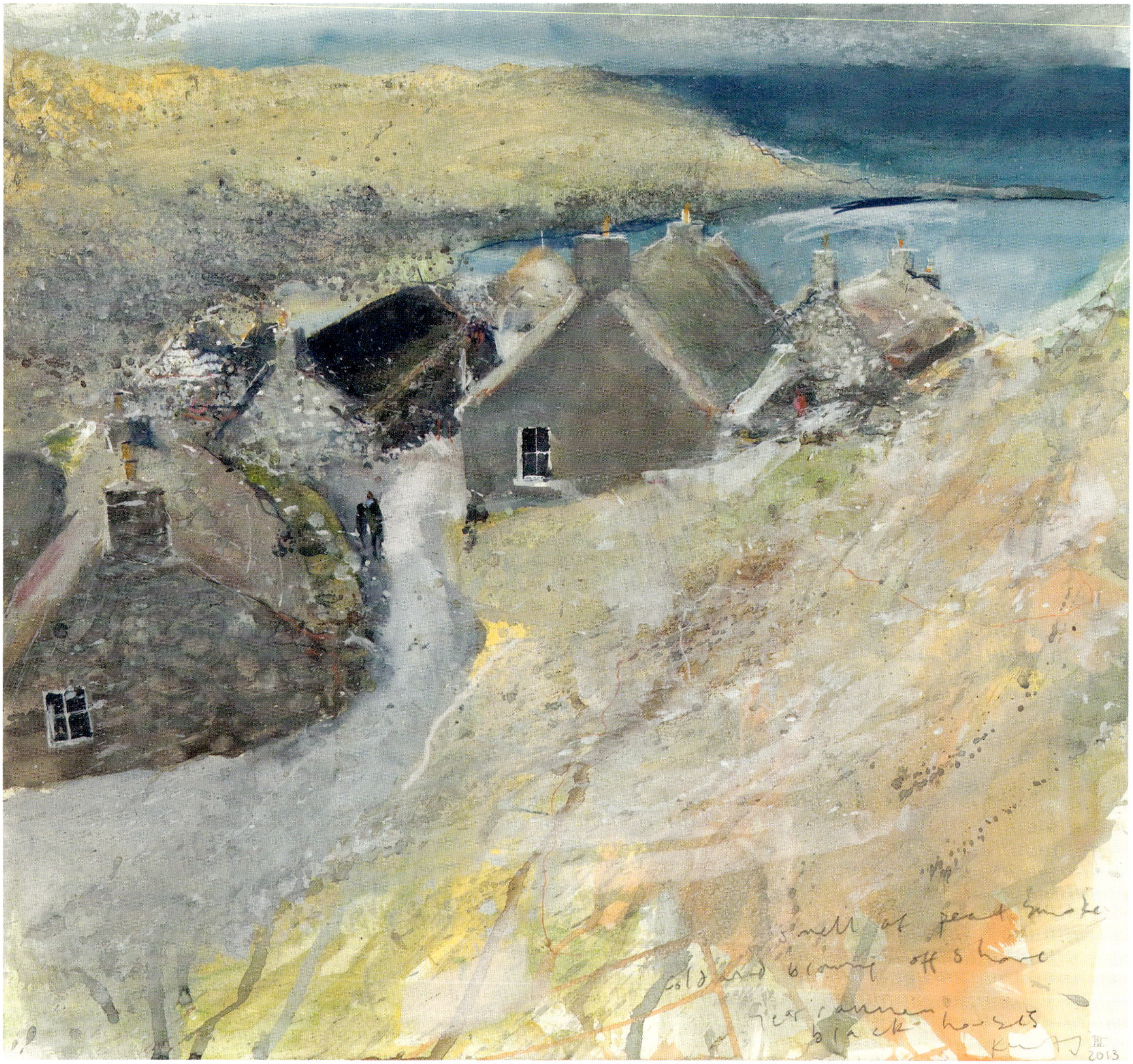

82. **Smell of peat smoke, cold wind blowing offshore. Gearrannan black houses**
March 2013 • mixed media on paper • 57 x 62 cm

28. Na Gearrannan, Isle of Lewis

John Stephens

My life seemed to have lost its way somewhere among the 25 miles of corridors which were the boast of the Teaching Hospital. Was it a mistake to have become a student again? To get some distance and I hoped perspective, I applied to the Western Isles to learn from the GPs there.

And suddenly space – Benbecula, its huge sky and a land of levels – shore, machair, causeways, moor. Always the wind, pulling, confronting. Visits to cramped front rooms, peat stoves, a slow exchange of information; finally a human scale. A coffin lowered, at the edge of the Atlantic, last rites in Gaelic held, then taken by the wind. Only sky, ocean, the very edge of existence.

On Lewis at Calanais I watched a bus bring new visitors. Groups moving among the stones, forming into patterns as solid and complex as the raised stones themselves. That night I was the only guest at Taigh Lata, the blackhouse hostel nearby. I woke in the pitch dark to see two human forms standing beside me, and where they connected an intense, visible certainty and calm.

These weeks brought me back, back to a sense of who I could be in my work, back to Rita, and later back to the Western edge of Britain, to Cornwall where we now live.

__John Stephens__ met Kurt Jackson working on a hop-farm when they were both at Oxford, Kurt studying zoology to become an artist and John studying languages to become a doctor. He lives in Cornwall with Rita from Holland and their children Olly, Zoe and Louis.

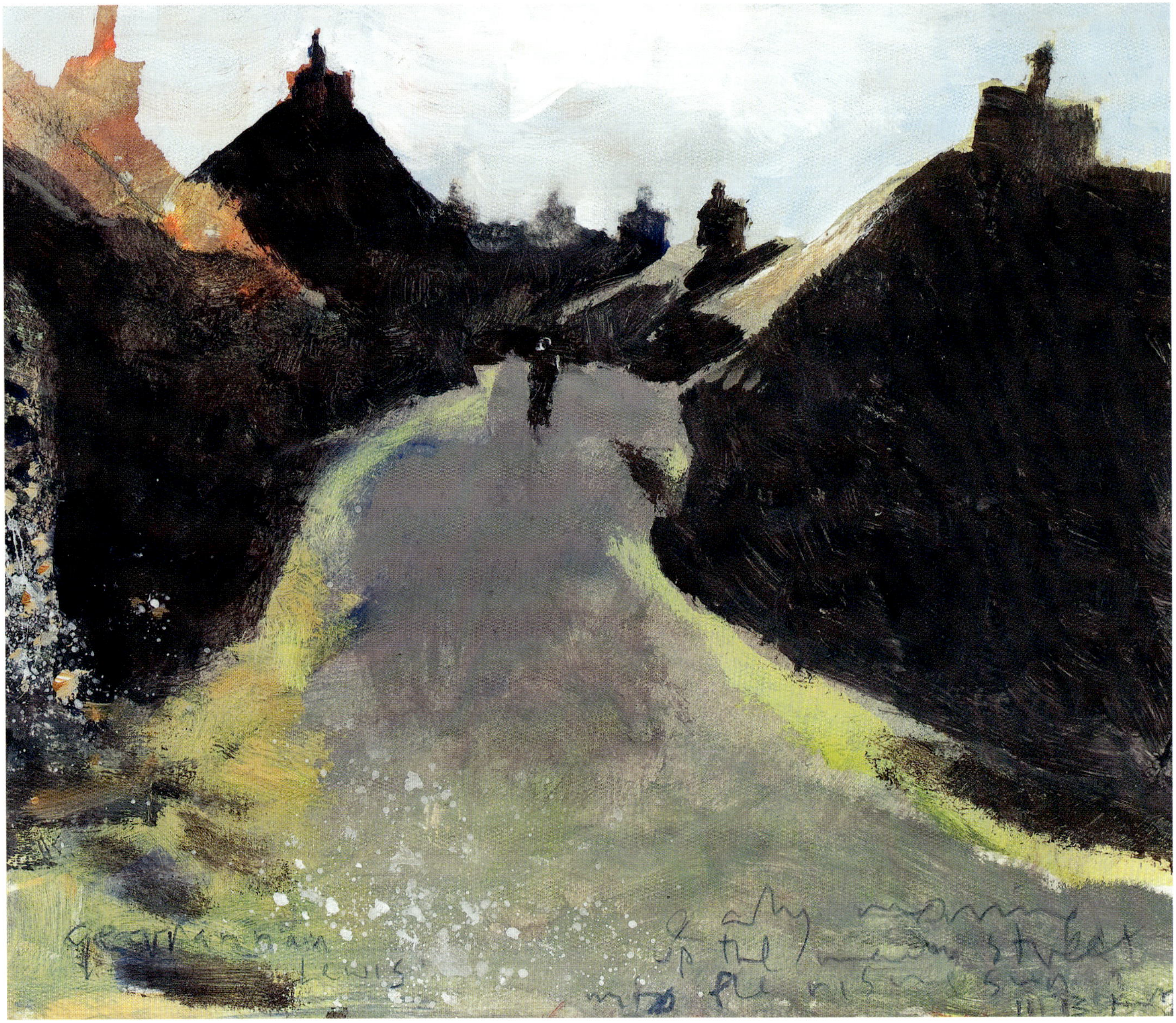

83. **Early morning up the main street into the rising sun. Gearrannan, Lewis**
March 2013 • acrylic on board • 16 x 19 cm

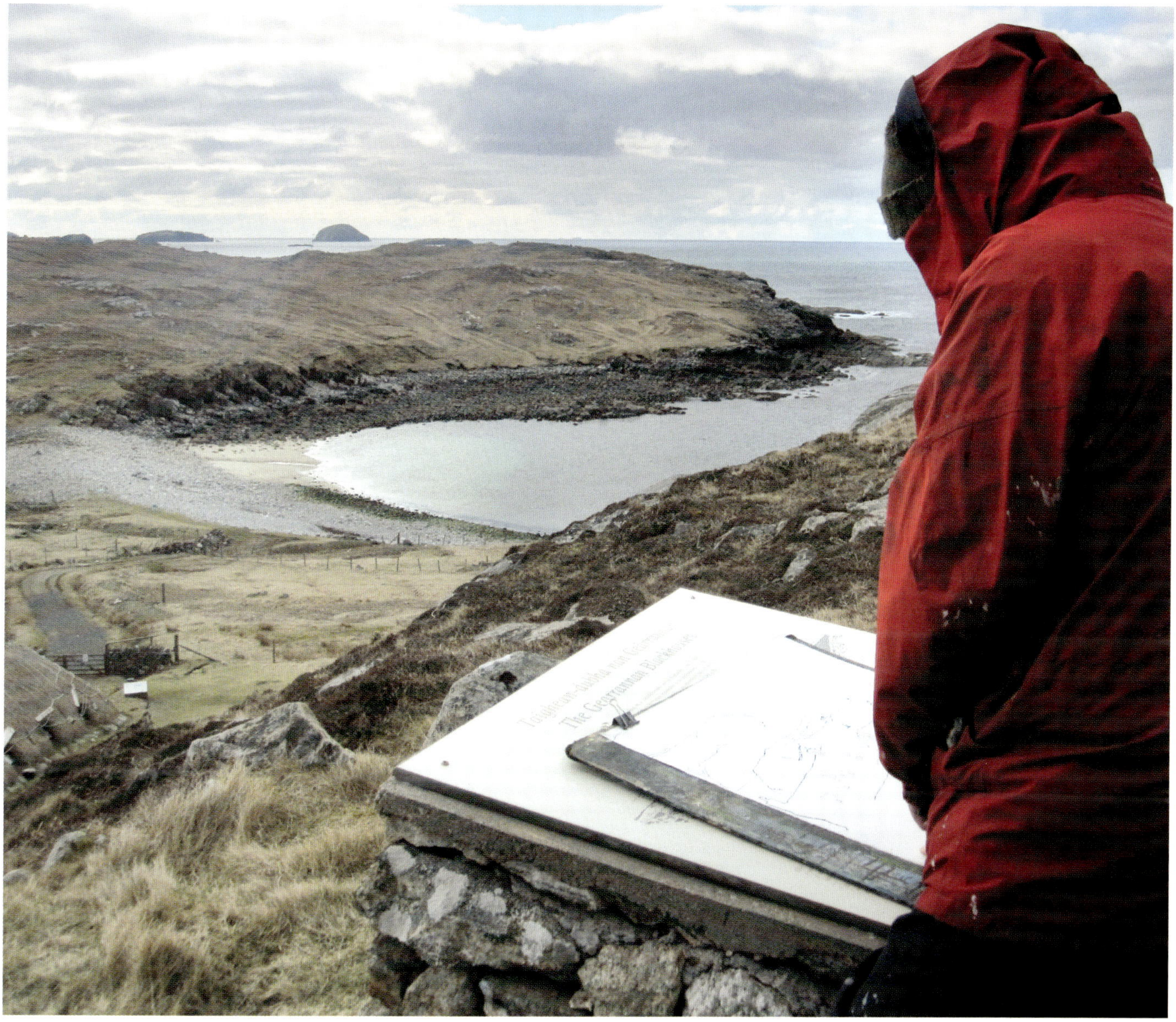
The Gearrannan Blackhouses

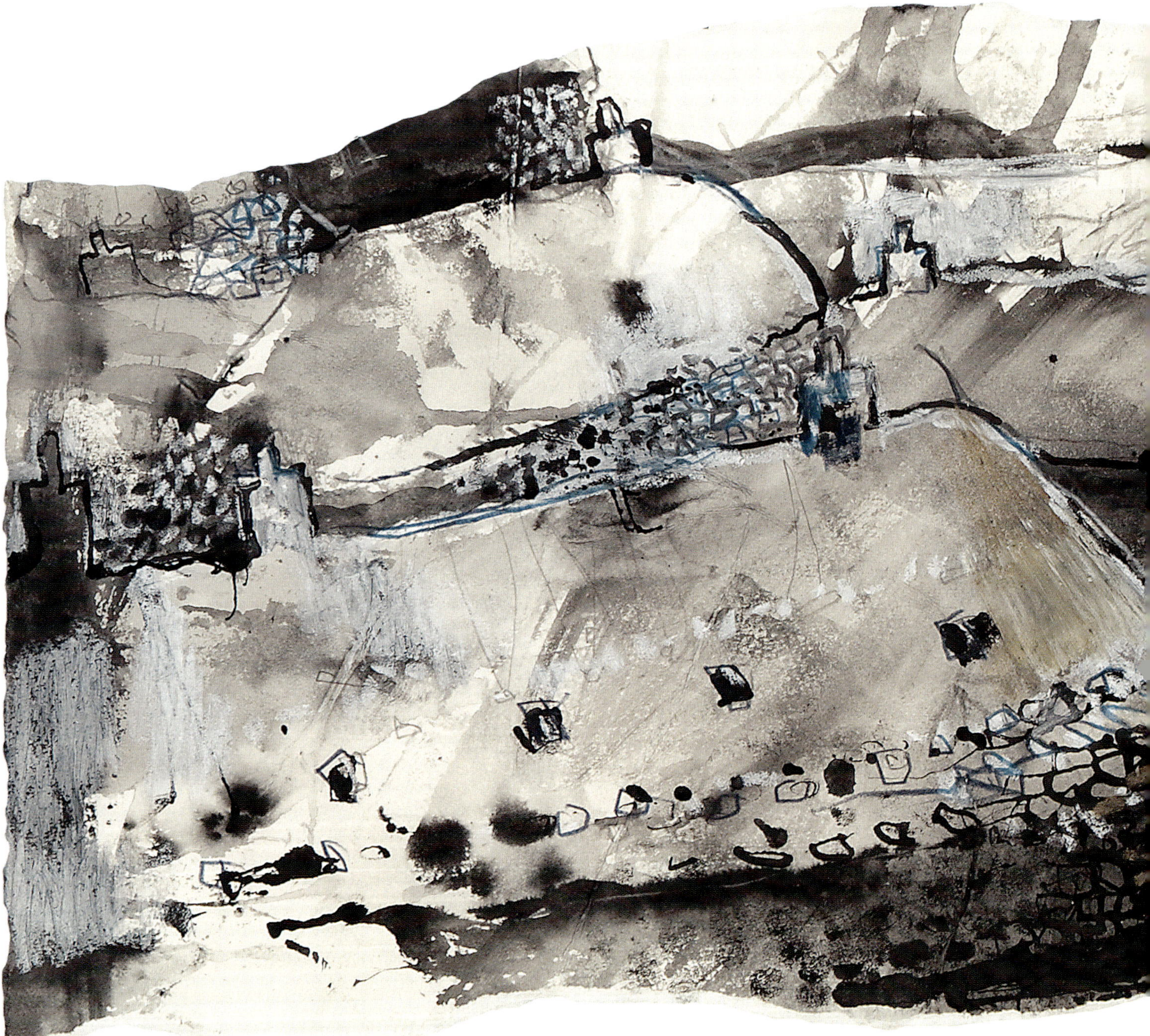

84. **The drawing that was snatched by the wind. Gearrannan**
March 2013 • ink, pastel and crayon on paper • 24 x 60 cm

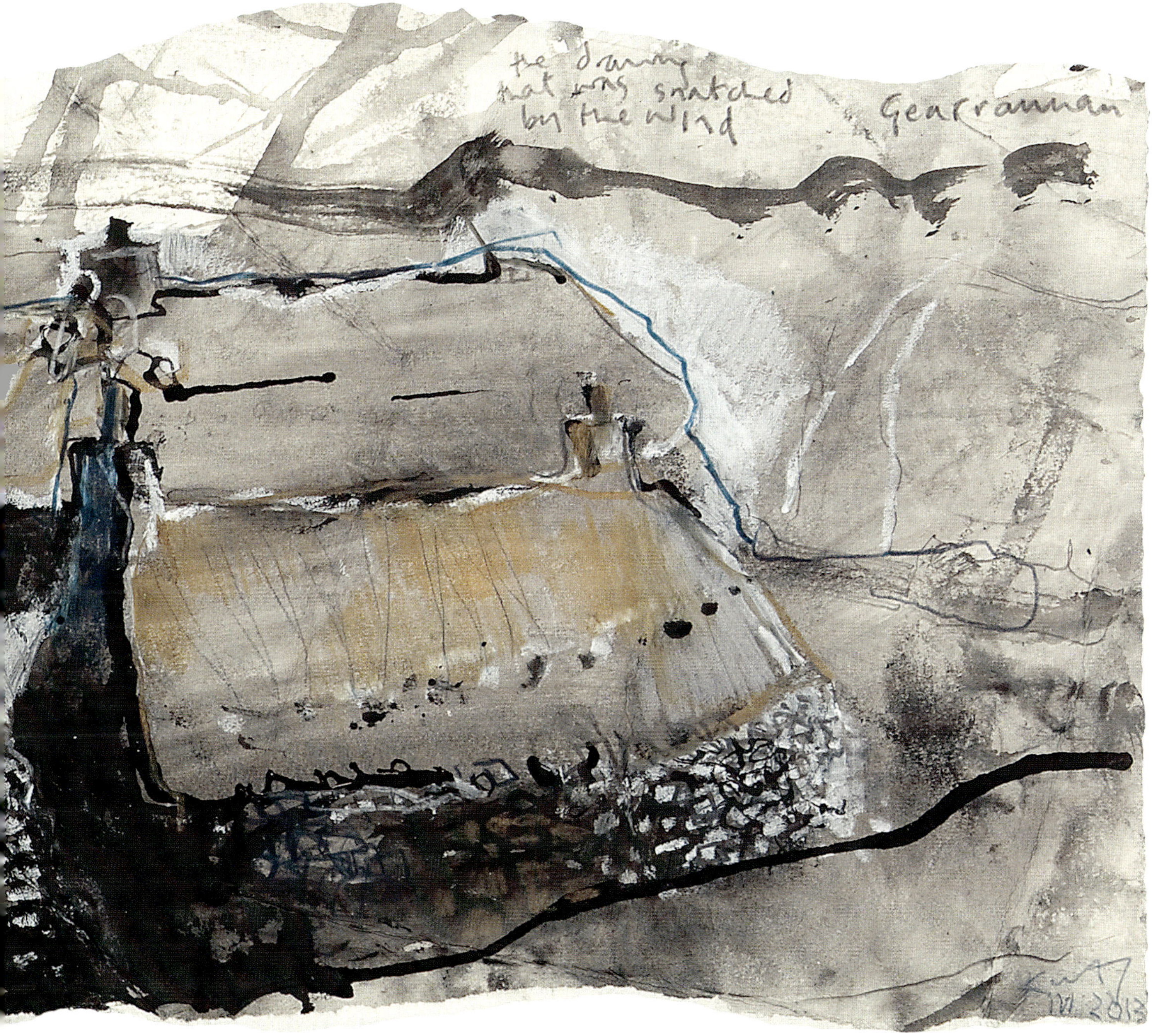
the drawing that was snatched by the wind
Gearrannan

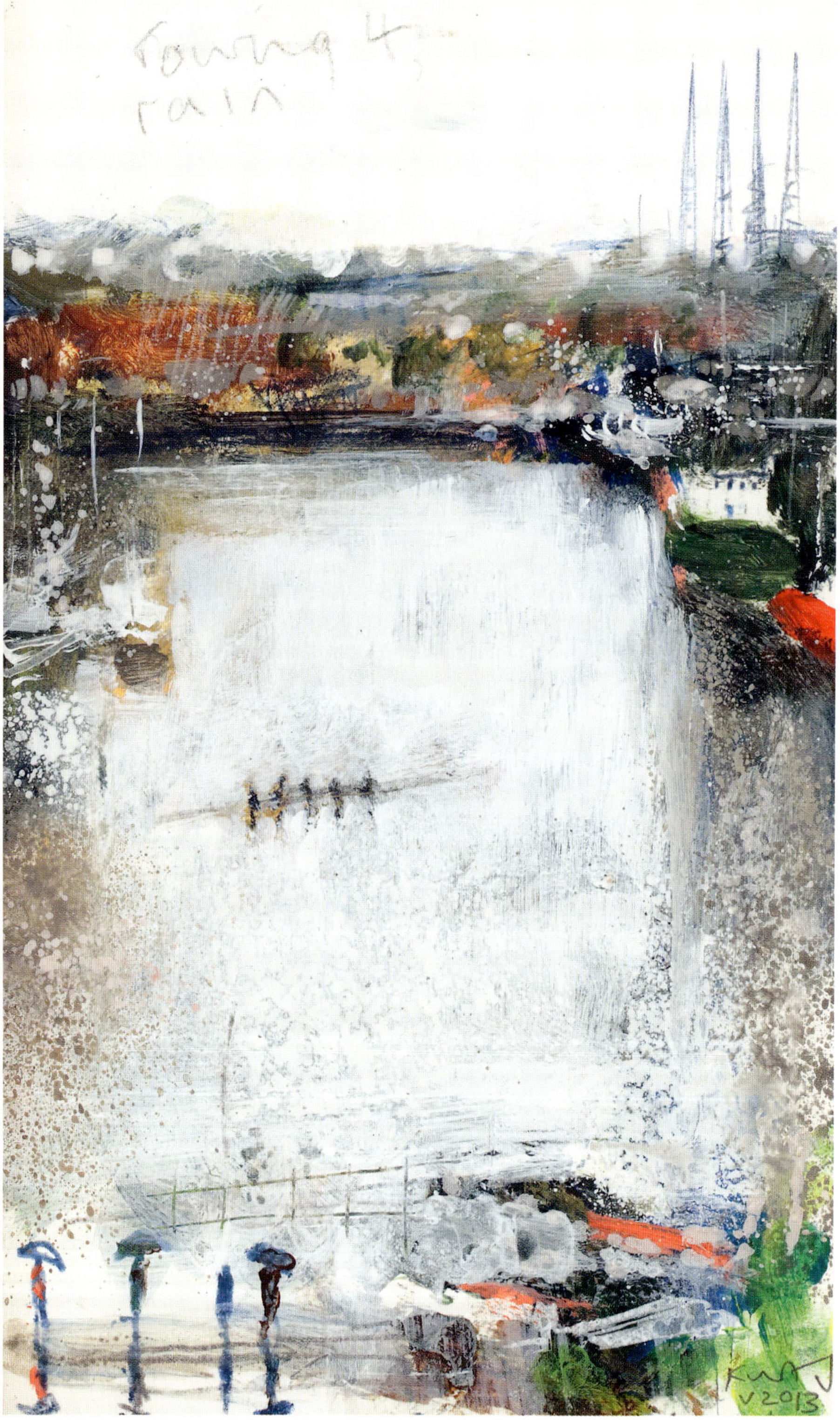

85. **Rowing four, rain**
May 2013 • mixed media on board • 24 x 14 cm

28. Looking out of my window, Spike Island

Helen Taylor

For almost four decades, my partner and I have overlooked Bristol's Floating Harbour. Such a romantic term for a body of water that is held at constant level by locks, constructed in 1809 to ensure ships could remain afloat in Bristol Docks on the tidal River Avon. Even though the 'floating' refers to ships which before its construction had been dumped onto the mud and rolled on their sides, I love the idea of this great artificial lake itself afloat as it daily soars and dips, rages and calms, bobbing along with its inhabitants – the large swan colony, cormorants and gulls, houseboats, ferries, rowing boats and gigs, as well as historic vessels.

From our window we glimpse in the distance Isambard Kingdom Brunel's sublime Suspension Bridge, and nearby the masts of the ss *Great Britain*, his great iron screw-propelled ship restored magnificently in recent years after a rescue operation from its 1886 grounding on the Falklands. Moored by the new Wapping Wharf commercial and residential development is the jaunty *Matthew*, a reconstruction of John Cabot's Bristol-built ship which took him to Newfoundland in 1497.

Thankfully, after 2012's disastrous wet summer drove the private ferry company into insolvency, the distinctive yellow and blue ferryboats have been returned to the water by a new public company. Most days gliding by is the *Bagheera* boat on which – in 2003 after 27 years of cohabitation – we celebrated our wedding.

Spike Island, where our house was built in 1867, is situated on a narrow strip of land between the Harbour and the 'New Cut,' William Jessop's ingenious tidal waterway that diverts the River Avon around the centre of Bristol to keep the Harbour water at a steady level for river traffic and large vessels. For a long time derelict and run-down, Spike Island is now part of Bristol's arts quarter, housing Spike Island Art Studios and Aardman Animation's headquarters, and boasting the refurbished ss *Great Britain* ship and museum. From the front of this house on the busy Cumberland Road, we look south to the Cut and Bedminster (once dominated by the Wills Tobacco Company). To the north, the Harbour is a relatively tranquil scene, punctuated by the sounds of the Prince Street bridge swinging next to the Arnolfini Gallery, the swish of small boats, and the desultory chatter of customers at Bristol's most popular tiny waterside café, Brunel's Buttery.

In 1972, when I first came to Bristol, the Docks were impenetrable to casual visitors. Heavily bombed in World War II, noisy, busy and increasingly unprofitable, the ship building and repair yards went into steep decline, and in 1977 last-man-standing Charles Hill's shipyard closed months after launching the beer tanker, *Miranda Guinness*. In recent years, ramshackle sheds and warehouses that embodied the Docks' rich history have been knocked down or burned, to be replaced by bland blocks of houses and flats, complemented by new houseboat moorings, the family-friendly Museum of Bristol 'M Shed,' and waterside restaurants, kiosks and ice-cream vans. The Docks – renamed 'Harbourside' – have become a centre of heritage, leisure and consumerism.

We photograph obsessively. In winter, it's a series of etchings: dramatic lowering skies and dark shadows with building and boat silhouettes, sometimes a breath-taking snow scene with the harbour frozen over and the Harbourmaster cutting a passage with his little boat for vessels and birds. In spring and summer, especially during events such as the Harbourside Festival, or at weekends when the lovingly restored steam railway offers rides, it's like a busy film set.

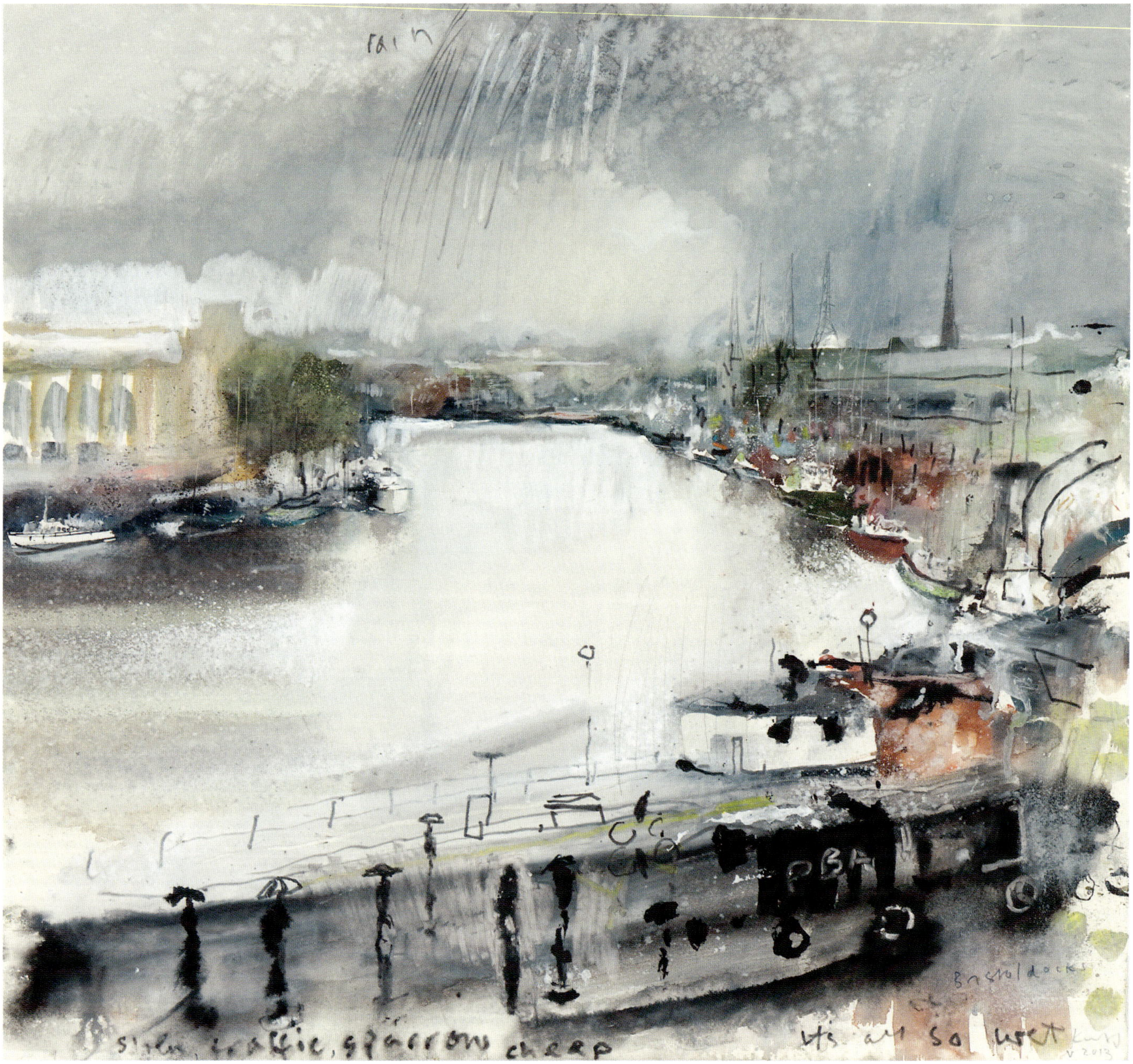

86. **It's all so wet. Bristol Docks. Sirens, traffic, sparrow cheep**
May 2013 • mixed media on paper • 57 x 62 cm

Locals and tourists mingle on the *Matthew*'s Avon Gorge cruises; swimming Newfoundland dogs demonstrate lifesaving in the water; visitors stride, jog, gig-race, kayak or cycle along the Harbour. Occasionally, on windless days, the Harbour is an absolutely still lake of golden-brown water that makes your heart stop.

The sounds, smells and quality of light change daily. Couples and children quarrelling. The steam train puffing clouds of smoke into our garden. Screaming seagulls swooping onto junk food remnants. Rock bands performing outside Lloyds building at the curve of the Harbour. Bacon frying mouth-wateringly below us at the Buttery. The water sparkles and dazzles in summer, while in winter there is a sludgy peacefulness about a Harbour gently rocking its houseboats, ferries and rowing boats, with walkway lamplights and apartment and office lights in the blocks opposite making ghostly reflections through damp mists and darkness.

__Helen Taylor__ is professor of English and humanities arts and culture fellow at the University of Exeter. She has published widely on women's writing and the literature and culture of the American South. She is an honorary fellow of the British Association of American Studies.

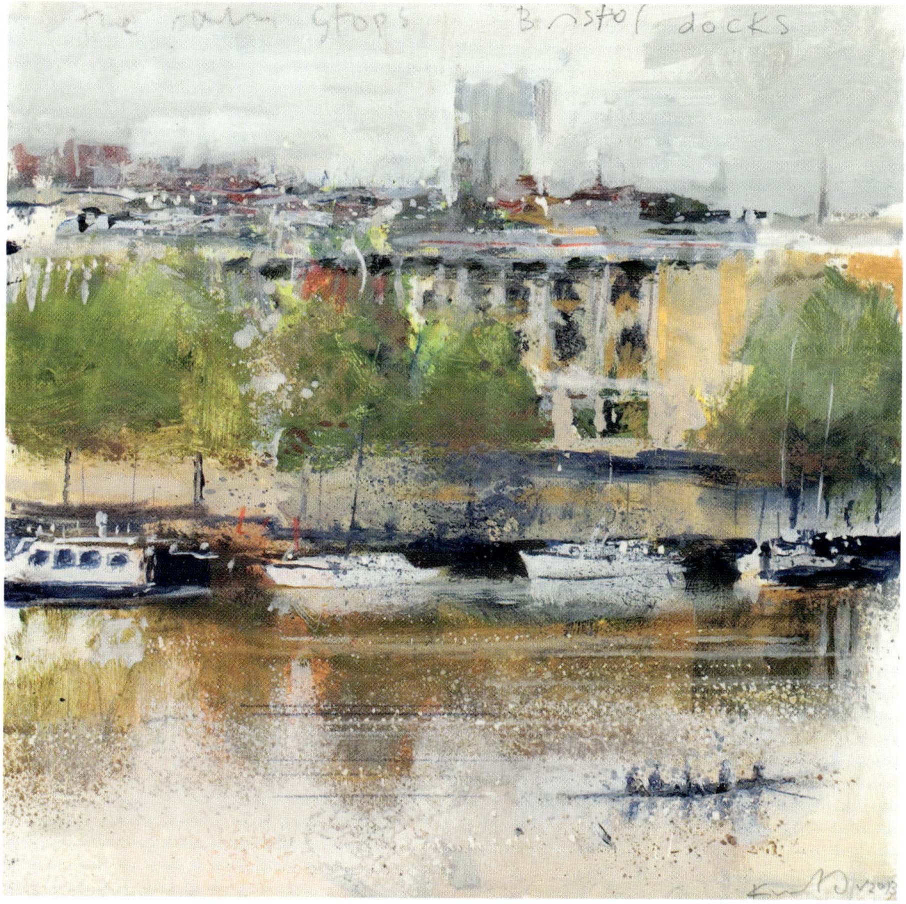

87. **The rain stops. Bristol docks**
May 2013 • mixed media on board • 21 x 21.5 cm

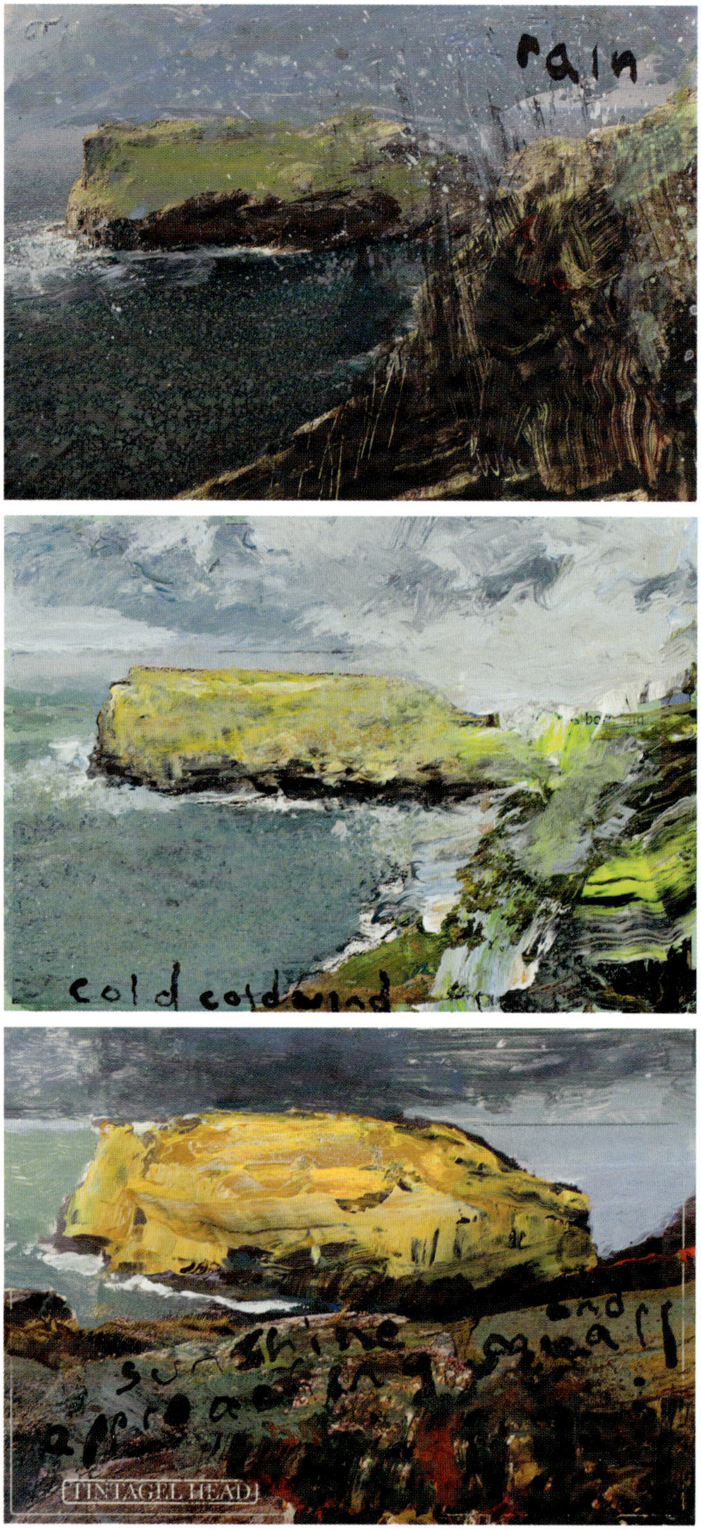

88. **Rain; Cold, cold wind; Sunshine and approaching squall**
February 2013 • mixed media on postcards • 11 x 16 cm (x3)

Tintagel Castle

Charles Thomas

The best and perhaps the most informative, view of Tintagel's so-called Island – and I say this as one who has been there countless times over a great many years – is a short distance east along the cliff path, not far from the car-park by Tintagel's medieval parish church. The first, I guess obvious, question to ask yourself is: Why is this handsome parish church so far from the main street of Tintagel village with all its pubs and Arthurian-souvenir shops? Well, the village itself, whose real name until the late 1800s was Trevena, probably goes back to the 12th–13th centuries and it still contains a few antique buildings like the National Trust's handsome Old Post Office. Tintagel church, on the other hand, today at the edge of a very large graveyard, but actually within a much smaller and older oval embanked enclosure: this we excavated (as an archaeological project) in the 1990s. We found the remains of Christian burials dating from about AD 500, dated by associated pottery, and also the stone foundations of an earlier church, smaller, perhaps 9th–10th century.

The best interpretation is the Tintagel Island, in the Roman period and some centuries on, was occupied – possibly seasonally rather than permanently – and was accessible by a natural land bridge or narrow neck from the mainland. By the Middle Ages this has eroded to the point where some kind of wooden bridge was necessary; more of the neck fell away, leading to a present English Heritage concrete path and stairs (which, so geologist claim, may well collapse a century on from now).

The full story, as far as we know it, of Tintagel, arguably Cornwall's most important site and the setting for the King Mark, Tristan and Isolde legends (not originally for 'King' Arthur, probably a North Briton and here a 12th-century introduction) is in my book *Tintagel – Arthur and Archaeology* (Batsford/English Heritage, 1993).

It seems almost certain that, after Britain's Roman period of the first four centuries AD, there arose a native kingdom of Dumnonia, covering Cornwall, Devon and most of Somerset. It had no fixed centre, but a series of occupied strongholds; one such was Tintagel, accessible as a small port (Tintagel Cove, the beach below the ticketing office and restaurant) and used for several hundred years as a spot where Mediterranean imports – wine and oil in pottery containers, fine table-wares – were perhaps traded for ingots of streamed tin from the Cornish hinterland.

It's also clear that, at the end of the Roman period, there was some small official centre here, perhaps a tax-collecting office. And then in the 13th century Richard Earl of Cornwall, chose both the Island and part of the adjoining mainland as the site of a dramatic, if somewhat pointless, castle, masonry remains of which are still visible.

Enough of that; I'm concerned here with the view. Most of the views of Tintagel Island are drawn or photographed from the eastern side, from above the cove or from the headland with its vast late-Victorian hotel. But the place I've chosen to recommend to Kurt, who has seen more of Cornwall than I've ever done, is the optimum in all weathers. In sunshine, blue sky, miles of sea and coast, a wealth of bird-life, it's tremendous. And in stormy weather one appreciates how the sea has eroded, and will go on eroding, our northern coastline. There is a long sea cavern, so-called Merlin's cove's little beach – and waves crash into and along it. Spray can be hurled up a hundred feet and more. I love most of my native Cornwall, and have plenty of special places to sit and gaze; but, for an archaeologist and landscape historian, the cliff path southwest of Tintagel Island remains supreme. I'd like to think that if I reach the age of 90, like my late mentor Courtenay Arthur Ralegh Radford (first excavator of Tintagel in modern terms) at the same age I could be airlifted to the top of the Island by helicopter. And then, pushing up the daisies, I might learn even more of its secrets!

Charles Thomas, from a well-known Camborne mining family (Dolcoath, etc.), has been an archaeologist and local historian for most of his long life. He was the first professional director of the Institute of Cornish Studies, University of Exeter, and in the 1990s worked at Tintagel involving excavations. He still sees Tintagel as a place of magic and mystery.

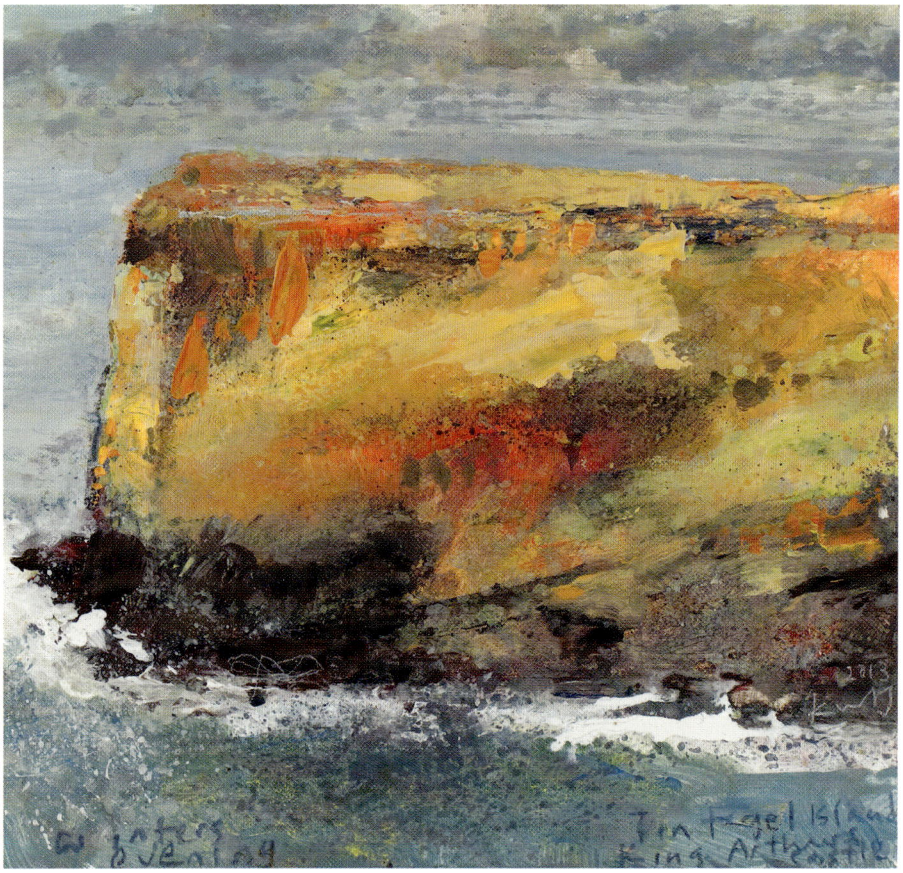

89. **Winter's evening, Tintagel Island**
2013 • acrylic on board • 18 x 19 cm

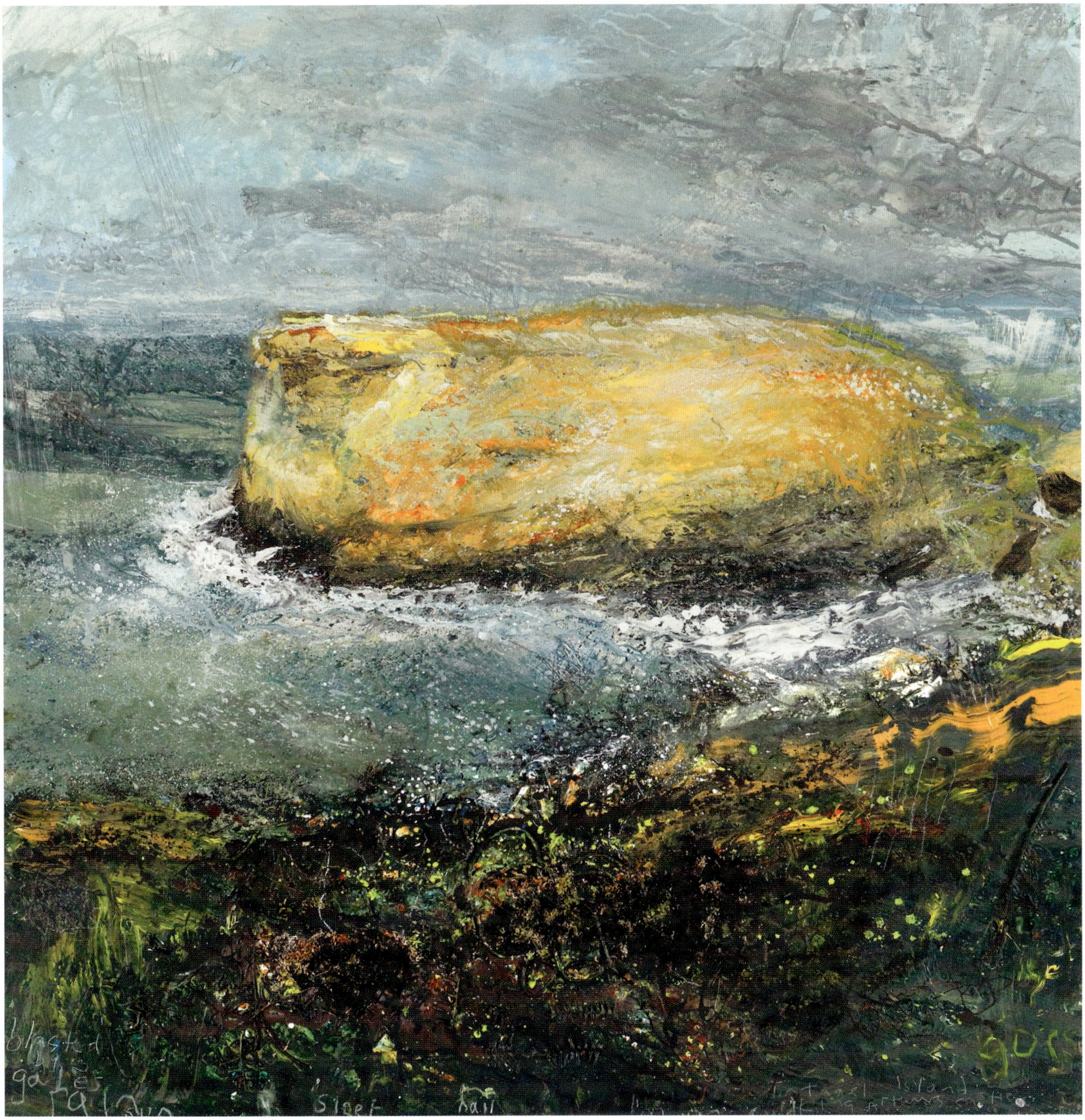

90. **Rain, sun, sleet, hail. Tintagel Island, King Arthur's Castle**
February 2013 • mixed media and collage on board • 81 x 82 cm

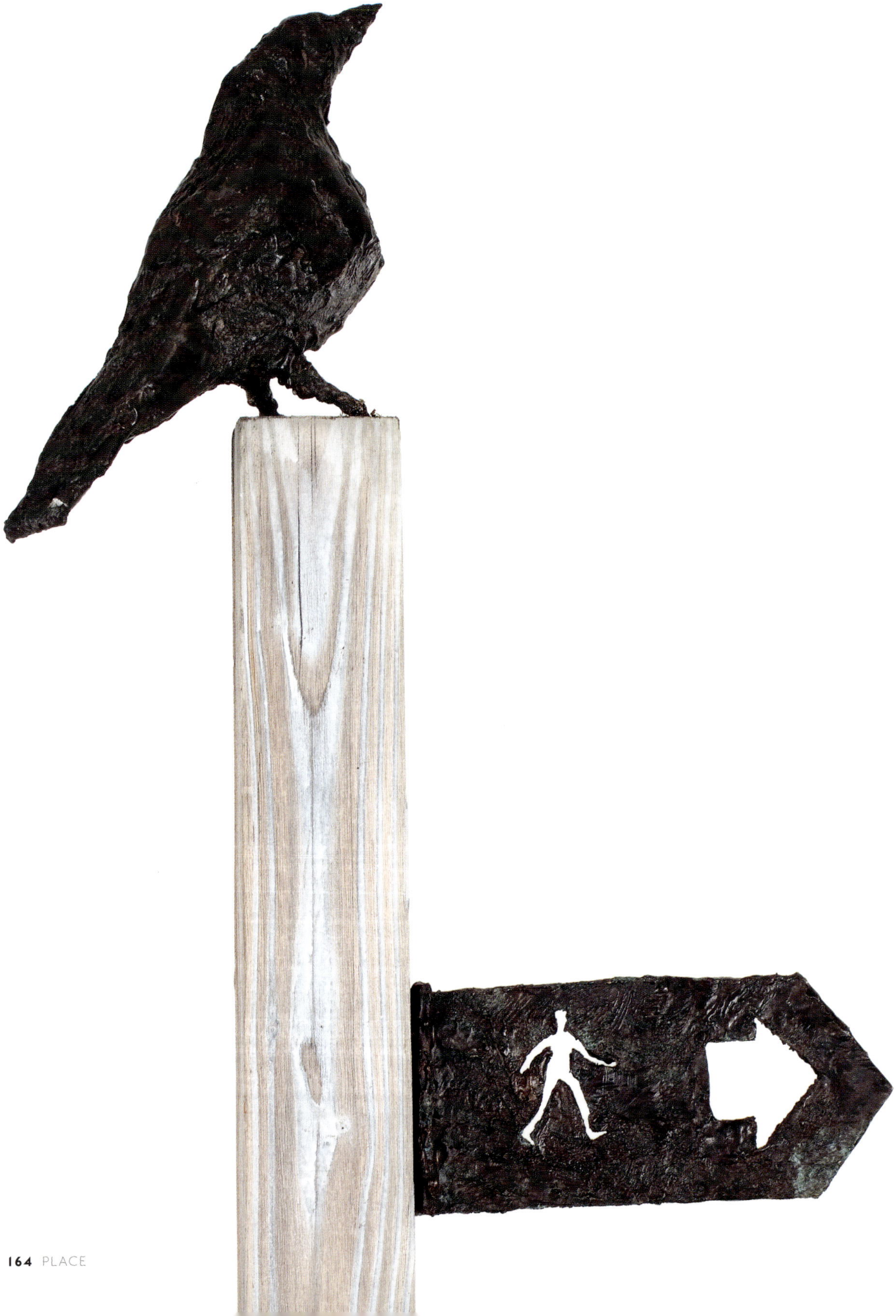

30. Vale of Llangollen

John Vidal

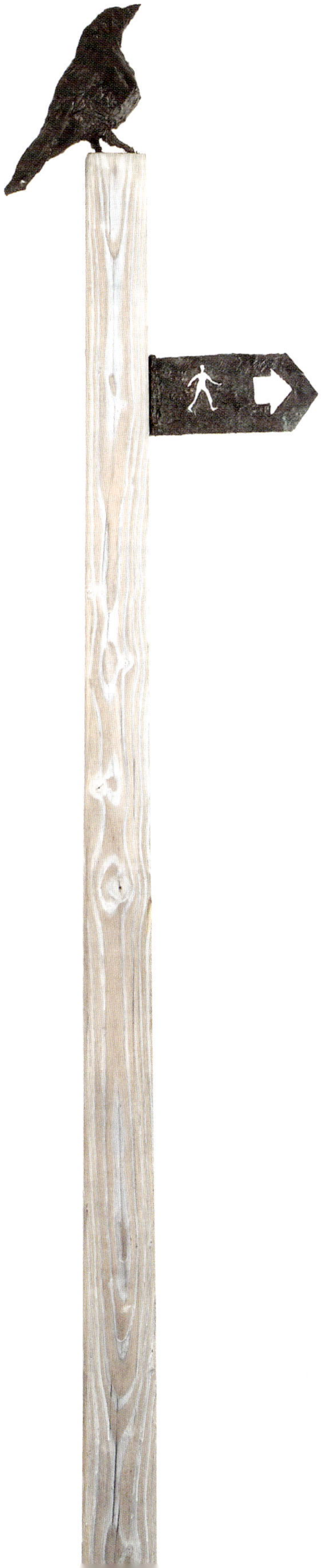

High above the Vale of Llangollen we roll in the bracken and stain our hands and clothes deep purple to collect the tiny whinberries. The bright Welsh sky is full of buzzards and skylarks. You can be up here on the wild moor all day and see only birds and sheep, feel only the lung-busting winds and lashing rain and forget that every step in this landscape traces 3000 years of human activity.

Over there, on the same level as the steep limestone cliffs we follow on the way to World's End, is the medieval Castell Dinas Bran which perches, ruined, on a much older iron age fort; above us is Eglwyseg mountain, pitted with old lead mines, shafts, stone circles and bronze age burial mounds; the tiny fields laid out below us in the Dee valley have not changed in 200 years. Stone and slate have been quarried here and taken to England for centuries; and those old twisted firs with their limbs leaning on the ground have always bent to windward and given sheep some shelter.

This is a complex landscape of valleys, crags, moors, forest and fields, all played by changing wind, rain and sun. It is familiar and loved because, while it is man-made, it is still human-scaled. No structure stands more than a few metres high, no path is wider than two people, no wall cannot be easily scaled or hill climbed.

Up here, man's works are sparse. The wind blows strong but there are no turbines in sight; a radio mast gives barely a signal; a steep road climbs to a distant pass but there is no sound of traffic; and far down below us is Llangollen and the river Dee but no sign of people. The land reflects humans, but every age has just left a scar and moved on.

Instead, the prospect from these moors always thrills. Far, far to the west are the peaks of the Berwyns and Snowdonia, and beyond them the coast, the sea and the promise of other lives. To the east, over the old border of Offa's Dyke, is the Shropshire plain – low lands full of bustle and bigger places that have long sent these valleys waves of settlers, armies, a new language and customs.

Up here, though, the wind is warm today, there's ivy in the rock cracks, lichen on the tree trunks and the oaks and rowans are covered in moss. The long, late summer clings on. It's been one of the best years for fruit. We snack on blackberries, pluck the damsons and the sloes, roll again in the bracken and watch the buzzards.

John Vidal lives between the Welsh borders and London where he is The Guardian's environment editor.

91. **Bran**
2014 • bronze and pine • 265 x 40 x 25 cm

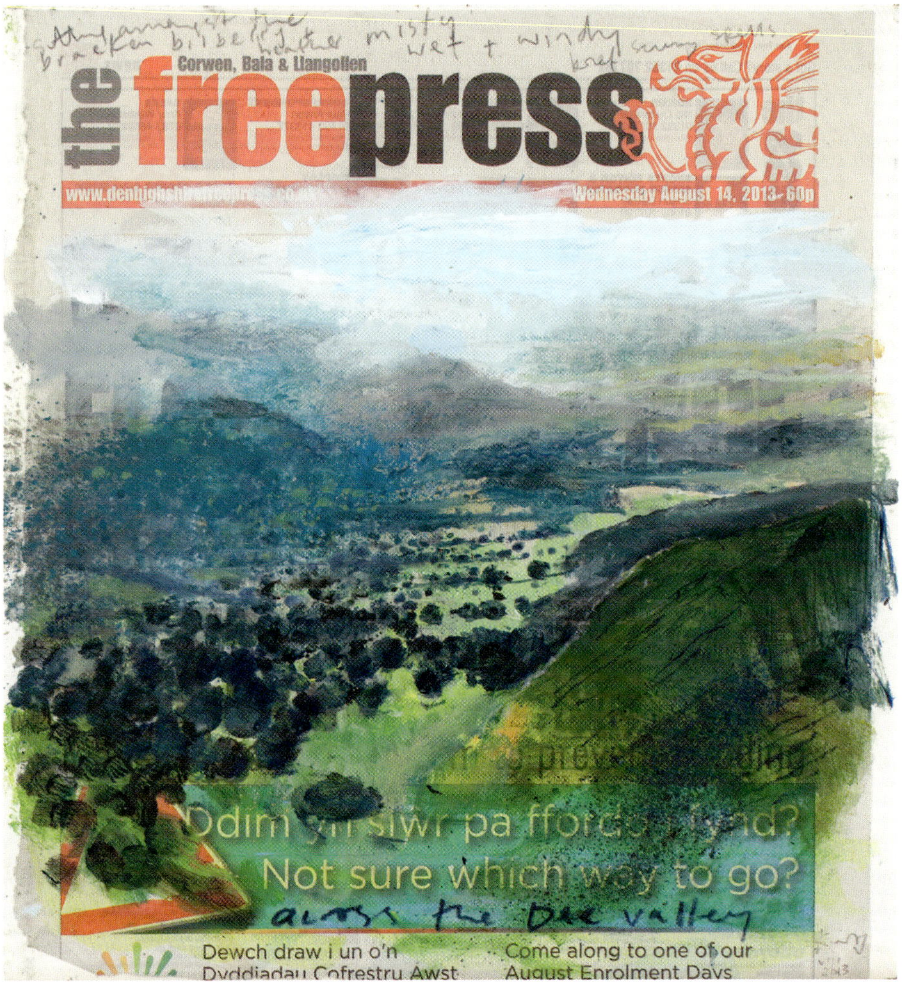

92. **Sitting amongst the bracken, bilberry and heather. Misty, wet and windy. Across the Dee Valley**
August 2013 • mixed media and collage on board • 32 x 29 cm

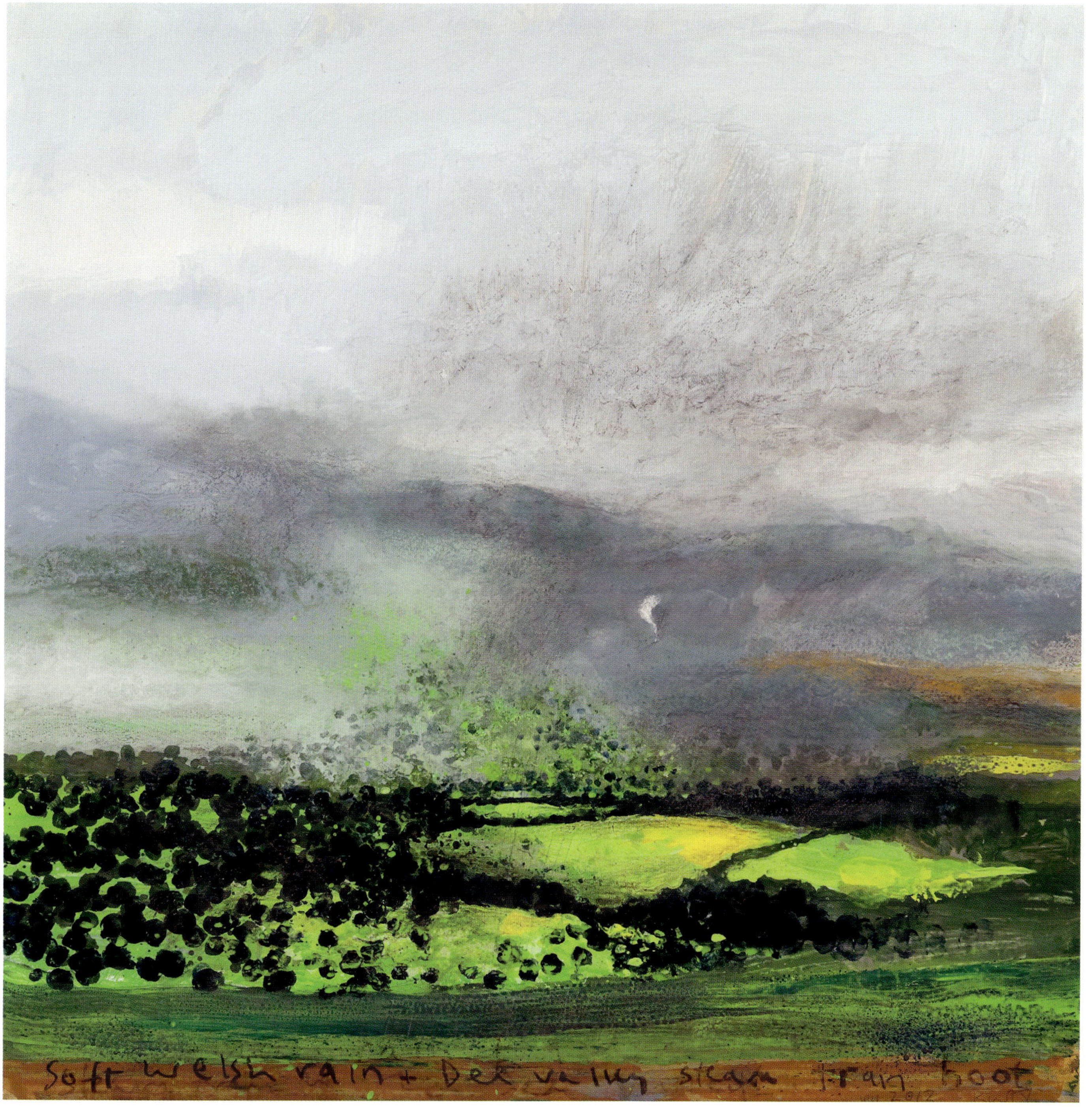

93. **Soft Welsh rain and Dee Valley steam train hoot**
August 2013 • mixed media on board • 59 x 60 cm

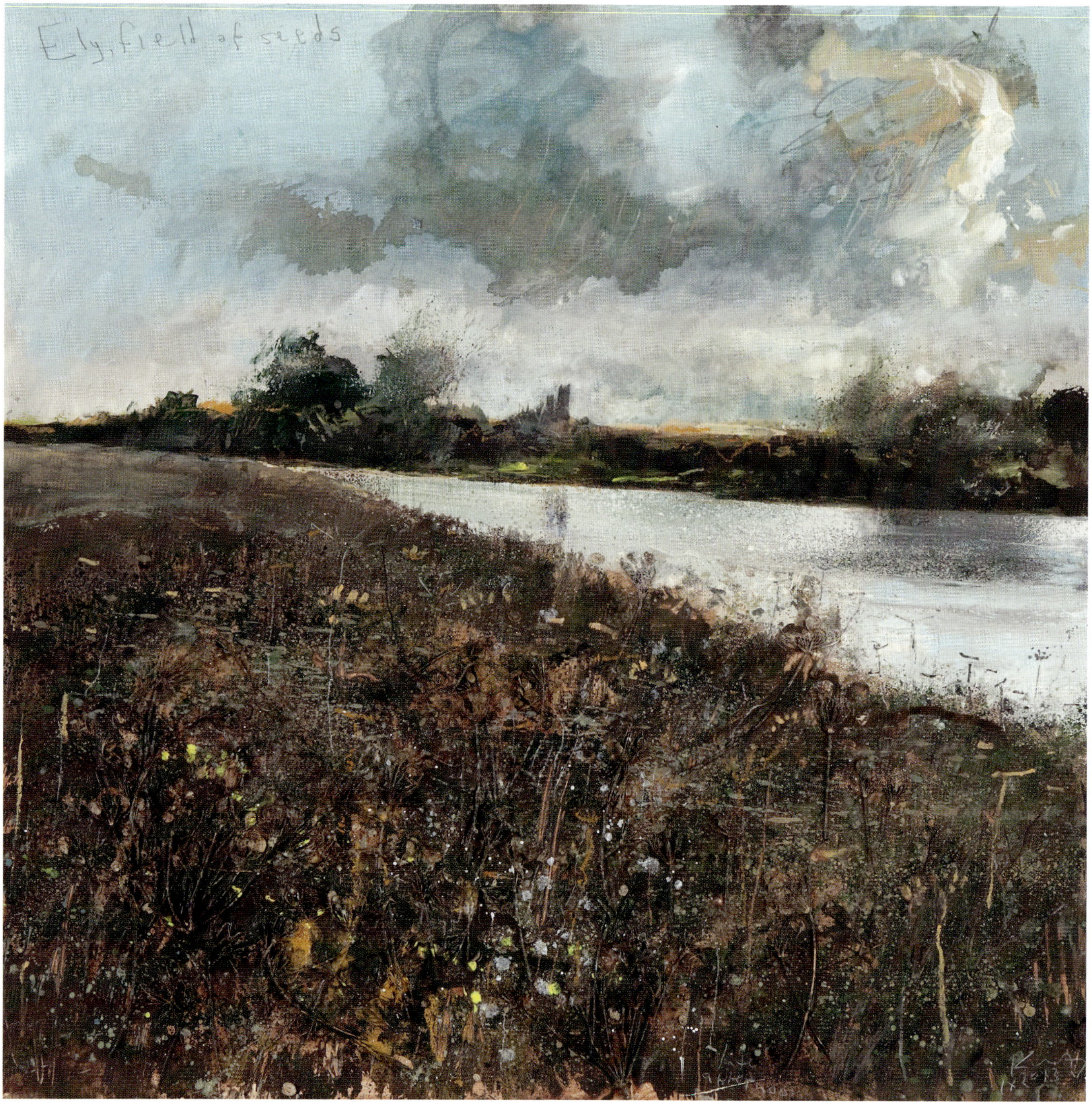

94. **Ely, field of seeds**
September 2013 • mixed media and collage on board • 58 x 60 cm

31. Ely, Cambridgeshire

Bob Wilson

We have a small traditional narrow boat called *Arun* on which I travel the canals and rivers with Cathy, my wife. We're off on it whenever we can find the time, or when city life becomes too much for us. Gliding up and down the waterways in the biggest garden of all – the English countryside. Summer of 2006 found us heading east through Peterborough, onto the fens and through to the Great River Ouse. The journey was adventurous. We negotiated ancient waterways cut through the peat as drainage channels and on through the locks. Then along a low fast tidal stretch and down onto the Great Ouse. So it was a relief to sail into the safe haven of Ely, a jewel of a city perched on a hill dominated by the stunning Norman cathedral. What we had intended as a weekend visit ended almost a year later.

That same year we returned to spend Christmas onboard our boat. Ely was peaceful. The tourists who throng its streets in the summer months had departed. Peacocks, a wonderful Regency tea room serving hundreds of teas from around the world was closed and the huge antiques showroom housed in restored barns was silent. Our only companions were the horses who grazed the long grasses in the fields that surround the cathedral and the famous geese who act as if they owned the city.

On Christmas Day we left our friends, the two black mute swans, and slipped out of our moorings and headed south. The day was calm and the river was still. We had it to ourselves. Our little boat chugged along, its vintage Russell Newbury single cylinder engine puffing away in celebration of the day. On one side the river was guarded by a high embankment built as a flood defence. The other stretched into a long low water meadow.

On our return, in the low light of the late afternoon, a barn owl appeared over the tall grass of the water meadow. We watched as it swooped and dived until it picked up an evening meal in its talons. Then, as it flapped away, a buzzard suddenly appeared intent on stealing the owl's prey. Up and down they squabbled until the owl escaped, its meal intact. As I glanced at the still waters I could see the reflection of that majestic cathedral even though it stood some two miles away in the distance. It was a perfect day.

Bob Wilson *lives in London but takes every opportunity to escape in his narrow boat onto the canals and rivers into the biggest garden in the country. He works for Greenpeace where he produces events that are big, colourful and loud, to promote their campaigns.*

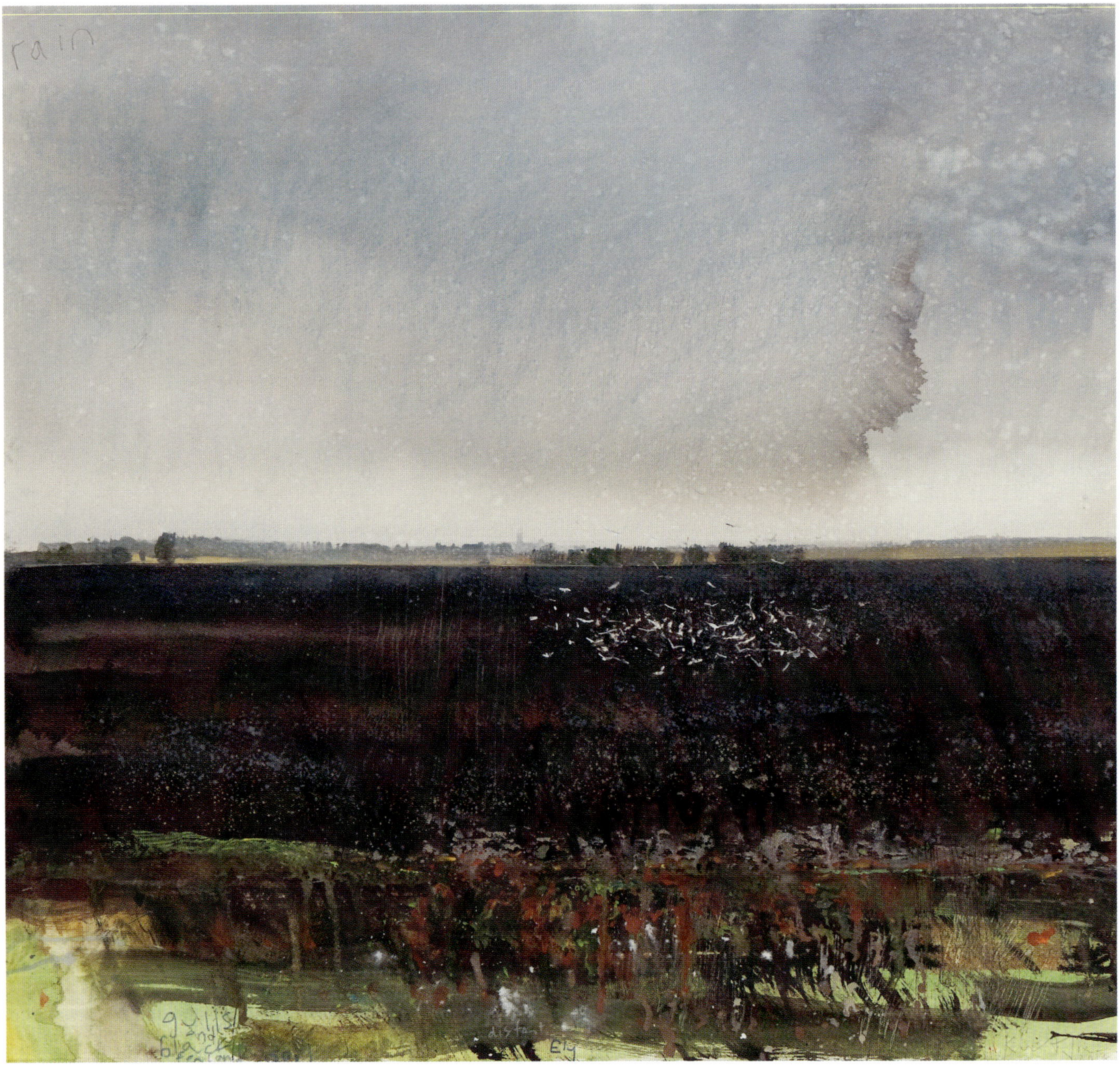

95. **Rain. Distant Ely, gulls and black fenland soil**
September 2013 • mixed media on paper • 57 x 61 cm

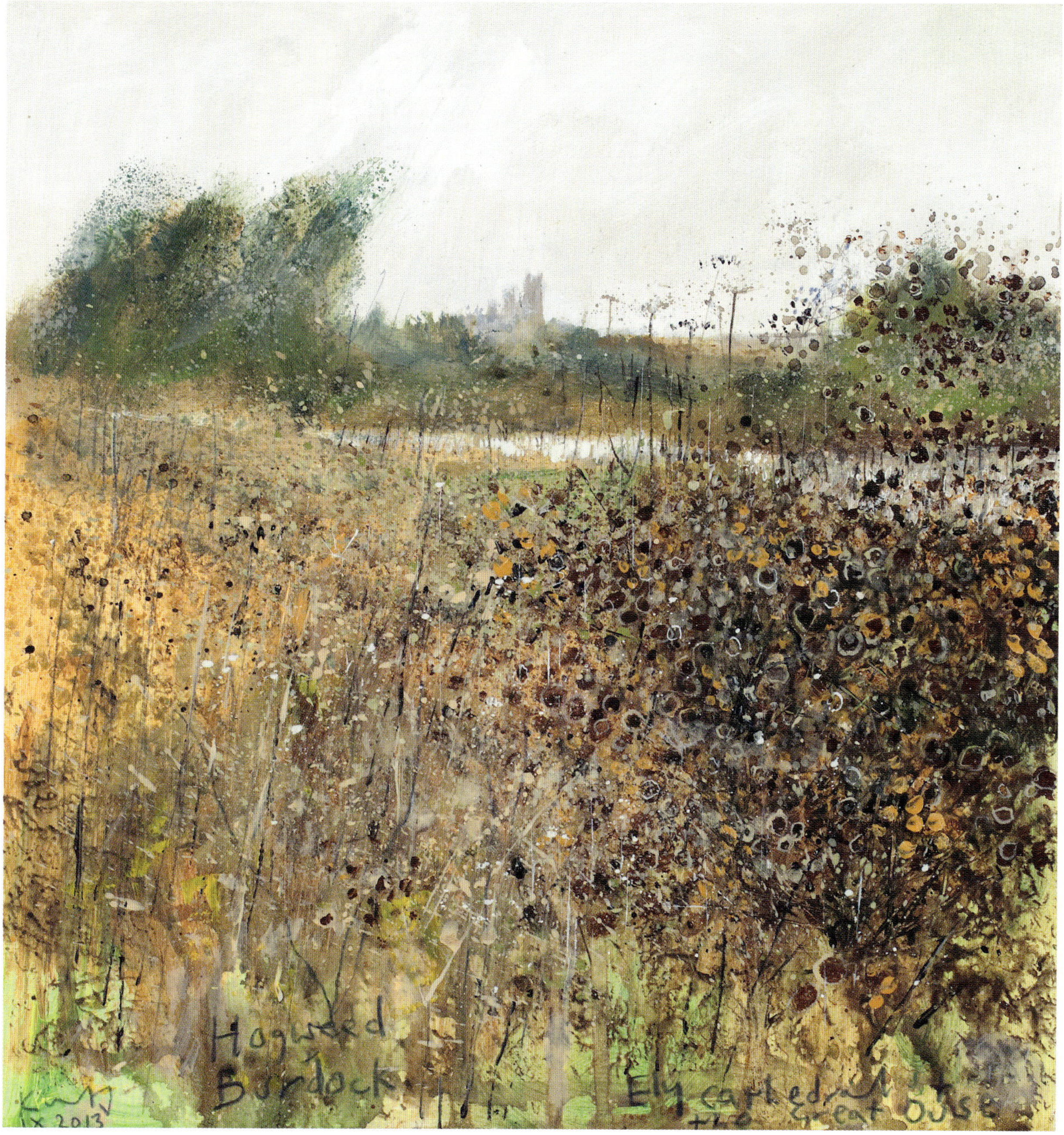

96. **Hogweed and burdock. Ely cathedral and the Great Ouse**
September 2013 • mixed media on board • 30 x 29 cm

Appendix

Selected solo exhibitions

2014

- 'Cargodna', Redfern Gallery, London.
- 'River', Horniman Museum, London.
- 'Place', Southampton City Art Gallery.
- 'Line caught and Local', National Maritime Museum, Falmouth.
- 'Archipelago: The Isles of Scilly, off Cornwall', Campden Gallery, Gloucestershire.
- 'A Bite of the Camel', collaboration with Rick Stein, Padstow, Cornwall.

2013

- 'The Thames Revisted', Redfern Gallery, London.
- 'The Burn', The Lighthouse Gallery, Glasgow.
- 'A One Mile Walk', Campden Gallery, Gloucestershire.

2012

- 'The Sketchbooks', Redfern Gallery, London.
- 'The Catacol Series: Paintings on Aran', Dovecot Studios, Edinburgh.
- 'The Fishermens Friend', with Greenpeace, National Maritime Aquarium, Plymouth.
- 'This Place: St Just-in-Penwith', Truro, Cornwall.
- 'Kurt Jackson & St Just', Royal Cornwall Museum, Truro.

2011

- 'Recent Work', Redfern Gallery, London.
- 'Kurt Jackson at 50', Falmouth Art Gallery.
- 'The Forth', Dovecot Studios, Edinburgh.
- 'Tree/Gwedhen', Truro, Cornwall.

2010

- 'Ardnamurchan', Dovecot Studios, Edinburgh.
- Book launch and exhibition, Osborne Samuel Gallery, London.
- Lorient Festival, Brittany.
- 'The Dart', Truro, Cornwall.
- 'A Taste of Glastonbury', Oxo Tower, London.

2009

- 'Forest Gardens', Messum's, London.
- Glastonbury Festival charity auction, *The Guardian* newsroom, London.
- 'River Avon, Part 2', Victoria Art Gallery, Bath.
- 'Enesow: An exploration of the islands of Cornwall', Truro, Cornwall.

2008

- 'The Lights of West Cornwall', Messum's, London.
- 'Wicken, a Threatened Landscape', charity auction for Friends of the Earth, Foyles Gallery, London.
- 'The Solent Project', touring exhibition: St Barbe Museum and Art Gallery, Lymington; Gosport Arts Centre, Hants; Quay Arts Centre, Isle of Wight.
- 'The Tamar', Truro, Cornwall.
- 'The Mining Paintings', Geevor Mine Gallery, Cornwall.
- 'Theatre Five', Royal College of Surgeons, London; Royal Cornwall Hospital, Truro.

2007

- 'Caroline and the Veg Patch', Messum's, London.
- 'River Avon, Part 1', Victoria Art Gallery, Bath.
- Glastonbury Festival charity auction, The Hospital, Covent Garden.
- 'The Cornish Crow', Truro, Cornwall.

2006

- 'Kardamili and Priest Cove', Messum's, London.
- 'Porth', Catmose Art Gallery, Rutland.
- Dundas Street Gallery, Edinburgh.
- 'The Thames Project', South Hill Park, Bracknell, Berks.
- 'Ponds, Pools and Puddles', Truro, Cornwall.

2005

- 'Below Carn Gloose', Messum's, London.
- 'Porth', Royal Albert Memorial Museum and Art Gallery, Exeter and Canterbury City Art Gallery.
- 'The Painted Etchings', Newlyn Art Gallery, Cornwall and Dundas Street Gallery, Edinburgh.
- Glastonbury Festival charity auction.
- 'Three Woods', St Barbe Museum and Art Gallery, Lymington and Royal Cornwall Museum, Truro.
- 'The Cornish Hedge', Truro, Cornwall.

2004–05

- Paddington Station installation.

2004

- 'River Drome and Samson, Scilly', Messum's,Cork Street, London.
- 'Porth', touring exhibition: Newlyn Art Gallery; Worcester City Art Gallery; King's Lynn Arts Centre, Norfolk.
- RGI Gallery, Glasgow.
- 'Two Woods', Victoria Art Gallery, Bath.
- 'The Cornish Estuary', Truro, Cornwall.

2003

- Messum's, London.
- Glastonbury Festival charity auction, *The Guardian* newsroom, London.
- 'St Michael's Way', Truro, Cornwall.

2002

- Messum's, London.
- 'Delabole Slate Quarry', touring exhibition: Penzance Geology Museum; Slate Valley Museum, New York, USA; Helen Day Art Centre, Vermont USA.
- RGI Kelly Gallery, Glasgow.
- Dundas Street Gallery, Edinburgh.
- Royal Cornwall Museum, Truro.
- 'Scilly', 'Priest Cove', Truro, Cornwall.

2001

- Messum's, London.

2000

- Messum's, London.
- Origin Gallery, Dublin.
- University of Exeter.

1999

- Messum's, London.
- Origin Gallery, Dublin.

1998–99

- 'Carnsew', touring exhibition: Falmouth Art Gallery; Worcester City Art Gallery; Lancashire Mining Museum.
- Cornwall Geological Museum.

1998

- Messum's, London.
- Twin town exchange, Concarneau Town Hall, Brittany.
- Origin Gallery, Dublin.
- Royal Cornwall Museum, Truro.

1997

- Darlington Art Centre.
- Rheda-Wiedensbrück, Germany.

1995–97

- 'South Crofty', touring exhibition: Camborne School of Mines; Penzance Geological Museum; Plymouth City Art Gallery.
- Doncaster Museum.

1986–95

- North Cornwall Museum and Art Gallery.

1984

- Robinson College, Cambridge.

Exhibited widely through the 1980s.

Selected group exhibitions

2014

- 'Power of the Sea', Royal West of England Academy, Bristol.

2013

- 'Wilder Shores of Love', Hilton Fine Art, Bath.
- 'Endless Summer', Royal Cornwall Museum, Truro.
- 'Picturing the British Tree', St Barbe Museum and Art Gallery, Lymington.

2012

- 'Landscape' Redfern Gallery, London.
- 'Endless Summer', Plymouth City Museum and Art Gallery.
- 'Sunday Times Watercolour Competition'.

2011

- 'Frameworks', Falmouth Art Gallery.

2010

- 'Exquisite Trove', Newlyn Art Gallery.
- 'Century', Plymouth City Museum and Art Gallery.

2008

- 'Africa Calling', Falmouth Art Gallery.

2007

- Presentation of paintings to Cornwall County Council collection.
- Art Miami, USA.
- Exhibition at Kew Gardens.

2000-14

- London Art Fair.
- Royal West of England Academy.
- Penlee House Gallery and Museum, Penzance, Cornwall.

2002

- 'Delabole Quarry', with Richard Long, Falmouth Art Gallery.

1994–2008

- Newlyn Society of Artists.

1994–97

- Penwith Society of Artists.
- City Gallery, Leicester.
- Hastings Museum.

1994

- Rheda, Wiedensbrück, Germany.

1982

- Three-man exhibition with brother and father, Maltings Gallery, Weathampstead, Hertfordshire.

Awards and residences

- Made honorary fellow of St Peters College Oxford (2011).
- Artist in Residence, Berne Shipyard, Bremen, Germany (2011).
- Elected honorary ambassador of Survival International (2009).
- Awarded honorary doctorate for contribution to the arts by the University of Exeter (2007).
- Residency at Treliske Hospital operating theatre, Truro, Cornwall (2007).
- Artist in Residence on Greenpeace ship *Esperanza* (2005).
- Artist in Residence, 'Live 8' at Eden Project (2005).
- Chair of Newlyn Society of Artists (2004–07).
- Artist in Residence, Glastonbury Festival (from 1999 onwards).
- Elected Academician, Royal West of England Academy (1998).
- Artist in Residence, Cill Riallaig, Ireland (1997).
- Artist in Residence, Cill Riallaig, Ireland (1995).

Broadcasts

- 'Moths', BBC 1, 'Inside Out', (23/09/2013).
- 'Tin', BBC 1, 'Inside Out', (15/12/2012).
- 'Cornwall's Rarest Tree', BBC, 'Spotlight' (2011).
- 'River Dart', BBC 1, 'Inside Out', (8/11/2010).
- 'Midweek', with Libby Purvis, BBC Radio 4 (28/07/2010).
- 'River Dart', BBC, 'Spotlight' (2010).
- 'Learning Zone', BBC 3 (2010).
- 'Spring', with Richard Mabey, BBC Radio 3 (2009).
- 'Kurt Jackson, A Picture of Cornwall', BBC 1 South West (2005).
- 'Kurt Jackson, A Picture of the South West', BBC 3 (2005).
- 'A Place in My Heart', Carlton TV (1998).

Public collections

- BBC
- Camborne School of Mines, Penryn, Cornwall
- Cill Rialaig Arts Centre, Co Kerry, Ireland
- Concarneau Town Council, Brittany
- Cornwall County Council
- Crown Court, Truro, Cornwall
- Edinburgh University
- Exeter University
- Falmouth Art Gallery, Cornwall
- Met Office, Exeter
- Ministry of Works, Republic of Ireland
- National Museum of Germany, Nuremburg
- Penlee House Gallery and Museum, Penzance, Cornwall
- Plymouth City Museum and Art Gallery, Devon
- Porthcurno Cable and Wireless Museum, Penzance, Cornwall
- Royal Cornwall Museum and Art Gallery, Truro
- Royal West of England Academy, Bristol
- Slate Valley Museum, Granville, New York
- St Barbe Museum and Art Gallery, Lymington, Hants
- The Steiner School, Hanover
- Tate Britain, London
- Tremough Campus, Cornwall
- Truro School, Cornwall
- University of Cambridge
- University of Oxford
- Victoria and Albert Museum, London
- Victoria Art Gallery, Bath
- Worcester City Museum and Art Gallery

Select bibliography

- Barrett, J, Turner, R and Walsh, A (eds) *Caught By The River – A Collection of Words on Water*, Octopus Publishing, London, 2009.
- Benington, Jonathan, 'The Avon Project', 2009.
- Cocker, Mark, 'Encounter: The visions of Kurt Jackson' in *The New Nature Writing*, Granta, London, 2008, vol. 102, pp. 22–26.
- Collins, Ian and Admiral Sir Jock Slater, 'The Lights of West Cornwall', Messum's, London, 2008.
- Crace, Jim, 'Enesow', 2009.
- Cross, Tom, *Catching the Wave: Art and Artists in Contemporary Cornwall*, Halsgrove Publishing, Somerset, 2002.
- Dubois, Marc, 'Theatre Five', 2008.
- Gaskell, Ronald and Jackson, Kurt, *The Cape*, Truran, Cornwall, 2002.
- Hare, Bill, 'Ardnamurchan', 2009.
- Jackson, Kurt, *A New Genre of Landscape Painting*, Lund Humphries, 2010.
- Jackson, Kurt, 'And', Falmouth Art Gallery, Cornwall, 2011.
- Jackson, Kurt, *Sketchbooks*, Truran, Cornwall, 2003–04.
- Jackson, Kurt, 'The Solent Project', St Barbe Museum and Art Gallery, Lymington, 2008.
- Jackson, Kurt and Livingstone, Alan, *Kurt Jackson Sketchbooks*, Lund Humphries 2012
- Jackson, Kurt, 'Three Woods', St Barbe Museum and Art Gallery, Lymington, 2005.
- Jackson, Kurt, 'A One Mile Walk', Campden Gallery, 2013.
- Jackson, Kurt, 'Archipelago', Campden Gallery, 2014.
- Lane, Stephanie and Maddern, Guy, *The Fine Art of Surgery – A collection of paintings, drawings and murals*, Royal Society of Medicine Press, London, 2012.
- Mabey, Richard, 'Forest Gardens', Messum's, London, 2009.
- Mallett, Francis, *Paintings of Cornwall and The Scillies*, White Lane Press, Devon, 1999.
- McCullough, Christopher and Packer, William, 'The Cornish Crow: An Vran Kernewek', 2007.
- Macfarlane, Robert, 'The Earth as it sees itself', Redfern Gallery, London, 2011.
- Marsden, Philip, 'The Trees of Cornwall', 2011.
- Nixon, Giles and Wallace, Catherine, 'Carnsew, A Working Granite Quarry in Cornwall', Falmouth Art Gallery, Cornwall, 1999.
- O'Brien, JA, 'South Crofty, The Last Working Tin Mine in Cornwall, Camborne School of Mines', Cornwall, 1996.
- Packer, William, 'Caroline and the Vegetable Patch', Messum's, London, 2007.
- Self, Will, 'The Thames Revisited', Redfern Gallery, 2013.
- Smit, Tim, The Thames Project, 2006.
- Taylor, John Russell, 'Porth', Newlyn Art Gallery, Cornwall, 2004.
- Think Books, *Icons of England*, Think Publishing, London, 2008.
- Warburton, Josephine, 'The Mining Paintings, Pendeen'.
- Welsh, Irvine, 'The Black River, The Forth', 2011.

Acknowledgements

The artist would like to thank the following for their involvement in this publication:

Caroline Jackson, as ever, for her companionship, enthusiasm and input throughout this project, Zinzi Tucker for her work as studio assistant, Fynn Tucker for the art photography, the writers for their involvement and written contributions, and the team at Sansom & Company. With thanks to the Richards at The Redfern Gallery, London.

PLACE